# HATCHET MEN

The Story of the Tong Wars
in San Francisco's Chinatown

# HATCHET MEN

### The Story of the Tong Wars
### in San Francisco's Chinatown

by

## RICHARD H. DILLON

Sanger, California

TheWriteThought.com

*To Dr. John E. Pomfret*
DIRECTOR, HENRY E. HUNTINGTON LIBRARY

**The Write Thought, Inc.**
1254 Commerce Way
Sanger, California 93657
559-876-2170
Info@TheWriteThought.com


Kindle ISBN: 9781618090492
ePub ISBN: 9781618090508
POD ISBN: 9781618090515


Library of Congress Control Number 2005925025

# ACKNOWLEDGMENTS

I am indebted to many people for aid and comfort in the writing of this account, including Librarians Allan R. Ottley of the California State Library, James Abajian of the California Historical Society, and book critic William Hogan of the *San Francisco Chronicle.* The Columbia University Press was kind enough to grant me permission to quote from pages 247-248 of Henryk Sienkiwicz's *Portrait of America*, edited and translated by Charles Morley and published by that press in 1959.

My greatest debt, however, is to Dr. John E. Pomfret to whom this volume is dedicated, and to the Huntington Library which he heads. Thanks to a research grant from that library, I was able in 1960 to lay the foundations of the present study in that outstanding historical research institution.

RICHARD H. DILLON

# Contents

Acknowledgments.............................................................. v

FOREWORD:
The Golden Mountains ............................................... ix

CHAPTER ONE
The Era Of Good Feeling............................................. 1

CHAPTER TWO
The Honeymoon Ends.................................................. 10

CHAPTER THREE
Pipes Of Peace ......................................................... 27

CHAPTER FOUR
The Six Companies..................................................... 36

CHAPTER FIVE
Sand Lots And Pick Handles........................................ 54

CHAPTER SIX
The Inquisition........................................................... 79

CHAPTER SEVEN
Salaried Soldiers Of The Tongs ............................... 110

CHAPTER EIGHT
Crusader Farwell...................................................... 143

CHAPTER NINE
Slave Girls.............................................................. 152

CHAPTER TEN
The Terror Of Chinatown.......................................... 167

CHAPTER ELEVEN
The Gray '90s.......................................................... 183

CHAPTER TWELVE
Little Pete: King Of Chinatown ................................. 216

CHAPTER THIRTEEN
Aftermath: Chinatown In Ruins.................................. 250

# FOREWORD:

# THE GOLDEN MOUNTAINS

*"The Chinese are quiet, peaceable,
tractable, free from drunkenness, and they are
as industrious as the day is long. A disorderly
Chinaman is rare and a lazy one does not
exist."*

—Roughing It, Mark Twain

KIPLING was right—at least, temporarily. East *was* East, West *was* West, and the twain did not really meet, as equals, in San Francisco for some twenty-five years after his now invalidated pronouncement of 1889.

For although some 30,000 Chinese resided in the environs of San Francisco's Dupont Gai, as the Chinese called Grant Avenue (old Dupont Street), and although they constituted a whole city within a city, they were never fully accepted during the entire nineteenth century. Indeed it was not until after World War I that first-class citizenship was extended to San Franciscans of Chinese extraction.

Much of this apartheid is to the discredit of San Francisco, of course. The general lack of such antisocial diseases as Jim Crowism and anti-Semitism in its history has unfortunately been cancelled out by a long and unpleasant era of anti-Chinese feeling. This campaign was carried on for decades by rabble-rousing demagogues for the most part, but not entirely. The more respectable politicians, members of the public in general, civic leaders, the pulpit and even the usually enlightened press were all guilty of bigotry and oppression. Of course there were many exceptions to this tendency, ranging from Reverend Otis Gibson to irreverent

Mark Twain.

But the blame for the apartness of the Chinese in Gum San Ta Fow (Big City in the Land of the Golden Hills) of some 75 or even 50 years ago does not rest entirely with the host community. For 50 years after the Gold Rush, Chinatown was the Celestial Empire's most far-flung political and cultural outpost. Chinatown was run, not by the Mayor of San Francisco, but by the Consul General of Imperial China and the Six Companies. (This was so until the fighting tongs moved in with a rule of terror.) The Quarter was not merely an ethnic enclave in the city, like the Italian sector of North Beach. It was truly China in San Francisco.

Much of the fault for the misunderstanding, the suspicion, and the lack of cooperation which existed between the two peoples and which kept them apart so long was due to the unwillingness of the Chinese to integrate—to even acclimate to the extent of modifying their dress or diet in their new environment. The reason was not, as Hinton Helper and others suggested, an outright hostility to Caucasians and their customs, based on a superiority complex. Rather, it was simply that the average Oriental did not—*could* not—pick up the language and customs of his new home, and frankly saw little reason to do so. He preferred to live with his own kind. He did not intend to stay. John would have remained an alien even had citizenship been thrust upon him at this stage of San Francisco's history. He might go so far as to trade his split-bamboo basket hat or skullcap for a wide-brimmed, black felt fedora, but he kept his old ideas and philosophies. Inwardly he refused to change. The so-called coolie was the alien par excellence. The term coolie gained wide acceptance as a synonym for Chinaman in the vocabulary of Americans. It was an Anglo-Indian word, not a Chinese term at all, and came from the Bengali or Tamil word *kuli* which signified "burden bearer" and which originally meant "bitter work." For a coolie it was much easier to form his own little China in the midst of bustling, confusing Fah-lan-sze-ko (San Francisco) than to undergo the psychological wrenching necessitated by the passage from one culture to the other. The typical Chinese immigrant of the 1850s wanted to remain in Ka-la-fo-ne-a no longer than necessary. When he had made his pile—perhaps $500—he would return home to his patient wife and family for a life of relative ease in Kwangtung. The typical Chinese in the Big City of the Golden Mountains was what the sociologists describe as a sojourner—here today and gone (home) tomorrow. John was just passing through. He did not want to be assimilated; on the contrary he preferred to be insulated from the *fan kwei* (foreign devils) all around him. He had one foot in Frisco but the other was still firmly planted in Canton. His great ambition was to make a lot of money and become a *Gum San Hock*—a returnee from the Golden Hills. While he was in San Francisco his one pressing desire was to be left alone.

The English traveler, Mrs. Algernon St. Maur, determined the real cause of the strained relations between Chinese and Caucasian San Franciscans early. She said: "The only real difficulty is that the Chinese do not make citizens. America wants citizens."

Police Chief George W. Walling of New York not only described the attitude of withdrawal practiced by Chinese immigrants, but also unconsciously betrayed the prevailing bias of Americans of that day against the puzzling newcomers. Walling said of the Chinese: "Suspicious as a man who finds himself in a den of thieves, he is ever on the watch, while he works, for some new manifestation of that American temperament which his own mind, dense with the superstition of many thousand years, can never quite understand."

The posters of Hong Kong which had led to his sailing to the Embarcadero in the first place had told John that California was a nice country without Mandarins or soldiers. Leery of these two elements of mankind, he steered clear of the few Yankee Mandarins (officials) and soldiers (policemen) he saw. He did his best to blend into the landscape, like a chameleon. But the Chinese was so *outré* because of his costume, coiffure and habits, that even in as diversified a city as San Francisco he stood out starkly.

In the last 50 years the people of San Francisco have tried to make up for the shoddy treatment meted out to the city's great minority group during the first 50 years of its existence. There is no doubt that the city has taken Chinatown to its heart, and the affection is sincere. But more important to the metamorphosis of Chinatown since 1850, or the bloody tong-war days of 1880, is the fact that somewhere along the way—at some unknown day and hour, at some invisible line in time—the majority of the residents of Chinatown decided to stay; to become Americans.

The sojourners became a minority. Slowly and surely San Francisco began to win over the larger segment of its Oriental population. It was as simple as that—and as complicated. No one can put his finger on any particular individual who took the lead, any more than one can ascribe the change of attitude to a given year. It was a gradual process of change—of unwitting acclimatization. But acceptance and integration were not easy decisions to make for those involved. Even after death the ties with China were strong in the Chinese. Hence the shiploads of bones and ashes of the dead which year after year left the Embarcadero bound for Hong Kong. For example, when the French ship *Asia* sailed in January, 1858, she bore the embalmed bodies of 321 Chinese. When the great American clipper *Flying Cloud* followed her in February it was with the bulk of her cargo consisting of the corpses of 200 Chinese Argonauts. There were no older or stronger family, clan and homeland ties on the face of the earth than those in Chinese society.

The tragedy of the mutual suspicion and misunderstanding which developed between the two groups, each so aloof from the other, was not immediately evident. It came particularly in the 1880s and 1890s as a last spasm of the symptoms of *apartheid,* just before the belated trend to Americanization on the part of the Chinese and to tolerance and acceptance on the part of the Americans. Misunderstanding created a social vacuum between the two peoples. This void between Little China and Frisco remained unfilled for a singularly and inexplicably long period of time; when it was filled by inrushing elements they were the forces of evil. The criminal class in Chinatown was small in the 1860s, just as it is today in the 1960s. But suddenly about 1880 it burgeoned and fattened and multiplied like some ugly cellular disturbance of the body politic. Held in check by the overweening prestige of the Six Companies, it burst its bonds when the Six Companies suffered a severe loss of face (*mien tzu*) in the '90s. The leaders of respectable Chinatown gambled— and the Chinese are a nation of gamblers—on the unconstitutionality of the Geary Act. Under the leadership of Chin Ti Chu, president of the Sam Yup Company, the people of Chinatown were told not to sign the registration documents instigated by the provisions of the act. The Six Companies' leadership was humiliated when the plan of peaceful resistance crashed down around their queues. The Geary Act was held to be

xii

constitutional by the Supreme Court. Thanks to Chin and the companies, thousands of law abiding Chinese had become technical law violators by their boycott of the alien registration offices. The Six Companies' officers found their prestige and moral strength crumbling with their loss of face. The fighting tongs, biding their time until just such an opening should occur, exploited it and seized control of the Chinese community.

The result was the shocking phenomenon in American history of internecine war in a racial ghetto—the bloody tong wars of San Francisco's Chinatown. Chinese preyed upon Chinese solely. It was a weird class of civil war; a struggle for power among bad men with the good people of Chinatown the pawns and the prey. Only Chinese suffered from the violent depredations of the hatchet men—the hired killers of the fighting tongs. They sized the police and city up correctly; kept "a family affair," the police would not interfere too positively. A policy of *laissez faire* had worked well in Chinatown since 1850. There was little reason to change it.

The good people of Chinatown, who were the great majority, found themselves bullied and terrified by a handful of well-organized criminals who aped the very white hoodlums who oppressed them. This new Chinese criminal element borrowed the worst features of the two civilizations which collided on Dupont Gai. From old China they took the code of an eye for an eye and familial responsibility for the actions of an individual. Thus the feud and vendetta code of China and the importance of saving face—at *all* costs—was transplanted to San Francisco. The boo how doy (literally "hatchet sons") distorted old traditions to their own ends. From the Americans they took hoodlumism, as gangsterism was called a century ago. But the hoodlum-inspired riots and head crackings of the 1870s were child's play compared to the deadly guerrilla warfare of the tongs. From city hall the hatchet men picked up American style crooked politics, long popular in the city by the Golden Gate. The elements of blackmail and graft were available to them from both cultures. Conditioned to violence by almost three decades of hoodlumism and anti-coolie crusading, the *boo how doy* took violence as a way of life.

The typical law-abiding Chinese of San Francisco was also well adjusted to a climate of violence, thanks to the mob bigotry and hoodlumism which surrounded him. But to make matters even worse he had a built-in susceptibility to gangster rule because of certain weaknesses of his philosophical makeup. These frailties—thousands of years old and inbred—invited attack by such antisocial forces as the fighting tongs. The Chinese was subtle, reticent and stoic. He had an elaborate defense mechanism for the swallowing of insults and abuse. A qualitative analysis of the Chinese immigrant would have revealed a blend of positive Confucianism, with its respect for law and order and authority, and negative Taoism, with its "old roguery," as Lin Yutang has termed the tendency to take the line of least resistance. It was a precarious balance at best, with the latter philosophy's cynicism and skepticism usually winning out over any individual's reform ideas.

It was only the Confucianism which Reverend Otis Gibson saw when he too quickly praised the Chinese newcomers for "the natural docility of their character... [and] respect for superiors; for all those who occupy positions of honor and power."

John was no idealist or reformer. Idealism belonged to youth, and China was old—centuries old by 1850. Taoism served the Cantonese *émigré* like a morphia. This opiate philosophy benumbed his outraged sense of decency and helped him to survive during crises; to endure—but never to overcome—misrule. He did not try to remake life or even to reshape it a little, but rather to bend with it.

The emigrating Chinese brought to San Francisco his traditional distrust of courts, officials and lawyers. In the Old Country 95 percent of all legal troubles were settled out of court. The clerk's office in China was handed down from father to son or else bought and sold. It was far more than a mere sinecure. It was an opportunity to practice what the Spaniards call *el mordido*—the bite. This bite, graft or squeeze was practiced also by the police, by officials, judges and witnesses in China. The immigrant fully expected the same conditions to prevail in Fah-lan-sze-ko. (He was often right.)

John was devoid of what Caucasians called public spirit. His outlook was self-centered and family-centered. Teamwork did not exist in his vocabulary. The new immigrant brought many virtues—pacifism, tolerance, industry, contentment—but he did not bring personal courage in the Western sense. He did not battle for his rights. Used to the bandits and war lords of China, he was not surprised when the goon squads of the tongs took over Chinatown. He did his best to make no enemies, to turn the other cheek, to dodge the ruffians as best he could.

For all his joining of societies, John did not tend to band his friends together to protect the weak or the law-abiding. Though the Chinese was supposedly a humanist of a high order by long tradition, to Americans he seemed to lack completely the virtue of compassion. He seemed to accept the murder of his neighbors as predestined—not something to fight. He was family-minded and club-oriented, but he was in no sense social-minded. His civic consciousness was nil. Civil rights were an un-fathomed mystery to John. He was used only to a world ruled by Face (not the same as honor, alas), Fate and Favor. This trio came to rule Chinatown, deadening justice, law and democracy. It was more pernicious than tyrannical, being in a great measure self-imposed because of habit and tradition. With even his virtues working against him, it is no wonder that the San Francisco Chinese, under the pressure of the fighting tongs, made self-preservationand not progress or freedom the keystone of his philosophy.

With the partial collapse of the Six Companies in the mid-'90s, the cult of detachment or disaffiliation in Chinatown became more pro-nounced. John virtually hid in his warren. He bowed down and waited for the storm to rage and die. His attitude can be called selfishness, cow-ardice, pacificism or stoicism; whatever it was it embodied a surrender to the old Chinese proverb—"It is better to be a dog in peaceful times than a man in times of unrest." A child of the most misruled nation on earth, his instinct and tradition would not allow him to act otherwise.

Only the Chinese Native Sons (later the Chinese-American Citizens' Alliance) tried to adjust to the new rhythm of living found in San Fran-cisco. These new short-haired, Americanized Chinese abandoned their old way of life—or at least much of it—in order to create a new life. It turned out to be an amalgam of the two—something like the Spanish and Indian admixture which has become Latin American civilization. These men had a choice of old Imperial China, new Republican China—still in the offing—or America. Overwhelmingly they chose America. The hatchet men, the exceptions to the rule, broke all Chinese tradition as it pleased them and borrowed only what was convenient from Taoism. They were the most extreme examples of the Cantonese—quick-tempered, pugnacious and adventurous. From the Northerners of China they scavenged a contempt for fair play. Since many, probably most, of the hatchet men were from the Chinese lower or criminal class, they were uneducated and less inclined to follow the old dictates of obedience, gentility of behavior and abhorrence of violence, even if they were aware of such civilized deportment. Among the Cantonese the tong men were the rugged individualists, yet paradoxically they banded together the tightest of all. They got things done, and ironically they were often better liked by Americans than law-abiding Chinese because of their cultural mobility. Little Pete, the well-known rackets' boss of Chinatown in the '90s, was a case in point. Dr. Rose Hum Lee pointed out that Kwangtung has not only been noted above all Chinese provinces for its progressive and adventurous people but also for its troublesome folk. There was no shortage of the latter in Chinatown and none more deadly—even on the Barbary Coast or the docks of the Embarcadero—than the swaggering bullies of the fighting tongs.

The blood brotherhood of the tongs ruled Chinatown from the 1880s until the earthquake of 1906. During this period the highbinders or hatchet men took over control of the tongs from the more peaceful membership. It required a motley, chaotic and disorganized alliance of forces to finally eradicate them. These forces came mainly from the Chinese community. The police and the courts were in a great measure responsible for the crushing of the tongs, but it was the long-abused Chinese people themselves who really won the battle. They began to fight back quietly by identifying themselves as Americans, by participating in government, and by respecting and obeying Yankee notions of law, order and justice rather than their own extra-legal codes. The courts gave them an opportunity to seek justice before American juries and to place their trust in the American bench and bar. The police offered protection. Although it was hard to forget the old system of corruption, the humble people of Chinatown began to place confidence in the police department. Before, they had always viewed the patrolman on his beat with suspicion; he was a potential oppressor rather than a protector.

If the Chinese were going to stay and raise their families as Americans, they had to abandon the old codes of life which conflicted with American law and which made possible—even *necessary*—the constant

xvi

series of vendettas which in turn bred highbinders and murder. The people of Chinatown finally realized this. They made their decision, and the hold of the tongs on the quarter was forced to slacken.

The American community, on the other hand, offered the Chinese more respect and understanding as it outgrew its stupid bigotry. The Chinese Exclusion Act of 1882, not exactly a model piece of legislation *in toto,* was a powerful third force which cut down on the importation of fresh highbinders and which banished gunmen, and kept them out as undesirable aliens unless they were smuggled in.

As the hatchet men killed one another off or were jailed, the older men began to regain control of the tongs. There were more family men in Chinatown too. The san doy, bachelor, no longer ran the town. The Six Companies—the welfare organization based on the immigrants' provinces of origin—regained the powerful position it had long held. The family associations began a renaissance. The Chinese-American Citizens' Alliance began to grow in numbers and strength. Many members were Christians and not just "rice Christians" (converts who embraced Christianity only because of mission handouts), and they were appalled by the bloodletting in Chinatown. Many lived outside the Quarter and felt about the tong wars as any other horrified San Franciscan felt. The Chinese-Americans were not subjects of either the Consul General or the illegal tongs. They were Americans and their numbers had leaped from but one percent of the country's Chinese population in 1870 to 10 percent in 1900—some 15,000 individuals ready to rally against the dead hand of tradition as represented by the killer tongs.

Finally, the tongs themselves had had enough. In 1913 they created a Peace committee which secured an armistice. Their power was declining as that of the mercantile class, Chinatown's quasi elders, rose. Chinatown was eventually united against the hatchet men as implements of the old way—the wrong way—of settling disputes. But the Americanization process had to grow out of a blood bath of two or three decades before the old customs were thrown off.

The tong wars continued sporadically until as late as the 1920s. But the heyday of the *boo how doy* was over. In that last era they took on some of the coloration of Chicago gangsterism. They died out later on New York's Pell, Mott and Doyers Streets than on Dupont Gai. There are still tongs in San Francisco and other American cities—the On Leongs, Hip Sings, Ying Ons, Chee Kongs, Bins Kongs and Suey Yings—but most are benevolent or merchants' associations now. Their vendettas are political and bloodless. Some people, like Dr. Rose Hum Lee, caution that the tongs may try a comeback in two areas—narcotics and Communist subversion. A revival seems unlikely, but wary eyes are always kept on them by law-enforcement agencies.

The manner in which the American-Chinese community has integrated into our society so fully, bringing us so much to enrich it, is a testimony to the worthiness of these people to full citizenship. They had to overcome enormous obstacles in order to reach the position to which they are now welcomed.

From the 1880s until the earthquake and fire of 1906 wiped out ghetto Chinatown, San Francisco paid heavily for its sins of commission and omission. This book attempts to tell the story of the high cost of bigotry and intolerance. It is no condemnation of San Francisco's Chinatown nor of its citizens, past or present; it is a condemnation of the criminal classes which flourished there. And it is, I hope, a very thorough condemnation of intolerance.

Richard H. Dillon
San Francisco
False Spring, 1962

# CHAPTER ONE

# THE ERA OF GOOD FEELING

*"The Chinese have invariably proved to
be, as a people, docile, sober and orderly,
thus exhibiting the proper traits of good
citizenship... However, they are becoming
more civilized (sic!) and refined by constant
intercourse with the white population and
many have added drinking and gambling to
their accomplishments."*

—San Francisco City Directory, 1852-53

SAN FRANCISCANS were horrified on Tuesday, March 6, 1900, at the
callous attitude displayed by one of the city's leading newspapers, the
*Call*. In reporting on the current tong war in Chinatown the newspaper
cast the account in the form of a sports story complete with a box score
of dead and wounded, as if the deadly vendetta were a soccer match. The
*Call's* gruesome tally revealed that in the three-months-old war, 7 men
had died and 8 had been seriously wounded. (The other team in this ma-
cabre and murderous three-cornered game—the police—had gone "hit-
less" with not one murderer captured during the Hop Sing vs. Suey Sing
war.) How could such a shocking event have taken place in San Francisco only sixty-two years ago? San Francisco was a world port and a
metropolis, not a grubby cowtown or mining camp. Yet gunmen roamed
her streets, or at least the streets of Chinatown. And what had gotten into
the hard-working, docile Chinese that such open warfare could rage in
the streets of the quarter?

This state of affairs did not erupt overnight. It was the product of almost fifty years of erosion of law and order in the Chinese Quarter. Almost from the moment the first Chinese alighted on the Embarcadero there had been within Chinatown a drift contrary to the trend in the city at large. In the city as a whole there was a steady tide setting on toward order and peace. It was a taming process with murders, duels and vigilance committees eventually becoming passé. But in Chinatown there was a cultural eddy and the reverse was taking place. Criminality was increasing like a cancerous growth. The tong wars came later to Chinatown than most people imagine, but the state of affairs which led the *Call* to run its cold-blooded box score was the product of many years of deterioration. To trace this course which led to the tong wars one must go back to the very beginnings of Chinese settlement in San Francisco.

Early San Francisco was not afflicted with tong troubles. This is not to say that Dupont Gai was crime free for the first several decades following the Gold Rush. Far from it. For where, in what Utopia, is there a city of up to 30,000 inhabitants without a crime problem? But compared to the '80s and '90s, the 1850s were at a time of a Pax Sinica. The immediate reasons for crime in Chinatown then were the obvious ones— human nature, opportunity and an oversupply of single men who were rootless males, without family ties, in a foreign land. They were ignorant of local language, customs and laws. To cap it, Chinatown did not have a police force of its own as an American city of comparable size would have had. True, the police on Chinatown beats tried to preserve law and order just as did those in Happy Valley, on the wicked Embarcadero, or the wickeder Barbary Coast. But many of the officers, particularly the "specials," or "locals"—the auxiliary police—had their paws out. And it was not for friendly handshakes but for cumshaw—tips.

The petty grafting of the police—at times not so petty—tended to shake the Chinese newcomer's confidence in the force. And if the cops on the Chinatown beat were honest, and most were tolerably so, who was to say what their lieutenants or captains—or perhaps the chiefs— were up to? As for the politicos hanging around city hall, the graft prosecutions and other scandals of late nineteenth and early twentieth century San Francisco speak volumes. There was no use looking to them for help.

Small wonder, too, that it took decades for the American-Chinese to accept the proffered protection of even an honest policeman. In nine cases out of ten be would be an Irishman whose family was of "the Chinese Must Go!" persuasion, influenced by Dennis Kearney or some similar agitator. If the cop on the corner turned out to be a special, he was almost sure to be in the employ of the criminal element and not likely to defend the decent people of Chinatown.

The wonder is that the officer on the beat did as good a job as he did. He was torn internally by the temptation of payoffs versus the desire to do his duty. At the same time he might be wholeheartedly in sympathy with the ostensible aims of a mob marching on Chinatown "to save American labor." Nevertheless he comported himself pretty well under the circumstances, even during the crisis of the summer of 1877. Graft and kickbacks or not—noncooperation by the oppressed people be hanged—he still did his job and saw to it, at the expense of more than one bloody nose of his own, that the hoodlums and self-styled saviors of the laboring classes did not get a chance to crack innocent beads, even if they wore queues. Credit is long overdue the Irish members who pounded Chinatown's steep streets where they were fair game for clubs of hoodlums and knives of highbinders. The common people made no outward show of gratitude toward their protectors. They almost seemed to wish to thwart the apprehension of the human leeches who fed upon them. On the other hand, the criminal classes tried to flatter the harness bulls, to make friends with them, and to *buy* them off.

Chinese and Americans were still uneasy strangers during the 1850s. Sino-American contacts prior to the Gold Rush were few. In 1800 the first Chinese had been brought to the United States to learn English. Eight years later a young Chinese performed on horseback in New York, and in the 1830s the first Chinese woman, Ah Foy, came to America. A juggler of 1842, Chong Fong was upstaged by another immigrant of the gentler sex who was exhibited as a freak on Broadway. In 1847 the junk *Keying* arrived and posed in New York Harbor for Currier and Ives, but only a handful of Chinese had ever seen the States before Jim Marshall spied gold dust in Sutter's millrace. That year of 1848, P.T. Barnum opened his Chinese Museum in New York, and California received its first Chinese settlers—two men and a woman landed from the brig *Eagle.* From this beginning a colony of 300 had grown in San Francisco

3

by December 1849, when they met in the Canton Restaurant on Jackson Street and chose Selim Woodworth as adviser, arbiter, protector and quasi consul for the Chinese in America. By the end of 1852, the 300 had become 25,000.

In the years immediately following 1849, the Chinese were welcomed to San Francisco as a quaint segment of society. They were considered colorful and docile and quite law abiding. When roughly handled in the mines or persecuted by the Foreign Miners' License Law, they often drifted down to San Francisco from the Mother Lode, to swell the population of Little China, as Chinatown was first called.

Little China was adjacent to Little Chile which became Sydney Town and later the Barbary Coast. A second Little China existed for a time at the foot of Frémont Street where Chinese wreckers squatted on the beach and broke up old hulks like the *Loo Choo,* which had brought Colonel Jonathan D. Stevenson's regiment of brawlers to Yerba Buena. A village of 150 Chinese fishermen huddled in the lee of Rincon Point not far from the mouth of Mission Creek. With their twenty-five boats they took 3,000 pounds of sturgeon, shark and herring each day, most of which they dried. Other colonies were located on Hunter's Point, in the South Bay, on the *contra costa,* and at China Camp in Mann County. But these were fish or shrimp camps where the men anchored their homemade junks, and merely satellites of Chinatown.

Dupont Gai became and remained the nucleus of Chinatown. Strangely, for a ghetto, old Chinatown grew up not across the tracks or as an outskirts shanty town. It blossomed in the heart of the city on high ground adjacent to Portsmouth Square—San Francisco's first civic center. The heavily crowded but substantial buildings occupied the very site of the founding of Yerba Buena, the parent village of San Francisco, if we except Captain William Richardson's temporary structure on the beach itself. The second building erected, that of Jacob P. Leese, was located on the corner of Dupont and Clay in 1836. Dupont was then called *calle de la Fundacion,* Street of the Founding. When Port Captain Richardson constructed his second building, in 1838, the adobe La Casa Grande, it was on a lot on the west side of Dupont between Washington and Clay Streets. The great fires of May and September 1850 swept over the area of Chinatown, and when people returned to live in the ashes more and more of them were Chinese.

With little crime or disorder in Chinatown, John and Brother Jonathan got along well in these early years. Evidence of the great affection—however short lived—of San Franciscans for their new Oriental neighbors was the celebration of August 28, 1850, in Portsmouth Plaza. Mayor John Geary, Reverend Albert Williams and Frederick A. Woodworth—like his brother Selim a sort of quasi consul for the Chinese community—gathered on a platform erected in the square. There they orated and then presented a number of religious tracts, papers and books printed in Chinese characters. The crowd listened in rapt attention to their speeches, translated into Cantonese by the interpreter Ah Sing. The mayor wound up the program by inviting the Chinese to take part in the funeral procession for President Zachary Taylor scheduled for the following day. They accepted with alacrity and gratitude. They were much honored by the gesture.

The next day the China Boys, as they were fondly called, formed up and marched in a procession to Portsmouth Square to hear Mayor Geary orate once again. The 1850 *City Directory* noted the appearance in the parade of the large body of the Chinese in their curious national costume as the most remarkable feature of the ceremony. The *Directory* ventured the opinion that this was the first procession in the limits of Christendom in which Chinese had formed such a prominent part. The next morning the China Boys presented Mayor Geary with an elaborate document in ornate Chinese calligraphy which read in translation:

August 30, 1850

To HONORABLE JOHN W. GEARY

MAYOR OF THE CITY OF SAN FRANCISCO

SIR: The China Boys wish to thank you for the kind mark of attention you bestowed upon them in extending to them an invitation to join with the citizens of San Francisco in doing honor to the memory of the late President of the United States, General Zachary Taylor. The China Boys feel proud of the distinction you have shown them and will always endeavor to merit your good opinion and the good opinion of the citizens of their adopted country. The China Boys are fully sensible of the great loss this country has sustained in the death of its chieftain and ruler, and mourn with you in sorrow. Strangers as they are among you, they kindly appreciate the many kindnesses received at your hands and, again, beg with grateful hearts to thank you.

The memorial was signed by Ah Sing and Ah He in behalf of all the China Boys.

Who would have dreamed that the sentiments pronounced by Justice Nathaniel Bennett that day would raise the curtain on a half century of intolerance and lawlessness? He said: "Born and reared under different governments and speaking different tongues, we nevertheless meet here today as brothers… You stand among us in all respects as equals… Henceforth we have one country, one hope, one destiny."

From that day on the Chinese took great interest and pride in participating in public affairs. They marched in various celebrations such as that of Admission Day in 1850. An ex-Philadelphian described their delegation in the Washington's Birthday parade of 1852 as the city's most orderly and industrious citizens.

In the same year Governor John McDougal urged that land grants be given the Chinese, since they were among the most worthy of all California's newly adopted citizens. H. H. Haight offered a resolution of welcome to them which stated that California took pleasure in their presence in such great numbers. The *Alta California* confidently predicted that the China Boys would yet vote at the same polls, study in the same schools, and even bow at the same altar as the rest of the city's citizens. Hinton Helper, the writer who did not like the Chinese because of their aloofness, was disgusted with the way the China Boys were "petted," as he put it, by the fond—almost doting—populace.

Symptomatic were the petty annoyances which began to crop up in San -Franciscans in regard to the Chinese. They simply could not understand, for one thing, why the Orientals clung to their traditional loose blue cotton blouses and trousers. There began to appear a bit of exasperated editorializing on this ridiculous point of the pajamalike garb of the

Oriental. Soon artists like Charles Nahl were commissioned by the *Wide West* and other papers to draw John in the native dress which sophisticated San Franciscans found so ludicrous. People began to poke fun at John, and Bret Harte's *Plain Language From Truthful James,* usually called *The Heathen Chinee,* became a best-seller.

By the end of the '50s only a handful of Chinese had Americanized to any noticeable extent. Frank Marryat found a few who wore patent-leather shoes, who cut their hair short in Caucasian style, and who could ride like the very Californians themselves. The San Francisco press noticed that several equestrian Celestials were taking the air on the Plank Road on weekends, with their "houris" by their sides. Norman Ah Sing, the baker turned volunteer Chinese Consul, even affected a stovepipe hat. But it was more than a decade before Reverend A. W. Loomis really began to notice signs of Americanization. Chinese hats, shoes and trousers were replaced with the American article by many, and queues began to vanish slowly. (The last one in Chinatown was that of Quan Hoy, who wore it till he died in 1936.)

A far more dangerous straw in the wind than satire was the xenophobia exemplified by Governor John Bigler's 1854 address in which he called all Chinese "coolies" and urged the State Legislature to pass a law to prohibit further immigration. The press did not recognize Bigler for the political bellwether that he was. They criticized his anti-Chinese sentiments as uncalled for. But soon the popular *Wide West* swung over to the governor, turning into one of the most violent organs of denunciation. Wild broadsides of editorials likened the Orientals to the plague. For the first time, direct allusion was made to their bad effect on American labor. Since the *Wide West* was reporting the "present stagnation of business" in other columns, the scapegoatism of the Chinese is obvious. The *Wide West* posed as highly shockable too: "It is more than we can endure that their females should parade the streets with painted cheeks, disgusting every pure-minded observer." (And doubtless titillating the pioneers.)

In its editorial the once stable paper went so far as to blame the Chinese for the crowded and filthy conditions belowdecks on the coolie ship *Libertad,* rather than blaming the greedy owners. The paper later came partially to its senses when it learned that 180 Chinese had died on the

7

vessel, chiefly from ship fever or scurvy, since leaving the China Coast. But though outraged by the inhuman treatment of the *Libertad's* cargo, the *Wide West* could not bring itself to attack the greedy shipowners and businessmen who waxed fat on the coolie trade. They were potential advertisers. But the paper did let loose a blast at the tenement property owners of Dupont Street. The paper thought, mistakenly, that these land-lords were Chinese who were profiteering by jamming more and more coolies into the already overcrowded rookeries of Chinatown. Actually the Chinese leased their property in most cases, and from white owners.

As late as 1873, Chinese owned only 10 of the 153 major pieces of property in Chinatown. (Even in 1904 they owned only 25 of the 316 major parcels listed.) City Assessor Alexander Badlam found only about $500,000 in personal property held by Chinese in 1875, and between $150,000 and $200,000 in real property out of San Francisco's total of $300,000,000. He reported Chinatown rentals to be high, but found that the Chinese had shown little disposition to buy property though they had to pay large sums for leases. The reason of course was that most Chinese still considered themselves sojourners rather than permanent settlers. They were just waiting for their ship to come in—to take them back to Kwangtung.

As the '50s rolled on, more and more coolies flooded into port from Hong Kong via the fast clippers now specializing in their transport. It was estimated that more than 20,000 Chinese arrived in 1852 alone. But one in ten sailed home the very same year, and the statewide population of Chinese was probably no more than 25,000. The Chinese were still unrepresented by a consulate, although such tiny countries as Meck-lenburg-Schwerin had consuls in San Francisco. So in 1854, interpreter Norman Ah Sing began to represent the Flowery Kingdom, unofficially, in San Francisco. The uncredentialed spokesman for 25,000 Chinese set up an office on Sacramento Street between Kearny and Dupont.

With some 25,000 Chinese in California, it would have taken a mira-cle of the first magnitude for none of them to be inclined to loose living or crime. There was no miracle; there *was* crime and prostitution. A dis-enchanted San Francisco took a closer look at the quaint Quarter which had sprung up in its midst. The city recoiled in somewhat theatrical hor-ror. Why, there was overcrowding there, and a general lack of sanitation!

It was obvious that there was no lack of crime, and to the city's feigned shock it found the Quarter crawling with fallen women.

Thus, ironically, the advent of the Chinese prostitute brought about the end of the Sino-Chinese honeymoon in San Francisco.

# CHAPTER TWO

# THE HONEYMOON ENDS

*"I think there is a class of outlaws among
the Chinese population here who give us a
great deal of trouble. There are also a great
many good men who are made to suffer for
the doings of the evil. Among our people,
if John Brown does wrong, he suffers as an
individual; but if a Chinaman does wrong,
the whole race suffers for the act of the
individual."*

—Charles Wolcott Brooks, 1876

THERE WERE few Chinese women in San Francisco in the '50s and
practically none of the decent variety. One of the first to arrive from
the Orient was the notorious Madame Ah Toy. The editors of the *Annals of San Francisco* chorused: "The lewdness of fallen white females
is shocking enough to witness, but it is far exceeded by the disgusting
practices of these tawny-visaged creatures."

Ah Toy proved to be a remarkable madame. When a complaint was
lodged against her Clay Street house of ill fame as a public nuisance, she
somehow abated the nuisance, without changing her line of business, to
the satisfaction of Judge R. H. Waller of the Recorder's Court. In any
case, she was discharged by the court. She must have enjoyed her visit,
for she soon returned. This time as an un-shingled advocate. Ah Toy
represented the defendant in a case, a little woman charged with kicking
and mauling a corpulent Chinese whose name the newspapers made into
Jonathan Nissum. The fat man claimed that the female had abused him

grossly. The press chortled, "Much to the inconvenience of his ample corporation." Ah Toy pleaded that her friend had been forced to thrash the plaintiff for welching on debts of honor. Ah Toy lost this 1852 case. Her friend had to pay a $20 fine and hear the judge threaten her with a second helping if she dared to batter the gentleman again.

During the last month of 1854, Ah Toy and her colleagues suffered from a police crackdown on the red-light district. A number of women were convicted—under a Grand Jury indictment—of keeping disorderly houses. In March 1859, she was again hauled into court, protesting that she had been innocently working on a bowl of rice with her chopsticks when she was arrested. The object of this harassment of harlots was to remove them from the major streets of the city, as a nuisance. It is hardly necessary to add that the object was not realized. Not in 1854, 1864, 1874 or 1884.... Of course the white Cyprians who enjoyed good police and city hall connections were not disturbed in this cleanup drive on vice.

In the mid-'60s the Chinese brothels were shut down tight—briefly. But 1866 was a special case. Chief Martin Burke was going out of office, being succeeded by Patrick Crowley. Burke wanted to make a big impression as a final gesture, so he cleaned up the town momentarily; or at least Chinatown. The California *Police Gazette* at this time hoped loudly that the force itself would be reformed, too, under the new administration. Too many men who were drawing a salary of only $125 per month were flashing diamond rings and sporting gold-plated revolvers.

In the 1850s and 1860s the slave trade was not the big business it became in subsequent decades. It merely offered an excuse for the city to strike out at the irritant which was Chinatown. To the city emerging from an era of good feeling, the trade in Chinese wantons was a source of annoyance but hardly an economic foundation for the terrorization of the Quarter by armed bands of killers. The handwriting was clear but it was in the hieroglyphs of old China, and city hall could not figure them out.

An overwhelming percentage of all Chinatown arrests between 1850 and 1870 were of harlots. In the fiscal year 1865-1866, for example, some 91 Chinese prostitutes were actually imprisoned in the county jail. Many more got off with fines or forfeiture of bail for the age-old misde-

11

meanor of "tapping at their windows"—that is, soliciting.

The cleanup of prostitutes was usually a perfunctory and meaningless gesture. The California Police Gazette, which enjoyed sensational cases while attempting to preserve an expression of outraged decency, said that the hounding of the girls of Chinatown was: "The usual offense, the usual bail and the usual result, bail forfeited. It is a pity officers could not find better employment than persecuting these poor Chinese slaves. Do they not know that these poor serfs were obliged to do as they do?" Even more fruitless was the arrest of customers, but this was done half-heartedly for a time, starting with the case of Antonio Juan Baptiste who was fined $20 for visiting the Pike Street establishments.

The city could hardly clamp down on Chinatown's prostitutes without brushing up against crime in general. There was plenty of criminal activity there, but no gang or tong wars. When there were instances of assault or murder—the latter extremely rare—it was usually a case of *cherchez la femme.*

But there were relatively few crimes of violence such as rape, assault, murder or even armed robbery in these early years of Chinatown's history. In comparison with the city which surrounded it, Chinatown was practically a haven of peace. (Frisco itself, on the other hand, was described in these terms: "Cases of political corruption, or party jobbing, or personal scandal, of ruin by debauching and gambling, by duelling and suicide, of squatter violence, or robbery and burglary, or assault and murder—these are nearly as plentiful as blackberries.")

Most so-called crime in Chinatown was ludicrous. The majority of arrests were for petty larceny—stealing bread, pipe, chickens, boots or scrap iron. Following this in number of arrests were cases of burglary and the carrying of concealed weapons. As late as the 1880s, when hatchet men were prowling the alleys, a great percentage of arrests of Chinese were for such atrocities as running liquor stores without licenses, peddling unstamped cigars, or fencing stolen hardware in Waverly Place's hock shops.

The real crime which existed in Chinatown generally fell into four categories: lotteries and gambling, no crime at all to many people; opium smoking, the Chinese equivalent of alcoholism; prostitution, again a social phenomenon not essentially criminal; and petty thieving. What we might call hard-core crime was difficult to find in the early decades. Chinatown was then, as it is now, a relatively law-abiding area of San Francisco.

There are no brothels or opium dens in Chinatown today; thieving is minimal; lotteries, if any, are discreet. There are a few confidence men, of course, but only gambling remains as a major "evil," with poker, *pai gow,* or Thirteen Cards having replaced the classic *tan,* or fan-tan. It is difficult to convince many blond Anglo-Saxon, church-going Caucasians—who join their Chinese neighbors on flights or bus trips to Reno's gaming tables, like commuters—that Chinatown is, by reason of gambling, still a den of iniquity. Arrests are still made of those who prefer a game chancier than placid mah-jongg, but the officers who pull off such raids are apt to be labeled "spoilsport police inspectors" by the press.

What makes the small number of American-Chinese arrests today even more remarkable is that these-people have acclimatized, or Americanized, with such a vengeance in the last quarter century that one would expect them to be more like the typical gringo Californian—used to an occasional brush with John Law. For California is still fairly lawless territory. Of every 100,000 persons in the state, there are 137 in prison today. This compares with 70 per 100,000 in Wisconsin and a mere 20 per 100,000 in granitic New Hampshire.

A hundred and more years ago California was far wilder than it is now. The city of San Francisco, alas, had no Hogarth to depict its innumerable gin lanes, but even wicked London could not boast a Shark Alley and a Murderer's Alley as Frisco eventually did. The time was not yet ripe, however, for Chinatown's blood bath.

The historian Herbert Howe Bancroft called the thirty years of the city's history from 1847 to 1877 "the Augustan Age of Murder." But he was not referring to Chinatown, where the strange inversion of criminality prevailed. The exact number of homicides committed during this period will never be known, but the Sacramento *Union,* in applauding the actions of the second San Francisco vigilance committee, stated that there were 1,400 murders in the six years 1850-1856. On the other hand, Bancroft recorded that in the thirty years following 1847 there were only 16 legal executions and 8 extra-legal (Vigilante) hangings in San Francisco. Among the two dozen criminals who had the rare honor of actually suffering capital punishment for their crimes—for not having friends in high places—there were two Chinese. Chong Wong was executed in 1866 for the murder of his mistress, and another murderer, Chin Mook Sow, was hanged in 1877.

The first vigilance committee took up only one Chinese case. On a complaint of Ah Sing and Lip Scorn, the Vigilantes deported Ah Low and Ah Hone and their property—two prostitutes—because of their supposed evil influence on the Chinese community. Charges were soon preferred against Sun Co and Ah Oeh by other Chinese as word got around of this convenient extradition service. The committee of vigilance quickly realized that it was being victimized by a conspiracy. Refusing to be used by one faction in Chinatown against another, it washed its hands of any Chinatown affairs.

According to Bancroft, no class of people benefited more from the activities of the vigilance committee than the "Guests of the Golden Mountains." The bullies who were accustomed to maltreat the Chinese were forced to lie low or leave. The Chinese merchants were so grateful to the 1856 committee for the change in social climate brought about by the crackdown on the lawless crowd that they subscribed $1,000 to the vigilance committee fund. As a testimonial of their appreciation, the committee rendered the Chinese a formal vote of thanks for their contribution.

For years well-meaning citizens and the press had deplored the outrages perpetrated upon arriving coolies by water-front hoodlums. Finally on the evening of July 17, 1869, a Vigilante-like group was formed by a large body of citizens meeting in a Fourth District courtroom. Their express purpose was to create a society for the prevention of abuse of Chinese. The society elected officers and pledged that a party of men would be on the Embarcadero for the arrival of the next steamer bearing coolies. It set up its own six-man police force and made public its constitution. The preamble of this document proposed the protection of the Chinese, since the municipal authorities were unable to halt the hoodlums' attacks, which the society termed a disgrace to American free institutions, to civilization and to Christianity.

Unimpressed by the good intentions of the group, the California *Police Gazette* lampooned it as a society for the prevention of cruelty to Chinese. Then the newspaper's editor sarcastically begged for the creation of similar societies to protect the Irish, the Germans and the Americans. Though most of the roughnecks who picked on the Chinese were Irish and thus Catholics, the leader of the Chinese Protective Society was the very prominent (French Canadian) Roman Catholic printer, Edward Bosqui. The organization operated about a year, spending some $6,000, but the Chinese had little faith in it and gave it only $600. It was soon dissolved.

A good index of the degree of bigotry in a city is the record of punishment of minority-group criminals. The evidence suggests that there was little or no racial bias, as distinguished from overt hostility, in San Francisco's early years. In the main, Chinese evildoers were treated to the same brand of quick frontier justice in the '50s as any other group. The one exception to this rule was when San Francisco's first chief of police, James Curtis, tried to humiliate Chinese criminals as well as to punish them. For a brief period Curtis not only sent them to the chain gang, like whites and Negroes, but also cut off their queues. The first three trophies of war—the pigtails of Ah Sing, Ah Bing, and Ah You—Curtis hung on the railings which decorated the city hall; after the old Spanish custom of mounting the heads of malefactors on pikes on city or castle walls. Curtis said of the swaying queues, "They are a warning to all Celestial evildoers."

Judge Lynch was in the chair during the 1850s, but the Chinese outlaws of California were treated no better and no worse than their brothers of the Coast whose skins were a different color. In San Francisco, lynchings were few and none of the victims was Chinese.

Although they were treated quite fairly by even the drumhead courts of the lynchers, there was already a growing bias against the Chinese. Bancroft revealed it when he expressed a low opinion of the first immigrants from China, saying that while there were good Chinamen and bad Chinamen they were mostly of the latter category and highly skilled in robbing sluice boxes, to boot. The common punishment for these Chinese claim jumpers, incidentally, was nothing so drastic as a lynching bee. True, a rope was used on them but it was only laid on their backs to the tune of fifty lashes. Their queues were sometimes amputated too.

A good way to size up the class of citizenship enjoyed by a minority group is to examine the swiftness and surety of punishment visited upon those who prey on them. The Negroes in the South over the last hundred years, for example, simply have not received the "separate but equal" amount of justice and protection given the whites. In San Francisco and the West of a century ago the situation vis-a-vis the Chinese was better. It was less good in the mining camps than in the cities. In the Mother Lode entire Chinese communities were sometimes forced by mob pressure to pack up and move out. Usually violence was not employed, but the threat of violence was always there.

When a so-called Celestial was the victim of a criminal attack, however, the forces of law and order—both legal and extra legal—extended their protection to him. In this respect the Chinese were more fortunate than the California Indians and about as well off as the Sonorans and native (Mexican) Californios. Even San Francisco's Asian harlots had rights. When John Badger struck and knocked down a *chinoise* daughter of joy, he was arrested and convicted of assault and battery. He got off no more easily than Ah Choy, the madame with the penchant for beating up her girls. She was convicted in July, 1859; Badger in September. And observe the other side of the coin. In May of that year Ah Chong was arrested for assault and battery after kicking a white youth. He was quickly discharged, however, when it was shown that he had been assaulted by the young hoodlum and had only retaliated in kind.

Chinese in the mines were definitely second-class "citizens," but they were regarded as human beings, not as animals or slaves as was sometimes the case with Negroes even in the West. Thus, when in 1851 a Mexican murdered a Chinese in Drytown he was lynched (clumsily, with a log chain) on the handiest tree. When a Frenchman named Raymond murdered a Chinese at Big Bar on the Consumnes River in 1852, he was tried by a jury of twelve white men and hanged for his crime. Mickey Free, one of the Sydney Ducks who plagued San Francisco until driven out by the first vigilance organization, met his end at Coloma for robbing and murdering thirteen Chinese, among numerous other crimes.

Arrests were not always the same as convictions. There were a number of men who preyed on the Chinese and escaped with the practically nonexistent penalties. The most shocking example of a breakdown in justice, in regard to Chinese in California, occurred in 1871. A mob mur-

16

dered twenty-one Chinese in Los Angeles. Thirty-seven of the mob were indicted by the Grand Jury but many got off with sentences as light as 6 years, and even 2 years, of imprisonment. The reason for the paucity of convictions as compared to the plenitude of arrests of those abusing the Chinese was mainly political, as might be expected. Governor Frederick F. Low spelled it out himself in an interview he gave historian Bancroft: "You cannot get a police court here to convict a hoodlum for beating a Chinaman today, before an elected judicial, because the hoodlum and his friends will have the vote and the Chinaman has not, and cannot."

Though Bancroft was no close friend of the Chinese in California, he did denounce vigorously the outrages committed upon them. Rightly, he placed the largest share of the blame on foreigners and mainly on the Irish immigrants. These were the very people who only a few years earlier had been persecuted themselves by the Know Nothings and others. It was the same old story; instead of the two bottom layers of society working together to better their common fortune, the next-to-the bottom class turned on the lowest group and visited upon it the most vicious kind of bigotry. Bancroft, however, was probably guilty of snobbery when he asserted that he had yet to find one instance when attacks on the Chinese were not roundly condemned by all of the "decent" people of the community.

Where Bancroft saw most of the early Asiatic immigrants as sluice robbers, Albert Deane Richardson, the popular New England essayist, leaned far overboard in the opposite direction. He had nothing but praise for them as law-abiding citizens. Richardson knew that their treatment in California had offered them unusual provocation to crime. He saw that the law which forbade their testifying against white men in court had aggravated the great disadvantage at which their ignorance of English placed them. The New England writer claimed that some of the Chinese confined in California jails were wholly innocent of the offenses for which they had been sentenced. Richardson called attention to the fact that notwithstanding all the provocations offered them, the public records of the state showed that the percentage of Chinese convicted of crimes was much lower than that of other foreigners. In fact, he said, it was only a bit higher than that of the native-born population.

The percentage of criminals which the Chinese managed to muster varied widely, and wildly, from orator to orator depending on his point of view and school of statistics. A California State Senator begged to differ with Richardson, claiming that as high as 17 percent of all criminals in California were Chinese. But he ruined his bombshell by also padding the total Oriental population in order to make the immigrants appear to be more of a menace to red-blooded American labor than they actually were. The legislator claimed that they constituted 25 percent of the entire population. Charles Aull, turnkey at San Quentin Prison, brought out a formal report in 1876 which somewhat weakened the Senator's stand, but which did not substantiate Richardson's claim. Aull found that of 1,145 convicts in the penitentiary, 198 were Chinese.

Richardson was particularly shocked by San Francisco's unwillingness to accept the testimony of an Asian in court. He learned that a ruffian could shoot down a Chinese in cold blood before a thousand others, and if no white man witnessed the deed the murderer would go scot free. He thought this double standard of justice in California was a burning shame, especially since it took place in a state which he felt was characterized by a love of justice and fair play. He was right, of course. Not only did it foster a climate kindly to criminals, but it also drove the decent people of Chinatown still further away from what should have been their natural hope and refuge—the American system of courts.

The lack of crimes of violence in Chinatown during these early decades lulled the police into inaction. They soon developed a casual attitude toward the minority clustered around Dupont Street, contenting themselves with an occasional descent on the bordellos of the district. In some respects this hands-off policy is to the credit of the city. Despite hard feelings between the two communities, there was never a pogrom—not even in the critical year of 1877. Chinatown was a ghetto but it was not a walled ghetto of people brutalized by the police. (The only actions remotely resembling police-state methods occurred in the early nineties with the tong raids of Lieutenant Price and others of the Chinatown squad in which tong headquarters were deliberately destroyed.) The damaging effect of this attitude of the police was that it allowed the city within the city to substitute extralegal institutions for the normal American agencies of law, order and justice. This paved the way for the rise of the tongs. One clan or company pressured another, rather than resorting to the legal arbitration of a controversy. These customs hardened into a system of face-saving exaction of revenge. When the pacifying hand of the Six Companies became palsied after the Geary Act loss of face, the system got completely out of hand, was taken over by the criminal element, and resulted in the series of tong wars which appalled America.

Bancroft, writing in the 1870s, did not yet identify the problem as tong rivalry and conflicts but he did point out that as a rule the Chinese were able to manage their own trials and punishments, administering justice among themselves even to the execution of offenders. He also remarked on their ability to keep their proceedings covered from the eyes of the law. This statement of the historian added up to a tacit approval of the brutal and unjust system arising in Chinatown. It paralleled the sentiment in city hall and among the public at large. Neither Bancroft nor any of his fellow San Franciscans could foresee the horrible consequences. The city was pleased with the apparent lack of crimes of violence in the squalid, crowded Quarter. The Hall of Justice and city hall were willing to go along with the sunny optimism of Reverend Otis Gibson who proudly proclaimed, "The Chinese excite less riots and commit fewer assaults and murders than almost any other foreign element among us. There is a class of bad Chinaman who do such things, but in far less proportion than is done by their labor competitors from Europe."

Despite Gibson's whitewashing, the plain truth is that Chinatown was not entirely unacquainted with crime before the rise of the tongs. Chinatown had criminals from the very beginning. There were a number of bribery cases, for example, in the Recorder's Court by the fall of 1854. There were so many, in fact, that Charles Carvalho had to be appointed to the court as Chinese interpreter to take care of John's running afoul of the law. Bribery cases continued over the years, a major one being the attempt of Ah Quoy to "buy" Special Officer Benjamin S. Lynes in 1866. Some of the Chinese bunco artists were quite skilled in their trade too. There were those who cut up the cuttlefish in their shrimp nets to sell them to gullible Frenchmen as California frogs' legs. Fishermen also operated cookie cutters on the wings of skates and sting rays, stamping out pseudo-scallops for the market place. But these were more instances of sharp business practice than out-and-out criminality. (After all, Caucasians often have revered far bigger scoundrels, including stockjobbers, land-fraud tricksters, robber barons and railroad swindlers as proud pioneers of the West.) A favorite Chinese trick was deteriorating or sweating coins. They would pass gold pieces which they had worn or shaved down to a slightly smaller circumference than when minted. (The edges were not yet milled to prevent this practice.) The Chinese would keep the flakes of gold they peeled off in pokes, just like gold-dust. In 1859, Chinatown was flooded with spurious Mexican dollars—bogus varieties of the medium of exchange in the Far East. These particular "dollars Mex" were dated 1854 and made in China. They had never seen a mint in either Manila or Mexico City. In July, 1870, two Chinese were arrested for counterfeiting bills of the Bank of India.

Yet even with the padding of the statistics on Chinese criminality by arrests of amateur counterfeiters and bunco steerers—and for such trivial offenses as violation of the Cubic Air Ordinance (sleeping too many in a room), or for peddling without a license, the Chinese as a group managed to stay out of trouble in quite remarkable fashion. In 1876 the New York *World* commented on the fact that California's prison statistics showed the average of crime among Chinese to be lower than for any other segment of the population. Very few indeed were hardened and vicious criminals like the murderer-rapist-thief, Ah Fook, finally arrested in 1866 after a long career of crime; or the treacherous servants, Ah Say and Ah Sam, who bungled the murder of Mrs. Saufley in Oakland. These latter two were about the only Chinese with heinous enough crimes on their hands to rate a rogue's-gallery woodcut portrait in the California *Police Gazette*. Chinatown, in the 1850s and '60s, got little newspaper space, much less a real headline in the scandal-mongering Gazette. Yet in the 1890s the sector would do a *volte-face* and secure a seeming monopoly on murder.

The patient and long-suffering Chinese, both on the raw mining frontier and in cosmopolitan San Francisco, rarely resorted to violence in the '50s and '60s. They seldom even defended themselves when attacked. Hence the frequency with which they were abused by cowardly hoodlums. An exception was made to the rule in 1855, when a party of three ruffians near Greasertown, south of San Francisco, asked a Chinese for some water. While he was obliging them one of the men, William Link, drew a pistol and fired at him. The ball struck John in the wrist but he instantly drew a revolver and shot Link dead. The rest of the gang fled. The Chinaman was arrested but after an examination of the case was acquitted. Normally, however, this handiness with firearms was restricted to the criminal class in Chinatown. For the most part the law-abiding Chinese preferred to put up with the indignities and even physical attacks of hoodlums with a stoicism and pacifism which was much remarked upon. It was not until 1874, for example, that another such story broke in the newspapers. In that year a Celestial beat off four roughnecks, singlehanded, to the delight of the San Francisco press. But basically John was a peaceable man. This made all the more unexpected and horrible the senseless butchery which would take place within a few decades. No one, certainly not the police, could guess that in a few years the cobbles of Chinatown's alleys would be slick with the blood of the innocent as well as of the guilty.

Until about 1880, there was no special name for Chinese criminals. The terms highbinder and hatchet man came late. While giving testimony during the 1870s in regard to evildoing in Chinatown, Special Officer Delos Woodruff answered a question from the bench by saying, "A lot of highbinders came to the place—" The judge interrupted him with a gesture of his hand. "What do you mean by 'highbinders?'" His honor queried. "Why," replied Woodruff, "a lot of Chinese hoodlums." The judge persisted, "And that's the term you apply to Chinese hoodlums, is it?" "That's what I call them," responded Woodruff.

From that time on, Chinese murderers, pimps, blackmailers, gunmen, professional gamblers and toughs of all kinds in San Francisco began to be known as highbinders. It was not necessary that they be tong men, though most of them were. When they took to assassinations with hatchets and cleavers the other term, hatchet man, was born. The word highbinder had apparently been used to signify a member of the Irish *banditti* as early as 1806. It was used in New York and Boston as a synonym for hoodlum and was probably extended to Chinese bad men by New York police. As late as 1876, the word tong itself had little usage. Reverend Otis Gibson, testifying that year before the Chinese Immigration Committee of the California Senate, stated that the Hip Yee tong controlled

7

the brothels of Chinatown. He carefully distinguished the organization from all of the Six Companies by describing a tong as more like a labor union, such as the washerman's guild. Policeman Alfred Clark also explained the term to the State Senators, insisting that the Six Companies had nothing to do with the slave-girl trade. He reported that it was under the control of the Hip Yee tong. Later Gibson changed his mind and attributed proprietorship of Chinatown's gambling dens to the Hip Yee tong and the whorehouses to the Po Sang tong. In any case, the public was exposed to the term tong, a word which would one day chill every citizen's spine. Also, the testimony of Gibson and Clark demonstrated that Americans were still confused over the role of the Six Companies.

Crime in Chinatown, as the years wore on toward the tong-war decades, remained an individualistic matter except for the tong combines which ran the gambling houses and red-light district. In his 1859 annual report the chief of police asked the Board of Supervisors to appoint a special committee to investigate the evils of Chinese prostitution. But he said nothing about organized gang warfare in the Quarter.

Yet even as early as 1854, ominous portents of the protection racket of future tong troubles were being heard. The editors of the *Annals of San Francisco* noted that whereas the Chinese were generally peaceable and contented folk who seldom troubled the authorities, there were a few secret societies among them which grossly oppressed their brethren. 'The police have attempted to interfere," said the *Annals,* "and to protect the injured, though seldom with much effect. The terror of these, lest vengeance should somehow befall them from their persecutors, has generally prevented full disclosures of the unlawful practices of the secret societies."

The *Wide West* also sniffed something rotten in Chinatown: "Those among them who have the opportunity are continually levying taxes for some inexplicable purpose on those of their countrymen who are able to pay them and afraid to refuse. The only reason they themselves are ever known to give for the various disturbances that arise among them is the existence of a secret society of which no member ever was seen, or known to exist, by any of the received rules of evidence."

On October 6, 1854, police hurried to the hotel kept on Dupont Street by Ah Kuang. There they quickly quelled a disturbance, arresting a number of Chinese who were attempting to extort a fine for the benefit of the Triad Society. Here was the secret society whose existence the *Wide West* doubted. The police were still in the dark as to the evil they were trying to combat. They did not know that the seeds of future tong wars were already sown in such actions as the riots at Ah Kuang's hotel.

Although it is commonly said there were never any tongs in China itself, only in America or other outposts of the Chinese, this is mainly a pointless quibble over semantics. Kenneth Scott Latourette estimated twenty-five years ago that fully one half of the adult male Chinese population belonged to one or another secret society. The San Ho Hui, or Triad Society, alias the Hung Society and the Society of Heaven and Earth, was a secret organization of real power in China. It was primarily a revolutionary political movement formed to oppose the Manchus. But it was destined to do more than just play a role in mainland disturbances such as the Taiping Rebellion of 1850-1864. It fathered all of the fighting tongs of San Francisco. This progeny differed in that their announced reasons for existence were as benevolent or legal-aid societies rather than as political parties or revolutionary clubs. But in action they were almost identical; they were secret pressure groups not at all unwilling to stain their hands with blood to reach their goals.

Five months after the Triad Society raid, on the last day of March 1855, the Grand Jury of San Francisco (unwittingly) took another anti-tong measure by indicting Charlie Ah You for assembling parties of armed men for the purpose of disturbing the peace. But things then quieted down and the coals of the tong wars smoldered on for another seven years.

In the summer of 1862, a leak developed in the wall of silence and secrecy which surrounded the fighting tongs, growing in strength every year. The police were asleep, lulled by the stereotype of the docile Chinese. Had they read one of the valley newspapers they might have learned something of what was going on beneath their very noses in Chinatown. On one of those typically mot, blistering days of summer in the Central Valley a typesetter laboriously composed an announcement which had been paid for and sent up from San Francisco. He cursed as, fumbling to spell correctly the unfamiliar "heathen" names listed at the end of his sweat-stained sheet of copy, he composed the piece.

*Richard H. Dillon*

When the Sacramento *Union* hit J Street, the Capital's main thoroughfare, it carried the item buried back among the advertisements for Japanese salve, corner saloons and Sitka ice. It read [there were not yet six companies in the union]:

FROM THE PRESIDENT DIRECTORS OF THE FIVE CHINESE COMPANIES OF CALIFORNIA

The deceased, Yu Kow, was a See Yup man. He was connected with a bad gang. Speaking the English language well, he chose for his victims those of his countrymen who were ignorant of the foreign tongue. These he oppressed. He made fish meat of them. Innumerable were his dark deeds, injurious to life and property, sometimes committed in clear, shining day, often by stealth at night. Placed as the leader of a large gang [tong], he intimidated his victims, who were afraid to accuse him before the courts. And if ever accused, the gold and illicit gain of his villains were placed at his disposal, thereby enabling him to employ eminent counsel to escape the punishment of the law.

Verily, he was a wicked man!

It was our intention united to have accused him, for crimes committed, before the tribunals of justice and by getting him punished, save our countrymen from receiving further injuries at his hands. But who can fathom the excellent principles of Heaven! The evil leader fell, assassinated. This was indeed a great happiness for his countrymen. But his followers, animated with bad hearts, are striving now to cause innocence and excellence to suffer. They wish to confound virtue with crime. They arrested Chu Pak, charging him falsely with having aided in the murder of Yu Kow. They charge that he wrote a letter and sent money to Wong Yuen to accomplish the deed.

How easily they could have forged one and submitted it to the presiding officer of justice for scrutiny! But for what ends? They know full well that it would be impossible for the American judge to detect the written Chinese characters. The Chinese alone are able to distinguish the different handwritings of their

24

countrymen. They, therefore, well knowing this fact, forged a letter with no other purpose than evil and to lead justice astray. Such are the false schemes, the black plots, of this wicked gang.

But we, the Head Directors, are well acquainted with the defendant, Chu Pak. He is considered amongst the men of the Four Districts [See Yup) as the most upright For the long period of six years he presided as Chief Director, Master and Trustee of the Company, and his conduct throughout has been pure and excellent. His great virtues are known to all and farspread. During his term of Directorship, he had occasion severely to correct and reprimand Yu Kow for his evil deeds. For this, Yu Kow never forgave him but harbored in his heart a spirit of revenge and hate. All of a sudden, Yu Kow was murdered and his followers, because he fell, preferred false charges against Chu Pak. This is perjury and oppression. Behold the facts!

But we, the Head Directors, bowing our heads down, place our hope in the clear discrimination of the officials of justice, trusting that after a strict investigation, they will save the innocent from receiving wrong, thereby defeating deceitful plots to the great happiness of our merchants and people.

Wherefore we, the Head Directors of the Five great Chinese Companies of the State of California, deeming it our duty to expose wrong and evil schemes, do now publish these facts, submitting them to your high intelligence and praying you to pass a righteous judgment in the perusal of the same.


The ultimate fate of Chu Pak is not known today but the "black plots of this wicked gang" continued long after the Five Companies alerted their clansmen in Sacramento. The tong machinations continued and eventually seized control of the Chinese Quarter.

But long before the tong evil itself—the heart of the matter—became apparent to police and public, the curse of opium caught the eye of the authorities. They did not realize that it was, with gambling and prostitution, an economic foundation for the fighting tongs quietly building their strength underground. But the evil of opium which police and Federal authorities exposed in the '60s and later, was in itself enough to shock the entire community and attract the attention of Washington.

# CHAPTER THREE

# PIPES OF PEACE

*"Just as drunkenness is the curse and
bane of American society, just so opium
smoking is the curse and bane of the Chinese
people. Just as depraved, unprincipled white
men will open groggeries and drinking
saloons, in order to enrich themselves by
the certain ruin of their neighbors, just so
depraved, unprincipled Chinamen in order
to enrich themselves will open dens for
the certain ruin of their neighbors by the
consumption of opium."*

—Reverend Otis Gibson, 1876

IN ALL THE furor over coolies flooding the city from the wharves of
the Embarcadero, few San Franciscans in 1861 even noticed the arrival
of the clipper *Ocean Pearl* from Hong Kong. She bore no troublesome
coolies. All she carried was a cargo of rice and tea—and fifty-two boxes
of opium. These turned out to be Pandora's boxes for San Francisco.

The '60s saw the rise of the opium-den evil while the slave-girl traffic continued to mount toward a high point in the last two decades of the
century. But aside from these problems, the Civil War decade proved to
be a more or less peaceful period in Chinatown and something of an Indian summer to the era of good feeling of the 1850s. It was fortunate that
this was so. In 1861, the San Francisco police force was greatly under-
staffed. It totaled a mere 30 men. Only 7 men could be detailed to patrol
duty at a time, and 2 of these were kept busy guarding the wharves of the

Embarcadero. That left but 5 policemen—"Fearless Charlies" in the argot of the times—to protect a city of 80,000 souls. While hoodlums were amusing themselves by lassoing newly arrived coolies as they came up the streets from the docks, the San Francisco press was lamenting that "No civilized city on the globe ever had such meager protection, and yet, thanks to the vigilance of our policemen, no city was ever so orderly as San Francisco this day, even though a large proportion of it consists of the worst materials which ever composed a community."

The pressure of the press on the Board of Supervisors brought results, and the force's strength was increased from 30 men to 40. But the population rose too rapidly for the force to catch up. In 1863, Chief Martin Burke had only 56 regulars and 37 undependable specials. With this small band he tried to keep order in a city of 83,000 to 103,000 population, including drifters from the Seven Seas, shanghaiers on the Embarcadero, and ex-Bowery blacklegs on the Barbary Coast. It was a blessing the tong wars did not erupt in 1863. As it was, the first real anti-Chinese riot occurred that year on August 4. A party of Chinese employed by a contractor to grade a lot near the sugar refinery were driven off the job by a group of Irish laborers. It was not serious but it was symptomatic of things to come.

In the East, 1864 was the year of the fall of Atlanta. But in San Francisco it was the Year of Opium. The importation and smuggling of the drug into San Francisco became not only a plague but very big business. On January 16, a large lot was brought in on the ship *Derby*. It was seized by the authorities. On April 22, another shipment arrived and it, too, was captured as attempts were being made to smuggle it ashore from the bark *Pallas*. On June 19, revenue officers seized a large consignment of the drug hidden in eggs.

Reporters of the sensational daily press sank their teeth into the opium story quickly. The degradation of the opium dens was soon as good for a story in San Francisco as a shipwreck on Point Reyes. There is no doubt they were a sickening social institution. Estimates of the percentage of the Chinese population of the city who used opium ranged from 16 percent to 40 percent, with sots, or far-gone addicts estimated to range from 10 percent to 20 percent. But there is good reason to believe that many opium denizens adhered to the habit with no more insane passion or ill effects than the John Doe who clung to his bottle. Whatever the physiological case against opium smoking, it *did* bring in big money. And it thereby attracted and bred criminals and crime. One might almost say of opium that its side effects were the more deadly. With gambling halls and brothels, opium dens supported the fraternity of brigands who plagued the Chinese Quarter for years.

The correspondent of London's *Cornhill* magazine who signed himself "Day," visited California in the '80s and wrote that he never saw a street fight or other disturbance in some thirty trips to Chinatown, but he noted many opium dens operating openly in spite of the law prohibiting the sale of the drug for smoking. He observed wryly, "Occasionally, when the police are short of funds, they make a descent on some of the dens but, as a rule, the proprietors are left unmolested."

Almost everyone who was literate at all appears to have left behind him a description of the typical San Francisco opium den. Reverend Frederic J. Masters wrote: "The air is sultry and oppressive. A stupefying smoke fills the hovel through the gloom of which the feeble yellow light of three or four opium lamps struggles hopelessly to penetrate. There are two or three wooden beds covered with matting and each is furnished with lamp and pipe. Three Chinamen lie curled up on the beds, one taking his first puffs, the others in different stages of stupefaction. The room is about fifteen feet by ten feet, ceiling and walls black with years of smoke. We have been in this den about five minutes and no one has spoken a word. It is like being in a sepulchre with the dead."

New York Police Chief George W. Walling's description of the effects of opium read: "Reveries, dreams and stupefaction do not come with one pipe. Again and again the smoker cooks his lump of opium, packs it into the bowl and lazily watches the smoke curl up around the lamp. After awhile the pipe drops from his nerveless hand and there is a glaze on his eyes which are half-shut like a dead man's. His head falls upon his breast and he is in that opium trance which is either paradise or hell according to the degree of his indulgence in the narcotic."

Trust Mark Twain to describe the sot and his pipe both colorfully and succinctly. He wrote: "Opium smoking is a comfortless operation and it requires constant attention. A lamp sits on the bed, the length of the long pipe stem from the smoker's mouth. He puts a pellet of opium on the end of a wire, sets it on fire and plasters it into the pipe much as a Christian would fill a hole with putty. Then he applies the bowl to the lamp and proceeds to smoke—and the stewing and frying of the drug and the gurgling of the juices in the stem would well-nigh turn the stomach of a statue.... "

Evidence of the importance of the opium trade in the Pacific are the two wars forced upon China by John Bull to keep the trade booming. A whole fleet of swift vessels came to be called opium clippers—lean rivals of the tea clippers and Gold Rush clippers. San Francisco was their major American port of call. It became a market almost entirely for the prepared product but a little crude opium came in from time to time, to be refined (boiled) in Chinatown for local consumption.

Frisco bought only the finest opium—the Patna variety from India. With only 6 or 7 percent morphia, it was superior to the acrid-tasting Persian or Turkish opium whose 10 percent of the alkaloid induced headaches and skin rashes in its consumers. The opium was prepared by the Fook Hung Company in Hong Kong, a well-to-do firm which paid the Colonial Government $200,000 to $300,000 per annum just for the privilege of doing business. The refined smoking opium—a dark fluid of the appearance and consistency of molasses—was put up in five tael tins which sold in San Francisco for $8 each.

The Burlingame Treaty of 1868 between the United States and China held that no Chinese resident of the United States or American resident of China might import opium. But nothing was said of the keeping of opium dens. It was not until the 1880s and 1890s that strong legislation began to be applied to the problem. Earlier, an honest and efficient Customs officer lost his job and nearly his life when his efforts to expose the enormity of the racket led him too far down the trail. Like many other crooked big businesses of the nineteenth century, its ramifications extended far beyond the confines of Chinatown. By a section of the State Penal Code, denkeepers eventually were made guilty of a misdemeanor punishable by a $500 fine and 6 months in jail. A few keepers, and even customers, were locked up in the 80s, as a result. Since San Francisco was the American capital of opium debauchery, the city's Board of Supervisors also joined the attack. Their 1890 ordinance made even visiting an opium den an act punishable by a fine of from $250 to $1,000 and a jail term of 3 to 6 months, or both. By 1892, white visitors to opium dens were being given jail terms of 3 months and no option of a fine. Reverend Masters, however, reported fewer and fewer Caucasians as denizens of opium joints as the century wore on. Opium like the tong wars, was a Chinese problem. It attracted Caucasians briefly for what later would be called "kicks," but as a sociological or health problem it never amounted to much except for the Chinese. It was a problem which the Chinese community solved with surprising ease and dispatch. Opium was never a big problem after the 1906 earthquake and fire.

But none of the legislative maneuvers stamped out opium. Prior to 1887, the opium provision of the Burlingame Treaty was not even enforced. An immense quantity of the drug was shipped through the Golden Gate to the wharves of the Embarcadero. In late 1886, agents suddenly swooped down on a $750,000 shipment and seized it. During the following February, Congress passed an act to prohibit the importation of opium by Chinese. Surely this was one of the most healthy of the various acts promulgated to harass the Oriental minority. What this actually meant was that Chinatown's needs would have to be met in the future by smuggling and by white firms fronting for Chinese customers. These companies placed large orders for the drug, supposedly for medicinal purposes.

The Deputy Collector of Customs estimated that between 1884 and 1892, a total of 477,550 pounds of prepared opium entered San Francisco. Despite the efforts of hard-working Customs men, half of all the opium imported entered the Golden Gate illegally. Factories in Chinatown where the crude opium was refined were raided. Smugglers were apprehended. The Government increased duties from $6 to $10 a pound on the prepared product. The result was failure. From an average of 60,000 pounds per year, the illicit traffic increased to 100,000 pounds a year by 1888. The Government struck at the trade again in 1892 by placing a $12-a-pound duty on the drug to literally price it out of existence except for legitimate medicinal purposes. But the situation showed no signs of improvement. In fact it grew worse.

The Grand Jury horrified the decent population by reporting that "white girls between the ages of thirteen and twenty are enticed into these opium dens, become regular habitués, and finally are subject whol-

31

ly to the wishes of the Oriental visitors."

An anonymous police captain confirmed the Grand Jury's report and said darkly, "It is only we detectives who know the extent to which the opium habit has caught on amongst high-toned women in San Francisco. And the trouble is that the high-spirited and most adventurous women seem to succumb first."

The attacks on the traffic continued. Late in 1896, a $200,000 shipment arrived on a steamer for H. R. Davidson, an accountant of the Bank of British Columbia. Two new Custom agents, completely unknown to Bay area narcotics smugglers, were sent for. They were Caleb West of Washington and Leslie Cullin of Oregon. The two men discovered not only the supplier, Rosano & Company, but tailed the shipment and found its true destination to be the firm of Kwong Fong Tai. The Collector of the Port, John H. Wise, then stepped in and ordered all opium in port—from $300,000 to $400,000 worth of it—into bonded warehouses. Even with the ubiquitous smugglers working around the clock, the price of the poppy-seed paste doubled in San Francisco.

The San Francisco *Call,* about this time, estimated the number of opium rooms in the city to be 300. Most were in Chinatown, bearing red signs over their doors reading in Chinese calligraphy PIPES AND LAMPS ALWAYS CONVENIENT, or similar phrases. But some were in other sections of the city. They served some 3,000 hopheads or opium fiends, as the addicts were usually called. The newspaper would have had to be the size of *The New York Times* just to have listed and described the innumerable holes in the wall, garrets and subterranean huts which were opium dens. The *Call* contented itself with the more notorious dens, especially those which catered to whites.

Blind Annie's Cellar was one such den still frequented by Caucasians. It was a noisome sinkhole of depravity between—and below—718 and 720 Jackson Street. Ah King's place at 730 Jackson Street was probably the most notorious of all those resorted to by white hopheads. Hop Jay's smoking establishment was on the second floor of a tenement which was so outstandingly filthy that waggish reporters dubbed it the Palace Hotel.

Other dens clustered on Waverly Place, Church Alley, Washington Alley or Fish Alley, and on Duncombe Alley. This last was a narrow cavern from Jackson Street to Pacific Street and the Barbary Coast. Its doors bore no numbers, nor were any habitations listed there, but midway along the dank and slimy passage was a hidden opium hang-out.

One of San Francisco's great journalistic scoops was the expedition of Frank Davey, the crack photographer of the *California Illustrated Magazine.* He invaded the filthy dens under the guard of Officer Chris Cox and took the first flash photographs of them. His was one of the first photo-stories to appear in the San Francisco press. His pictures and those of the Department of Public Health document the degradation of the opium dens, all of which were wiped out by the quake and fire of 1906. They never made a comeback, and opium ceased to be a major problem. But it was the change in mores of the Americanizing Chinese rather than the crackdown by officials—or even the physical destruction of the dens by the holocaust—which brought an end to the opium evil. The American-Chinese abandoned opium before they jettisoned their pajama-like costume, their queues or even their concubines.

While opium was growing into a major problem for Federal agents and police the latter found their hands increasingly full with anti-Chinese hoodlumism. Trouble broke out on this new front in 1865 with the first serious anti-coolie riot. A mob of laborers drove off a party of Chinese who were at work excavating a lot south of Market Street. The crowd swelled to some three or four hundred men, marched on Tubbs & Company's ropewalk, and drove the firm's Chinese workers away. Only two Chinese were hospitalized, luckily, after the mob stoned the workers. The most seriously injured person was the ropewalk's foreman who had tried to protect his Chinese workers. He was knocked down, his lip and eye cut and his chest badly bruised. Chief Patrick Crowley led his men to the scene of the riot and personally dispersed the toughs. He arrested the mob's leaders on charges of riot.

There was nothing funny about the riot to those law-abiding Chinese concerned, but one defendant brought a bit of humor to an otherwise grim courtroom when he hired J. P. Dameron as his attorney. The latter employed all the tear-jerking tricks of the shyster in his pleading. At one point he cried out oratorically, "Did not our forefathers destroy Chinese tea in Boston Harbor? Why, Sir-r-r, these Chinamen live on rice, and, Sir-r-r-, they eat it with sticks!" This was too much even for the culprit Burke. He forfeited his $50 bail and took off.

Judge Alfred Rix handed the ringleaders stiff fines of $500 and sentences of from 90 days to 11 months in jail. This swift punishment only served to spawn another anti-coolie meeting at the American Theatre and the formation of anti-coolie clubs in each of the city's twelve wards. Worse, after the brave show of justice presided over by Judge Rix, the rioters were liberated by a decision of California Chief Justice John Currey on writs of *habeas corpus* based on legal defects in the commitment judgments. Most of the press stood by the Chinese, calling the Potrero district riot "a murderous and disgraceful onslaught." Reporters pointed out that one of the laborers, supposedly driven to riot by starvation, had no trouble digging into his levi's and coming up with $500 when his fine was pronounced. The *Alta California* blamed the miscarriage of justice on the inadmissibility of Chinese testimony in court—"the laws of California are such that the most intelligent Chinamen in the community could not testify against a white assailant, even if he were the vilest cutthroat who ever disgraced San Quentin with his presence." Ironically, shortly after the Potrero riot, Chinese testimony was finally admitted, but only in the county court.

As the decade of the '60s waned the Chinese population began to rise rapidly in numbers. The signal for the increase was Leland Stanford's clumsy swing at the Golden Spike at Promontory Point. With the East Coast linked to the West Coast by rail, thousands of "Crocker's Pets," as the Chinese gandy dancers were called, began to drift down to San Francisco. Drifting with them were hundreds of unemployed Irishmen from the Union Pacific Railroad. Some of these Chinese newcomers sailed for home, some went to Texas and Massachusetts, but most stayed on in Chinatown. At the same time a new wave of immigration developed out of Hong Kong. On May 13, 1869, alone, 1,276 Chinese arrived on the Embarcadero from the S.S. *Japan*. The new, big steamers brought them in like cattle, jammed below-decks. The City Directory guessed there were 8,600 Chinese in San Francisco at the end of the '60s. The Federal census figure was 11,817. Most accurate was the figure of the Chinese Protective Association (the Six Companies)—17,000.

Like a corollary to the increase in Chinese population, there was an increase in anti-Chinese incidents and riots. The people of Chinatown found themselves between the jaws of a vise: the growing tong underworld in Chinatown itself forming one jaw; the mounting pressure of hoodlums, labor and eventually a large segment of the city's population, forming the other.

Thus it was no surprise that the decade went out violently. The year 1869 was one of turbulence. It really belonged to the bitter decade ahead rather than to the fairly peaceful '60s. On January 24, Tong Moon Yun was shot dead on Dupont Street. On February 8, the corpse of a Chinese girl was found under a house on Cooper Alley. The 9th of April saw Ah Kow, sentenced to death for the murder of one of his countrymen, cheating the gallows by suicide in his cell. Eight days later a riot broke out among the Chinese population and many men were wounded. On May 20, Customs officials seized a cache of opium worth $15,000 on the S.S. *China.* On June 2, Werner Hoelscher was shot down by a Chinese. And so it went. The prestorm lull was over.

Violence was on the increase even though the Emperor of China himself, via an envoy Chi Tajen, warned the population of Chinatown through its quasi government, the Six Companies: "Be careful to obey the laws and regulations of the nation in which you reside. If you do so and at the same time pursue your callings in accordance with the principles of right and propriety, success cannot fail to attend your labors, while a contrary course will infallibly bring on you failure and misfortune." The underworld laughed at His Majesty. Anarchy might have prevailed but for the calming influence of the Six Companies. They would preserve the peace for another decade. To understand Chinatown and its past, a knowledge of this organization—which kept the fighting tongs in check for so long—is necessary. The story of the Six Companies' success is the story of Chinatown's growth; the story of the Six Companies' failure is the key to Chinatown's shame—the tong wars.

# CHAPTER FOUR

# THE SIX COMPANIES

*"It is charged against us that the Six
Companies have secretly established judicial
tribunals, jails and prisons and secretly
exercise judicial authority over the people.
This charge has no foundation in fact. These
Six Companies were originally organized for
the purpose of mutual protection and care
of our people coming and going from this
country. The Six Companies do not claim,
nor do they exercise, any judicial authority
whatever, but are the same as any tradesmen's
or protective and benevolent societies."*

—"Memorial" of the Six Companies of
President U. S. Grant, 1876

THE "GOVERNMENT" of Chinatown during the nineteenth century,
*de facto* if not *de jure,* was a combination of the Chinese Consulate General and the Six Companies, particularly the latter. These agencies managed to protect the law-abiding people of Chinatown both from hostile outside pressure and from internal lawlessness, although the Six Companies' organization was suspected and accused of heinous activities by Americans who did not understand its history and role in the Chinese community.

There was never any deliberate mystery about the Chinese Six Companies. Yet the American press and public, confusing tongs and companies, long insisted on investing the organization and its six member companies with a mystery. The bemused Knights of Labor called the Six Companies "a sort of tribal government." But President Shong Gee of the Hop Wo Company made a clear-cut statement of the role of the Six Companies—which he termed, as a unit, "the Chinese Benevolent Association"—as early as 1870. He stated that the society's object was simply to assist Chinese to come to California or return to China, to minister to the sick, to bury the dead, and to return their corpses to their native land.

Originally the Six Companies (separately) were agents of the Chinese firms in Hong Kong which established the coolie trade to San Francisco from the Crown Colony. The pioneers of this emigrant trade were two Hong Kong portrait painters, Hing Wa and Wo Hang. There was nothing new about such companies as they were set up in San Francisco. From time immemorial emigrants had tended to form clubs in Malaya and the Philippines. Each province's group set up a *ui kun* or company house. It was as if the Californians in the Far East were to set up a chapter of the Native Sons of the Golden West, complete with lodge hall. The ui kun existed in China itself when Cantonese and Fukienese settled in Shanghai or Ningpo. In Canton, too, there were these halls for "strangers" from other parts of the empire. Since the Chinese were the most alien of aliens emigrating to California, they took special pains to band together for mutual aid and protection.

But the American public persisted in ascribing to the Six Companies all manner of evils, including the usurpation of American judicial processes among the Chinese people. The press, too, gave the companies mysterious and dictatorial (and nonexistent) powers. In later years newsmen continually confused the companies with the fighting tongs. The merchants who were being preyed upon by tong highbinders thus found themselves the targets of newspaper editorials, rather than the predators who waylaid them. To correct some of these misconceptions the Reverend A. W. Loomis wrote an article which was published in the first volume (1868) of the popular San Francisco magazine, the *Overland Monthly.* He listed the things which the Six Companies were *not*—plotting societies, despotic lawmakers, punitive organizations, hiring halls for coolies, slavers, or dreaded tribunals. In order to disabuse the public of its incorrect notions Loomis compared the Chinese companies to the

Order of Hibernians or the Scandinavian Association. He tried to hammer home the point that they were simply the benevolent or mutual-aid societies of one particular group of the foreign born. Loomis reminded his readers that the poor bewildered immigrant in a strange land had to lay over somewhere upon arrival in port. He could not walk out of steerage into the trail to Hangtown or Copperopolis. He needed a caravansary or hostel. This the companies provided with their San Francisco *ui kun,* a combination hotel and Travelers' Aid Society. Loomis reminded his audience that the Chinese were only temporary residents. This gave them all the more reason to stick together closely during their brief stay. Loomis emphasized that the Chinese never—or hardly ever—abandoned one home to go in search of another. When they went abroad, wives and children were always left behind to keep house until their return. Every man hoped to return home after having improved his worldly estate in foreign parts. Loomis could not know of the remarkable change that would take place. Around the time of the earthquake of 1906 or the fall of the Manchu Empire in 1912 the majority of Chinese temporarily resident in San Francisco decided to set down roots.

It was true, and Loomis readily admitted this, that the companies were not exactly models of democratic government. They were paternal. If despotic, their leaders were benevolent despots. These leaders—well-to-do merchants in almost all cases—set up the rules and regulations of the societies without vote or veto from the masses of the membership. They made assessments, not to enrich themselves but rather to acquire buildings for company headquarters and hostels. Governing of the group was left by common consent to a few leading businessmen or scholars, if any of the latter could be found among the immigrants. Nearly all newcomers joined their proper company but membership was optional. They wanted the security which the companies offered them. They wished to lodge with others of their own kind—men who spoke their language. In the *ui kun* they could sleep and cook until they got adjusted to the country of the Golden Mountains; until their plans could take shape. Then they were off to pick up the shining metal from the streams of the Sierra Nevada.

The single function of the Six Companies which led to more misunderstanding than any other was their arbitration of quarrels. They tried to settle disputes before they became too serious. If they could not successfully arbitrate the case it was taken to the American courts. A poor ignorant coolie would have been helpless in an American court in the 50s, so the better-educated, more socially acclimated and sophisticated businessmen acted—through the companies—as managers of the legal affairs of all Chinese settlers. This led to accusations by the press and public that secret and severe tribunals existed.

Another operation of the Six Companies which led to attacks was their issuance of what virtually amounted to exit visas for Chinese. To prevent the absconding of debtors, the Six Companies entered into agreements with shipowners. No tickets were sold to Chinese returning to their homeland unless they could present a certificate from the Six Companies. This certificate—actually a simple receipt—was their clean bill of (fiscal) health. This exit control was the one major area of power which the companies really did wield; therefore their motives in this area were particularly suspect. But among the merchant population, white and Chinese, this system was well liked. Creditors knew that bankrupts and thieves could not abscond. It made the Chinese live up to their reputation of being good financial risks. They had to pay their debts or they could not go home. The mass of the American public overestimated the extent of this control, however, and saw the company presidents as mandarins enslaving coolies.

Opposition to the Six Companies from the Chinese of California themselves was small. Little ever reached the ears of whites, although Loomis—who knew Chinatown very well—did report a few individuals who were disgruntled by the company system. The grumblers were men who found the assessments a hardship and who were convinced that they could do well without the shepherding of the Six Companies and its Meeting House of the Flowery Kingdom. Some alluded to the company presidents as "rice ladles," meaning they cost a great deal and were of absolutely no use to anyone. A few inferred that all funds raised did not end up being put to the proper use. By and large it appears that dues were spent on proper activities—paying salaries of company officials, purchasing fuel, oil and candles, paying water bills, assisting the sick to return home, buying medicines, taking care of coffins and funeral expenses, repairing tombs, and taking on the expenses of drayage and lawsuits. There were a few temptable Six Companies men, of course. A gentleman named Wong, elected interpreter for his society, used his key office to sell the company's house and to go home *to* retirement on the proceeds. He had been trusted thoroughly by both Americans and Chinese as the sole elected business agent of the company. The company repaid the money in full, got its property back, and made the Wong clan assume full responsibility for the individual's crime.

There were joss chapels, or temples, in the headquarters' houses but they were furnished by voluntary subscriptions. There were no priests in the company houses. The companies did some charity work, caring for the indigent, the sick and the disabled if they were not being helped by their relatives—the normal thing among the clannish Chinese. The gathering of the bones of the deceased for shipment home was not usually the responsibility of the companies. However, sometimes people from one district or another selected their company president to handle the business end of this transportation. These company heads, after all, had close ties with shipping firms. From time to time the Six Companies contributed funds to famine and flood relief in China. After the disastrous Johnstown Flood in Pennsylvania in 1889 they sent $1,000 for relief work there.

In 1850, the Six Companies' structure was begun with the formation of a single company to assist all newcomers to Chinatown. It rented a Sacramento Street room and called itself the Kong Chow Company. This catchall organization took in all the immigrants from 6 of the 72 districts of Kwangtung Province. These 6 districts contributed all but a fraction of the migrants to California. Probably 10,000 of the 12,000 Chinese in California in 1851 were members of the Kong Chow Company. The name was taken from that of the geographic area of China encompassed by the half-dozen districts.

The 62,000 Chinese who resided in California by 1868 were members, with very few exceptions, of one or another of the Six Companies which grew out of the Kong Chow Company. The 6 were the Sam Yup Company, the See Yup Company, the Ning Yuen Company, the Yeung Wo Company, the Hop Wo Company and the Hip Kat Company. Only two of them came to be known widely to the non-Chinese of the Pacific Coast: the See Yups and Sam Yups. But it was more of a case of euphony than importance gradients. Out of either laziness or bewilderment, Chinatown reporters for the dailies tended to place all Chinese into one or the other of these camps. When the tong wars erupted, the press often identified the combatants as See Yups versus Sam Yups, instead of naming the actual fighting tongs involved in the mayhem. It was also a convenient way of breaking down the many factions of Chinatown into two. The See Yups and Sam Yups did represent the two major dialect groupings of the immigrants. The See Yups spoke the common tongue of Dupont Gai; the Sam Yups, a more courtly Cantonese.

The Sam Yup Company was organized in 1851 by those Chinese who did not fall into the six-district structure of the Kong Chow Company. The name Sam Yup means Three Districts and it welcomed people from Nam Hoi, Pun Yue and Shun Tak, which embraced the city of Canton and its immediate environs. By the 60s, this company owned a somewhat dilapidated company house or lodgings on Clay Street above Powell and another building on Sacramento Street, but its business headquarters was in a rented office on Commercial Street. Sam Yup dues were higher than those of most of the other companies. There was a $10 initiation fee; a $10 fee for removing the dead to China; a $2 assessment to pay off the Sacramento Street property; a $3.50 charge for miscellaneous costs incurred by the company; and a 50ft fee for the legal-proceedings fund. Officers were few and not particularly well paid. An assistant and a linguist or interpreter got $60—$80 each per month; a servant and a messenger were paid about $40 each. Rounding out the staff were the executive secretary, or *tung see,* and the treasurer. These officers each received from $80 to $100 a month.

The See Yup Company was known for some time as the Kong Chow Company as well, since it was the direct descendant of the original single company of 1850. The *raison d'être* of this sociobenevolent organization was spelled out in 1853 in a company statement translated by Reverend William Speer. "In China it is common to have councils and in foreign lands *ui kun,* company halls. The object is to improve the life of our members and to instruct them in principles of benevolence." The See Yup Company was the Four Districts Company. It represented the area of Kong Chow which included the provincial districts of Yan Ping, Hoi Ping, Sun Ning (now called Toyshan) and Sun Wui. There were also some members from Hok Shan. See Yup fees were light. Only $5 in dues had to be paid if done immediately upon arrival. If payment was deferred the amount was $10. There was also a 50-cent assessment for the lawyers' fund. No dues were collected from the aged, the sick or the disabled. When the See Yups set up shop they took all of the Kong Chow Company's members except a handful from Hok Shan and part of Sun Wui.

The Yeung Wo (Masculine Concord) Company was organized in 1852. It soon had an old house on the southwest slope of Telegraph Hill as its caravansary while it secured property for a better headquarters. In 1868 it was busy building its new *ui kun* on Sacramento Street. The only assessments this company levied on its members were $10 for admittance to membership and $10 for the removal of the dead to China. The company reported 26,000 arrivals as of 1868, some 13,200 departures, and 1,000 deaths. Its members became more numerous in Hawaii than in California. The area from which the Yeung Wo drew was called Heung Shan (now Chungshan) or Middle Mountain. This took in three districts between the Portuguese port of Macao and the Sam Yup country. It constituted a sort of peninsula where the Pearl or Chu Kiang River emptied into the South China Sea.

The Ning Yeung Company was formed in April 1854 by the separation of 3,400 members from the See Yups. A dispute occurred in that company and all Sun Ning, or Toyshan, men left to form the new organization. These men came from the populous district west of Macao which stretched inland from the seacoast. Although it asked only a small entrance fee of $5, the company was well to do. It owned a three-story brick building on Broadway. In only two decades of immigration this company received 27,900 members. But some 7,800 departed for China, and about 1,000 died in California. According to the late American-Chinese historian, William Hoy, this became the most powerful of the old companies. In spite of the constant reference in the American press to the See Yup-Sam Yup rivalry, Hoy insisted that the See Yups wielded little influence after 1854 and none that the Ning Yeungs could not nullify. The enfeebled See Yup Company, after the Ning Yeung schism, actually metamorphosed into a merchants' association rather than a true district association. Only because the seven companies tended to be broken into two major dialect groupings was the See Yup name preserved in importance. Another splinter organization was the Hop Wo Company. It was formed a decade after the others by those Chinese, mostly of the Ong clan, who came from the Hoi Ping and Yin Pai districts southwest of Canton and north of the Ning Yeung area. They had been members of the See Yup Company but in that organization they had felt their interests were slighted. Later its membership was swollen by one-time adherents of the Ning Yeung Company who had come to the New World from the Toyshan district. A very large proportion of these newcomers were of the Yee clan. The building which the Hop Wos acquired was a rented one on Commercial Street. Their entrance fees and all other charges totaled a mere $7. Some 17,000 Chinese came to San Francisco and California in general from the Hop Wo districts by 1868. Of these, 300 died and 8,200 went back to Kwangtung.

The Hip Kat Company formed in 1852, later changed its name to the Yan Wo Company, the Association of Human Concord. It was made up of Hak Kan people, or "foreigners." (Hak Kah signifies "stranger families" in Chinese.) These were double emigrants; not only had they left South China for San Francisco but they had emigrated to Kwangtung from North China in the first place. The clannishness of the Cantonese was such that the Hak Kah were never accepted as true "southerners." Though they had scattered through the province in such districts as Bow On, Chak Tai, Tung Gwoom and Chu Mui, they all spoke the same dialect; one quite different from the regular spoken Cantonese. Their first San Francisco headquarters was not in Chinatown at all, but just South of the Slot—that is, south of Market Street. Their building stood in Happy Valley not far from the Palace Hotel of today. This first structure was destroyed in one of San Francisco's fires in 186S, and the company secured a Chinatown building to replace it, on Dupont Street between Washington and Jackson. The Hak Kahs contributed 5,800 arrivals to the total Chinese population by the end of the 60s. Of this figure they lost 2,500 by departure and 100 via reported deaths. Many of the men in this company were cooks, stewards and seamen; just as Sam Yups' membership ran to tailors, merchants and herbalists; and See Yups' to laundrymen, restaurateurs and small shopkeepers.

In the late 90s two more companies formed up, to bring the Six Companies to an actual total of eight. The Shew Hing Company, named for the region from which it drew—two central Kwangtung districts of Kao Yew and Kao Ming—also attracted members from two districts quite a distance to the southwest; Yang Kong and Yang Chun. Very shortly the last company was formed. It was the Yin Hoi Company and was composed of men from the Yin Pin and Hoi Woi districts who were pulling out of the Hop Wo Company. It was always small and weak and it did not last out the 90s. When it disappeared its membership merged with the Shew Hing Company, leaving the present total of seven companies in all. The Shew Hing Company kept on and took in companyless men from the Sam Shui, Tsing Yuen and Sze Wui districts—to end up representing more districts of China than any other company.

The district associations became very strong in San Francisco. In the city an individual's affiliation to his company took precedence over his clan association, any smaller district group, his trade guild, and (at first) his fraternal society or tong. Yet somehow this strength collapsed before the onslaught of the ruthless tongs.

The officers and committeemen of each of the societies joined to form a congress of the six. This organization, a sort of United Nations of San Francisco Chinese, is what is usually referred to, in the singular, as the Six Companies. Really a board of presidents of the half-dozen companies, this nonsalaried group maintained a rented headquarters at 709 Commercial Street. This supercompany, or coordinating board, was the real power in Chinatown until challenged by the fighting tongs. A concomitant, almost identical, organization was the Meeting Hall of the Middle Kingdom, or Meeting Hall of the Chinese People. Disputes which arose between members of one company were settled within that company, but disagreements among members of two companies or more were referred to the supercompany for settlement. Also, matters affecting the general interest of all Chinese in the city were discussed in the Six Companies' headquarters. A case in point was the importation of what were called "big-foot women" (peasant women with unbound feet) for immoral purposes. The Six Companies protested this traffic but lost the campaign to the vested interests.

One important function of the various companies was the keeping of rosters of members. These furnished what were probably the most reliable statistics on the Chinese population in California 75 or 100 years ago. Reverend Gibson, drawing on Six Companies' figures, quoted an 1876 total of 151,300 Chinese in all California. He broke them down by company affiliation in this fashion: Ning Yeung, 75,000; Hop Wo, 34,000; Kong Chow (See Yup), 15,000; Yeung Wo, 12,000; Sam Yup, 11,000; Yan Wo, 4,300. This total is very large and the figures may reflect either padding, or more likely, the failure to list the many Chinese who departed from California for China or who died.

In addition to the Six Companies, the clan associations and the nascent tongs, there were trade unions or workers' guilds in Chinatown. The strongest guilds were those of the washermen, cigarmakers and shoemakers. They were organized somewhat like American labor unions, to prevent destructive competition and to set up apprenticeship standards. They were, to some extent, benevolent and charitable institutions in that they took care of the sick and the dead of their membership. An interesting facet of these organizations—one which seems to fly in the face of the traditional frugality of the Chinese—was their method of handling surplus funds at the end of the year. Instead of carrying them over to the guild treasury for the next year's demands, the members spent them on one glorious round of feasting; starting the new year from scratch.

Thanks to the unifying influence of the Six Companies, the Chinese of San Francisco were able to reach President Ulysses S. Grant's ear— for whatever good it did—during the heyday of political manipulation of bigotry. In a "Memorial" to President Grant they pointed out that "it has often occurred, about the time of the state and general elections, that political agitators have stirred up the minds of the people in hostility to the Chinese. But formerly the hostility has usually subsided after the elections were over." They reminded Grant that they had wives in Chinatown, that there were perhaps 1,000 United States-born Chinese children, although it was generally against Chinese custom to bring virtuous women so far from home. The Six Companies' spokesmen added that the outbursts of violence against the Chinese in San Francisco did not encourage them to bring in their wives and families. (In New York there were *no* decent Chinese women as late as 1874, if we can believe *Harper's Weekly.* On March 7 of that year the periodical ran a story on the English, Irish and American girls who had married Chinese in Gotham. It reported, "There has not been a Chinese woman resident in New York for years.")

The Six Companies admitted to the President that unprincipled Chinese were bringing in prostitutes from China. But the petitioners claimed that the trade was begun for the gratification of white men. They were probably right in part in saying that the proceeds from "the villainous traffic" were going to enrich Americans. They reminded President Grant that their attempts to return prostitutes by steamer had been thwarted earlier by American shysters who flashed writs of *habeas corpus* to protect the "businessmen" involved.

"These women are still here," stated the memorialists, "and the only remedy for this evil and for the evil of Chinese gambling lies, so far as we can see, in an honest and impartial administration of municipal government in all its details, even including the police department. If officers would refuse bribes, the unprincipled Chinamen would no longer purchase immunity from the punishment of their crimes...."

This appeal did little if any good. The derision, the segregation and the occasional violence in San Francisco was not only able to continue as before but increased against the people whom the press angrily began to call pagans, heathens and Mongolians.

Apparently Reverend Loomis's article of 1868 simply did not take. Misconceptions multiplied. Senator Eugene Casserly inserted them into the Congressional Record in 1870 by warning his fellow solons against "the secret organizations, rules and regulations of the Chinese in the United States [The Senator was not inveighing against the still undercover tongs; he was after the companies]... From thirty to forty thousand men are controlled by an organization of mercantile houses in San Francisco known as 'the Six Companies.'" He warned his colleagues that "the system is most like one of the secret associations of the Middle Ages of which we have but a vague idea because they were shrouded in darkness, but which we know were as energetic and formidable as they were mysterious. It is," he concluded, "the most complete specimen of an *imperium in imperio* of which we have an example in the United States."

Casserly backed up his claims by lifting chapter and verse from an earlier report of a Legislative committee of the State of California. (The cycle would soon be completed; the 1876 State committee investigating the Chinese would cite Casserly's words.) Quoting from the report, he claimed that:

The Chinese are under a government as absolute and perfect as any that ever existed, which system of government is maintained and enforced in this State, so far as the Chinese are concerned, wholly independent, outside of and in derision of the authority of the State of California as well as that of the Government of the United States.

This system of government is maintained and enforced by what is known as "the six Companies" and is, in fact, in derogation of the dignity of our national and state governments and in contempt of their lawful authority. This Chinese Government in California has its offices, its tribunals and executions of its decrees. It has been demonstrated by the police authorities of our principal city that individuals have been repeatedly imprisoned in Chino-California prisons, flogged, beaten, otherwise maltreated, and their property confiscated under the authority and by the command of the Chino-California government, and there is no reasonable grain of doubt (though this is not susceptible of proof) that the death penalty has been frequently inflicted under the same authority. The peculiar habits and customs of the Chinese, together with ignorance of their language, has heretofore made it impossible for the ordinary civil force of the State (the utmost our citizens are able to maintain at their own cost) to break up this extraordinary, tyrannical and illegal organization.

It is obvious from these accusations, flung mistakenly at the Six Companies, that word of the increase of crime in Chinatown was leaking outside, no matter how well the tongs kept their secrets. The situation continued to deteriorate, and in 1876 an investigating committee of the State Legislature repeated Casserly's words, warning that tribunals were formed, taxes (blackmail, actually) levied, and men and women intimidated—particularly interpreters and witnesses in court cases. The committee was correct about the amount of crime in Chinatown but completely off in ascribing its origin to the Six Companies. It wove together the exit visa system of the companies with the criminal despotism of the fighting tongs and blamed everything on the Six Companies.

After accusing the Six Companies of exercising the death penalty upon disobedient Chinese and exerting a despotic sway over one-seventh of California's population, the committee backed down. "We are disposed to acquit these companies and secret tribunals of the charge of deliberate intent to supersede the authority of the State. The system is an inherent part of the fiber of the Chinese mind, and exists because the Chinese are thoroughly and permanently alien to us in language and interests. It is nevertheless a fact that these companies or tribunals do nullify and supersede the State and National authorities. And the fact remains that they constitute a foreign government within the boundaries of the Republic."

The publishers of the *Overland Monthly* decided, in 1894, to try again to illuminate their readers as to the real role of the Six Companies. They had Walter N. Fong bring the story up to date. Fong found that twenty-six years after Loomis's excellent article in the same magazine, the Six Companies' story still remained "as mysterious as ever to the average American citizen." He was not surprised that public and press accepted their information from inaccurate sources, for he knew that even as late as the mid-'90s few Chinese knew English well enough to explain the organization of the companies.

Before he wrote his article Fong checked his own knowledge of the organizations against that of the president of the Ning Yeung Company and the president of the joint Meeting Hall of the Middle Kingdom.

Fong chose to explain the Six Companies by comparing the situation in San Francisco to that in China where the clan organization was far stronger. Springing probably from ancestor worship, clans were organized of all Chinese descended from a common ancestor. Their genealogies might go back more than fifty generations. All clan members, who usually gathered together in villages of their own, called each other "cousin." In the clan those who reached the age of sixty automatically became Elders regardless of their rank or station. Also important in the homeland were the *Kong Ming* or Titled Scholars—men who had passed special government examinations. These, with the Elders, formed the officers of the clans. To aid them the clans elected secretary-treasurers. All eighteen-year-olds became "men" with a voice in the management of affairs. If quarrels developed among clan members petitions were sent to the Titled Scholars and Elders. The plaintiff and defendant met before them, and the case was decided, usually by a compromise. The traditional law held the heads of a clan responsible for the crimes committed by any member of a clan.

It is obvious that this tradition of arbitration of disputes influenced not only the Six Companies of Chinatown but the fighting tongs as well. It unfortunately helped to drive a wedge between San Francisco's American-Chinese and the judicial processes and agencies available to them for many years. Since there were too few of a given clan in any one mining camp in California, they grouped themselves there not by clans but by province of origin. To them this was the next best thing. Many were already used to this system of grouping. (In Hong Kong, for example, Sam Yups had tended to associate predominately with other Sam Yups, and See Yups with See Yups, because of their dialectical differences and somewhat differing customs.) When the miners drifted down to San Francisco from the Mother Lode they retained the district basis in organizing socially.

Fong explained the exit system—still a thorny issue—once again. Each homeward-bound person paid $9 to the Meeting Hall of the Middle Kingdom and $3 to his own company, plus $3 toward the expense of shipping the ashes of his fellow company men home. The returnee paid his fees at his company. He then received a receipt which a Six Companies' inspector picked up at the gangplank as he boarded ship. If an individual showed up at the dock without a receipt to surrender he could sait by paying the inspector his fees on the spot. If he refused—and refusals were practically nonexistent—the inspector, as Fong explained with some delicacy, would try "with the aid of American laws to keep him from boarding the steamer."

By the '90s, officers of the Six Companies served only one term. In the early days they had enjoyed unlimited terms of office, but some corruption had then crept in. At the end of the nineteenth century company heads were elected, alternating among the different clans of the company.

Fong found that he had to answer the same charges which Loom is had answered a quarter century earlier. He pointed out that, while American and Chinese employers might contract for coolie labor, the Six Companies never handled such contracts. The See Yup Company had angrily repudiated this calumny as far back as 1855 when it stated that "our company has never employed men to work in the mines for their own profit, nor have they ever purchased any slaves or used them here." Fong reiterated that the companies had no secret courts in which to try their supposed subjects either. The companies held meetings to settle disputes and to arrange for payment of debts, it was true. But the decisions of the Elders and Titled Scholars did not have to be accepted. If both parties did not accept the decree of the arbiters, the case was taken to the proper American legal agency.

There was one occasion when the Six Companies did pressure the whole Chinese community; this was when the Geary Act was promulgated. The Six Companies levied a special $1 lawyers' fee on each member and asked them not to register under the harassing act. In vain they were testing the constitutionality of the legislation which they were sure violated their civil rights. Public and government officials soon claimed that the Six Companies had ordered their "subjects" not to obey the law of the land.

There is no doubt that when the Six Companies spoke all Chinatown listened. For 99 percent of all Chinese in California came from Kwangtung, and—to refine it further—from only 21 of its 72 districts. The handful of nonmembers in Chinatown, hardly more than one percent of the population, were natives of Shanghai, Ningpo, Fukien or North China. The reasons for this great preponderance of Cantonese were many. One was the convenience and accessibility of *the* port for the coolie clippers and later the steamship lines between San Francisco and Hong Kong. Another factor was the well-organized companies of Cantonese in the Crown Colony, which actively recruited immigrants from their close-at-hand province of Kwangtung.

The reasons for the amalgamation of the six and more separate companies into one organization were several. In the first place it was easier for a single organization to protect the interests of Chinese in legal matters than for a scattering of small, independent societies to do so. No Chinese embassy existed in Washington during the early years of settlement, and no consulate in San Francisco. The heads of the Six Companies were forced to serve as spokesmen for the Imperial Government to its San Francisco subjects. A single voice had to be maintained. Another pressure to unite for strength was the rising threat of the antisocial organizations in the Chinese community—the fighting tongs.

Fong mentioned the formation of the Kwong Duck tong in 1852 as the beginning of the fighting tongs, but singled out the Chee Kong tong as the secret society most responsible for those activities for which Americans carelessly blamed the Six Companies. This tong, whose original aim was the overthrow of the Manchu Dynasty, had set itself up as a sort of *sub rosa* government and secret tribunal over the Chinese populace. All this was the case long before the 90s, Fong stressed, and neither tong—nor any of their rivals—had the slightest connection with the Six Companies.

The Meeting Hall of the Chinese People, or Meeting Hall of the Middle Kingdom, the *Chung Wah Kung,* was jointly presided over by the chiefs of only five participating societies; the See Yups did not join. Delegates to it were elected according to the size of each company in members. The official name for the six united societies was the Chinese Consolidated Benevolent Association, but Americans found this much too cumbersome and called it the Five Companies until 1862, and then the Six Companies. In 1901, the Six Companies incorporated under its proper name, the Chinese Consolidated Benevolent Association. In 1862 the meeting hall's name was changed slightly, to *Chung Wah Wui Kwoon,* but it still meant the same thing. (Different words were used to signify meeting place or assembly hall.)

At first an attempt was made to adhere to Chinese tradition by selecting a Chinese scholar—whenever possible—to head each district association. But scholars were so scarce in California that they had to be imported especially for the posts. Eventually the idea of scholar-presidents was abandoned in favor of merchant-presidents. They had the biggest voice and the biggest stake in Chinatown affairs. This change helped to create a sort of Chinese chamber-of-commerce image in the American mind in regard to the Six Companies. This still exists. The Six Companies is much more than that, of course, but this was the direction the district companies individually and jointly began to take. Ironically, they followed the lead of the weakest of the district companies, the See Yup Company. More and more, at least in relation to the American community, the Six Companies took on the tone of a mercantile association. It actually served as a chamber of commerce until 1910 when the Chinese Chamber of Commerce of San Francisco was organized.

The board of directors of the companies, composed of the company presidents, rotated the chairmanship. Each man served at least once during his term of office as head of his own company. From 1850 until 1880 there was an unwritten law that no member of a fighting tong could become a president of the Six Companies or of any of its half-dozen components. Unfortunately this rule broke down in the 1880s when the tongs usurped—from the Six Companies—the reins of control over the populace.

The companies, like the gamblers and pimps, had special policemen as guards and watchmen over their members' places of business. William Hoy discovered files of reports by these men attesting to their duties—mainly ejecting drunken sailors and soldiers from Chinatown when they became obstreperous in stores or annoyed pedestrians. The Six Companies also began a program of "publishing" (posting) the names of lawbreakers and offering rewards for information leading to their arrests and convictions. Eventually the highbinder tongs took over this practice themselves, arrogantly advertising for the heads of enemies c.o.d. on various blind walls of Chinatown buildings.

For fifty years the Six Companies fought the tong hatchet men, attempting by peaceful and other means to persuade the one-time fraternal lodges to cease their flagrant, illegal enterprises and particularly to give up the use of violence for settling disputes. But their appeals to return to the traditional arbitration of quarrels fell on deaf ears in the tongs. The latter had replaced the rule of scholar-presidents with the rule of the hatchet and the Colt revolver. It was a strange campaign which was waged within Chinatown. From their humiliation in 1893-94, when their anti-Geary Act crusade backfired on them and caused them to lose great face, the Six Companies seemed to lose all the battles. But eventually they won the "war." Part of this was because of its strong allies—a belatedly militant police force; a one-woman commando force in the person of Lo Mo—Donaldina Cameron; a Chinese community finally united against its criminal oppressors.

In 1913 the tongs gave up. A Chinese Peace Society was formed with representatives from all the rival tongs; an armistice was brought about; and an uneasy peace at last settled on Chinatown. Time had run out on the tongs as early as 1906 when they were burned out by the April fire. The Quarter had really outgrown them and they were never able to make a powerful comeback. The *juk sing,* as the alien sojourner disdainfully called his American-born Chinese neighbor, began to assert himself. Soon he had secured hegemony in the community and broken through the invisible wall of bigotry and suspicion which separated Chinatown from the rest of the city. The Six Companies played a major role in this "fraternization" process.

But before the Six Companies could emerge again as the unquestioned voice and leader of Chinatown it had to fight for its very life and for the populace whose *de facto* government it was. And it had to fight on two fronts. The tide of bigotry, "sand-lotism," rolled in on Chinatown first in the '70s. But shortly, within the Quarter itself, the Six Companies found a fifth column arising in the form of the lawless tongs. These were soon at the throat of the Six Companies as it tried to fend off Dennis Kearney and his sand-lot crusaders who were perennially marching—or threatening to march—on Chinatown with the avowed intention of burning it to the ground and driving the -Chinese into the sea.

The fighting tongs were able to grow rapidly while the Six Companies was distracted by the onslaughts of the sand lotters. The latter accidentally played a major role in the rise of the criminal element to power within Chinatown, and thus helped bring about the tong wars themselves.

# CHAPTER FIVE

# SAND LOTS AND PICK HANDLES

*"So long as the Chinese are here, I shall give them the most complete protection which my official authority can control or create. The humblest individual who treads our soil, of whatever race descended and irrespective of the country of his birth or the language which he speaks, shall not appeal in vain for the protection of the law, which is no respecter of persons."*

—Chief of Police Theodore G. Cockrill,
1874

ONE OF the early attempts of California boosters to seduce travelers into a visit to San Francisco was a book called *The Pacific Tourist*. It described the people of Chinatown aptly and accurately for such an ephemeral publication. It called them "the hated of Paddy, the target of hoodlums, the field of the missionary, the bomb for the politician to explode, and the sinew for capital." Equally observant and accurate was San Francisco old-timer John H. Swift when he said ironically in 1876 that, "In 1852 the Chinamen were allowed to turn out and celebrate the Fourth of July and it was considered a happy time. In 1862 they would have been mobbed. In 1872 they would have been burned at the stake."

It was during the '70s that the Knights of Labor did their best to ignite the bomb mentioned by *The Pacific Tourist*. They marched about with banners which read THE CHINESE MUST GO! The demagoguery were quick to pick up this battle cry as a safe political crusade theme.

After all, the target people were voteless. But not everyone was ready to join the hysterical crusade as yet. When the shoemakers of the city went militant, parading at anti-coolie rallies in uniform as the St. Crispin's Guards, the Sacramento *Union* called them "shallow blatherskites" and "a convention of fools."

But bigotry in the '70s was speedily transformed into violence and brutality. Chinese were vilified, run out of towns in the interior, and occasionally beaten. One so-called coolie died from the effects of a stoning in San Francisco itself in May, 1871. The Chinese in California found themselves occupying the traditional position of the Jews—the scapegoats of society. This was particularly true during times of economic stress, recession, depression or whatever westerners chose to call such hard times as those of 1873. The contributions of the Chinese in building the West as the "sinews of capital" in the mines, in the fields and on the railroads were quite forgotten. Nor were there distinctions drawn between good and bad Chinese. The law-abiding Chinese were ground between the hoodlums and bigots on one side and their own criminals and tong bullies on the other.

Violence did not wait for the depression of 1873. During February of 1870, a gang of boys attacked a Chinese washhouse on Mission Street. They broke all the building's windows and beat the workmen as they fled. Police Officer David Supple attempted to arrest the ringleader. They all turned on him, knocked him down, and kicked and beat him severely while a crowd of men stood around him, watching but not making a move to help the officer. By the time the hoodlums were finished a mob of 2,000 men had gathered to see the show. A riot seemed imminent. Chief of Police Patrick Crowley arrived on the scene and with his usual force and vigor—personally leading eighty officers in clearing the streets—he restored order.

To make matters worse and to lend quite unnecessary fuel to the mobs who wanted to "clean up" Chinatown by tearing it down or burning it down, the first bloody internal riot in the Quarter's history occurred on May 22. The trouble grew out of the rivalry among Chinese laundrymen. The protective association, or guild, of washermen met every Sunday in a joss house over gaming rooms on the corner of Sacramento Street and Oneida Place. Here, applications and complaints were heard and ruled

---

*Richard H. Dillon*

upon. The case of the Was Yeup Company came up. The firm stood accused of violating the association's districting rules by opening a new washhouse in a district already assigned to another company. The decision was against the interlopers. Soon there was a scuffle between partisans of the company and others in the assemblage. Cleavers, hatchets, knives and clubs were brandished and then freely used. The fight turned into a full-scale riot. The attention of outsiders was commanded when pistol shots echoed from the interior of the building.

Down on Pike Street, John Meagber, a thirty-six-year-old Irish officer, heard the reports. He whistled for help, and five special officers joined him. They entered the fray after sending a citizen to get more aid. Captain Patrick R. Hanna and four of his men rushed to the scene of the presumed slaughter, inviting a number of citizens met en route to join them. Hanna had fought his way through the door when the chief of police arrived with a number of detectives.

A Chinese stood at the top of the narrow stairs leading to the room now jammed with brawling laundrymen. He blazed away at the officers with a pistol, narrowly missing one and actually grazing his coat. When he ceased fire, Hanna ordered his men to charge and several bounded up the staircase while Hanna himself and a few others cut off the rioters' retreat from the building. The officers who rushed upstairs met with a rough reception but flayed about mightily with their clubs. Although the escape of the rioters appeared to be cut off, they still tried desperately to get away, plunging downstairs and trying to burst through the ring of policemen blocking their exit. Few succeeded, yet only 16 men in all were seized, of whom 3 were wounded. This was a small percentage of the estimated 125 brawlers. The others had all fled by upstairs windows and the roof. The captives were tied together in pairs. An enormous crowd, probably 3,000 people, had been attracted. Chief Crowley, fearing the riot might spread, ordered Hanna to clear the streets. The captain did so with only 4 or 5 men but they had to swing their batons liberally. Crowley later said, "In five minutes more, nothing short of calling out the militia would have quelled the riot."

About twenty or thirty shots were fired in the melee upstairs but none of the scufflers were killed. The police had three wounded men in custody and apparently a number more were among the great majority of rioters who escaped. The officers found—either in the room or on the prisoners' persons—four cleavers, two hatchets, one chisel and a solitary knife. Only two pistols were found—a six-shooter and a derringer. But some of the captives explained that the other pistols had been thrown from windows and picked up and hidden by the gunmen's women, waiting in the street below. The meeting room was a shambles. Its walls were pierced with bullet holes. All the furniture was demolished, including glass vases, ornaments and the joss or idol (from the Portuguese *deos, god*) itself.

The traditional violence of the city which surrounded the Chinese Quarter seemed finally to be reflected in Chinatown itself during the '70s. A year and a month after the first riot another fracas exploded in which a Chinese shot and mortally wounded one of his countrymen. In February, 1872, several Chinese were wounded seriously in a cutting affray on Jackson Street, and in May a Chinese was murdered by two whites on Clay Street. The worried Six Companies asked Hong Kong to stop further emigration to San Francisco.

These brutal attacks helped to cloud a horizon which was just beginning to clear a bit with the news that Judge Davis Louderback would receive Chinese evidence as fully admissible in his police court. Another offset to Louderback's action was the campaign of the city's supervisors to harass the Chinese. The '70s would prove to be a decade of official investigations, harassments and attempted harassments. Typical of this campaign was the single day's haul of forty-five Chinese arrested for sleeping in one room. This was a violation of the sanitary laws of the city in general and the Cubic Air Ordinance in particular.

1873 was the year of the mysterious Queue Ordinance. There is perhaps more confusion about this piece of legislation than any other in San Francisco's history. Today most people who have heard of it at all believe it was a ruthless law which ordered *all* Chinese to cut off their queues. Not at all. Supervisor Robert Goodwin simply put before the Board of Supervisors an ordinance which demanded the cutting of the hair—to within one inch of the scalp—of all prisoners in the city jail. Ostensibly a health measure like the Cubic Air Ordinance, the Queue Ordinance fooled no one. It was transparently a legalized annoyance and embarrassment foisted on the Chinese though it technically applied to all prisoners in the county jail. Goodwin was the author of another of the so-called Pagan Ordinances—the Disinterment Ordinance, which prevented the shipping of remains of the dead to China upon penalty of a fine of from $100 to $150. This was a blow at the religious belief of the Chinese. Deprivation of his traditional queue was definitely an unusual punishment, but it was not an antireligious stroke, as was commonly believed by most Caucasians. The queue had been imposed on the Chinese by their Manchu conquerors centuries before as a symbol of their servitude. But this hirsute symbol of slavery was transformed by the Chinese into a badge of honor and worn proudly. It was imbedded in tradition, in national custom—but not in religion. When the time was ripe (1912) for the overthrow of the Manchu Empire and the establishment of the Chinese Republic, the Chinese of San Francisco willingly and quickly cut off their queues and wore their hair in Caucasian style.

Much to the credit of Mayor William Alvord, he vetoed the Queue Ordinance as being cruel and unusual punishment. Alvord stated that the ordinance was conceived in the spirit of persecution and was "a special and degrading punishment inflicted upon the Chinese residents for slight offenses and solely by reason of their alienage and race."

Supervisor A. B. Forbes lined up with Alvord to oppose vigorously the Pagan Ordinances. "I have unhesitatingly opposed all the so-called anti-Chinese resolutions introduced at our meetings," he reminded his colleagues, "because I believe they originated in a spirit and temper unconstitutional, unworthy, reprehensible and calculated to stir up and incite a certain class of our population to acts of violence and bloodshed... The whole letter and spirit of these resolutions are illegal, narrow minded, contemptible and utterly unworthy of the sanction of this body."

Supervisor Stewart Menzies leaped to his feet and retorted hotly that Forbes was an idealist with no common sense in anything he said. Menzies asserted that California was fast becoming a province of China.

Supervisor Charles Story agreed with Forbes. He said, "It is idle for this board to pass an order that on its very face is unconstitutional." But the ordinances *were* passed. Alvord immediately vetoed them, saying in his veto message that: "In my opinion, minor offenses which do not belong to the class of crimes called 'infamous' should not be punished by penalties which inflict disgrace upon the person of the offender."

An attempt was made to pass the Queue Ordinance (called the Bob-tail Order and the Pigtail Ordinance) over the mayor's veto. This maneu-ver failed when five supervisors supported Alvord's stand.

The *Alta California* warmly applauded Alvord, pointing to the many papers from all over the country which had approved editorially and had commended the mayor for his sense of decency and his pluck in follow-ing the dictates of his conscience. But this victory of Alvord's was short lived. The Queue Ordinance was revived in the summer of 1876; this time it was voted through.

A rabid fan of the Bobtail Order was the Sacramento *Record-Union's* anonymous Chinatown correspondent. He almost immediately claimed the Bobtail Order to be a great deterrent to crime in Chinatown and pro-duced figures from somewhere to show a rapid 33 1/3 -percent decrease in Chinatown arrests. His paper, however, disavowed his attitude that Chinese toughs were "far more concerned at the loss of their tails than deprivation of liberty," and attacked the practice as a disgraceful act of low demagoguery and an appeal to the prejudice of hoodlums.

The *Record-Union* reminded its readers that no other paper had set itself more strongly against Chinese immigration. But it had never sanc-tioned, and never would sanction, any unjust or dishonorable treatment of the Chinese. The editor moralized, "We cannot afford to disgrace our-selves by stooping to the perpetration of petty persecution or by soiling our hands with any of those weapons of old-world bigotry and intoler-ance whose employment has already darkened the pages of history."

The viciousness of the Pigtail Ordinance was related to the great numbers of Chinese arrested. They were rounded up wholesale and jailed—and thereby were liable to have their heads shaved—for violat-ing the cubic air rule. Most were criminals in no sense. Others were hauled in for licensing violations of which they were unaware. Blatantly anti-Chinese was the laundry license ordinance, since the fee was set at only $2 for washermen who could afford a horse (mostly Caucasians) but at $15 for those (mostly Chinese) who could not.

By September, 1878, there were four $10,000 damage suits filed by de-queued Chinese and fifteen more being prepared. Honorable Lorenzo Sawyer, United States circuit court judge, thought that the amputation of queues was clearly unconstitutional. He was right. In the test case of Ho Ah Kow, originally arrested for violation of the Cubic Air Ordinance, versus Sheriff Matthew Nunan, the Chinese won. The act was invalidated in 1879, and the practice abandoned although an attempt was made to restore it at the state level when Assemblyman Thomas J. Pinder tried to get a bill through to effect such a penalty for arrested Chinese.

Two great scares of the 1870s—used to great profit by anti-Chinese politicians in whipping up crowds—were the rumors of smallpox and leprosy epidemics in Chinatown. Writer J. P. Buel, for example, was so frightened by the tales told him of the Quarter that he labeled it "a world's fair of festering rottenness." The first giant-sized rumor of Chinatown pestilence got its start when two smallpox cases were found in a Clay Street lodginghouse. The horrifying rumor which resulted grew in horror on April 16 when the corpse of a Chinese was found in a basket at the foot of Pacific Street. The rumors continued, but no epidemic came except an epidemic of crime.

In March, 1873, Reverend Otis Gibson read an appeal from the Chinese of San Francisco to the Board of Supervisors. It deplored the growing invective of the press and the exaggeration of any evil or misery existing among the Chinese people. (The Sacramento *Record-Union* went much further than the appellants. It accused San Francisco reporters of putting down every sore nose or chin wart in Chinatown as "scriptural leprosy.") The Chinese reminded the city fathers that China was opened to the West *by* the West and by violence. The signers ended the appeal by suggesting that all Chinese-American treaties be abrogated, that all Chinese leave the United States, and that all Americans leave China. But before they wound up their statement they reiterated the fact that their people were good Californians and for the most part peaceable and industrious. "We have kept no whisky saloons, have had no drunken brawls resulting in manslaughter or murder." For his own part, Gibson took a parting shot at the white protectors of Oriental pimps. He pointed sarcastically to the reputation of the Chinese as good debt risks by saying, "It is a matter of common report that Chinese villains have always paid pretty well for not being molested in their favorite pursuit."

As the situation continued to deteriorate—a Chinese was killed by hoodlums on May 22—the Sacramento *Union* (the former *Record-Union*) which had defended the Chinese in 1867 and even in the opening of the '70s, now did a complete switch and denounced not only Chinese immigration but Oriental settlers already in California. The paper attacked sanitary conditions in Chinatown—such as the constant rubbish in the street—and wrung its editorial hands over the threat of small-pox, leprosy and cholera *morbus.* It charged the Chinese with governing themselves by their own code, defying the police, and practicing crime, profligacy and '"heathenism."

Anti-coolie organizations mushroomed so rapidly that a People's Protective Alliance had to be formed in order to tell one crusader from another. It tied all the associations of bigots together in one huge Ku Klux Klan-like structure for more effective action. Both city and State authorities had now sidled over to open alliances with these growing groups. Not content with the barbarous Queue Ordinance, city hall got the chief of police to crack down hard on violations of the Cubic Air Ordinance. There were 75 arrests in May, 1873; 152 in July; and 95 in August. The Chinese did not pay their fines. They simply continued to violate the ordinance while in custody; they were jammed into jail cells. An additional harassment of the Chinese was an amending act (struck down three years later by the Federal courts) which empowered the State Commissioner to require a $500-in-gold bond of any female Chinese immigrant he thought might possibly be a "lewd or debauched woman."

The clergy split completely on the Chinese question. Father James M. Bouchard, who should have taken a liberal or humanitarian view (he was part Delaware Indian Jesuit) instead denounced the Chinese immigration as ruinous in a speech entitled "Chinamen or White Men—Which?" The Protestant Gibson gave a stirring "Reply to Father Bouchard" in Platt's Hall on March 14, 1873, and made a fine defense of the Chinese; one which was marred only by certain anti-Catholic asides which the good minister simply could not resist. It was such a fine speech that the Chinese not only sent him a letter of thanks but offered to pay all the expenses of publishing the talk.

Writers, too, split on the question. Most of the press went along with the anti-coolie crowd. Henryk Sienkiewicz, the young Pole to whom fame would come when he wrote *Quo Vadis,* was rather hard on the

Chinese in San Francisco. But his author's inquisitive mind at least led him to locate and indicate certain mitigating factors in regard to Chinatown's evils. When he warned people against visiting the Chinese theatre alone because of the pickpockets, he did state that a second reason was that white hoodlums gathered there. "Quarrels and fights frequently occur between the Chinese and the hoodlums, sometimes ending with the thrust of a knife," he warned. He also called attention to the widespread gambling of the Chinese and explained the prevalent prostitution by the fact that 9 out of 10 of Chinatown's inhabitants were men. (The 1880 census actually showed 71,244 Chinese men and only 3,888 Chinese women in California.) Sienkiewicz reported cases of polyandry in the interior but he saw that the solution for the social problem of the disparate number of men and women in Chinatown itself was resolved by prostitution rather than by polyandry.

Ironically, at the very time in the mid-'70s that xenophobia and hysteria reached a peak, the Chinese Quarter began to "arrive" as a tourist attraction. Chinatown fascinated Sienkiewicz, Sam Clemens, Mrs. Frank Leslie, Albert Deane Richardson, Helen Hunt Jackson, Horace Greeley and other famous travelers and writers. Only three years after the visit of the Polish novelist a tourist guide prepared for railroad travelers devoted thirteen pages to Chinatown. Its description, however, could not compare with that of Sienkiewicz:

> The north side of the city of San Francisco, beginning with Clay Street is occupied by the Chinese district. Were it not for the brick buildings built in the European style, it might appear to the visitor in this part of town that he had, by some miracle, been transported to Canton or Shanghai. A strange impression is made by these noisy, nimble people, dressed in uniform costumes with their yellow complexions, slanted eyes, and long pigtails braided of hair and black silk reaching almost to the ground... On the street corners stand serious looking policemen in grey overcoats with silver stars on their chests. Perhaps the only other evidences of American civilization are the omnibuses which are drawn over the hills that cover the district neither by horses nor steam but by hidden chains [cable cars].

During the '70s a much more powerful voice than that of Sienkiewicz spoke out in favor of the Chinese. It was that of Samuel Clemens. When Mark Twain spoke people listened. In *Roughing It,* Twain thundered:

> They [the Chinese] are quiet, peaceable, tractable, free from drunkenness, and they are as industrious as the day is long. A disorderly Chinaman is rare and a lazy one does not exist... He is a great convenience to everybody—even to the worst class of white men, for he bears the most of their sins, suffering fines for their petty thefts, imprisonment for their robberies, and death for their murders. Any white man can swear a Chinaman's life away in the courts, but no Chinaman can testify against a white man... They are a kindly-disposed, well-meaning race and are respected and well treated by the upper classes all over the Pacific Coast. No California *gentleman* or *lady* ever abuses or oppresses a Chinaman under any circumstances, an explanation that seems to be much needed in the East. Only the scum of the population do it—they and their children; they, and naturally and consistently, the policemen and politicians likewise, for these are the dust-licking pimps and slaves of the scum there as well as elsewhere in America.

*The Pacific Tourist,* that pioneer of the long line of California promotional propaganda, tried to scold the Chinese Quarter for its evils—such as addicts curled up like withered leaves in dingy opium dens—while at the same time it attempted to "sell" Chinatown to the curious traveler. This involved nimble journalistic feats. The editor pointed to the foul habitations of the Quarter, but then cited the personal cleanliness of the people. He also admitted their lack of pestilence and relatively low death rate. He settled on a forbidding but tempting picture of a squalid yet fascinating *coin* of San Francisco. He warned that only three to five years of the opium habit would wreck the strongest constitution and the noblest manhood, but then said that "exaggerated are the stories told of visits to these dens by youths and women of American descent for indulging in this vice... They are rare, and only of the lowest classes of the women." This image of a mysterious Chinatown both assaulted and captured tourist imagination from that day forward. The stereotyped picture remains to this day in the minds of many people who visit San Francisco for the first time. As they timidly advance into the heart of Chinatown by night they expect to see an opium den in the shadows, if not a bloody hatchet on the cobbles of a dark alley. Perhaps because their grandfathers read in the 1879 *Pacific Tourist* that "streets and alleys and labyrinthine windings not only such as we tread are theirs; they live and travel under ground and over roofs, up and down, until the cunning policeman is outwitted in following them." The editor, in his ambivalence, attempted to be reassuring, which only made matters worse: "A visit to the Chinese quarter may be made in daylight or by night and with or without a policeman. The writer has frequently passed through the alleys and streets of Chinatown without the protection of policemen, and never experienced the slightest indignity." Though he added, as if in haste, "but those desiring the protection of a policemen can secure the services of one by applying to the chief of police in the city hall. Compensation should be made privately. Two dollars and a half is a sufficient fee." Like the dailies, *The Pacific Tourist* unfortunately confused the tongs with the Six Companies and described the latter as settling their controversies by the use of hired assassins. As a final reassuring note, the editor suggested that in the office of the chief of police or any Chinatown pawnbroker's shop they could see the implements of murder of the hatchet men. He might also have added the police clerk's office—a combination lost-and-found department and petty arsenal—where among the small change and pocket knives abandoned by felons were such interesting tools as Chinese dirks, opium pipes, and the coat of armor left behind by highbinder Ah Chung.

G. B. Densmore singled out a particular Chinatown hock shop for scrutiny. In this establishment, on the east side of Washington Alley, he saw—just as the editor had predicted he would—all kinds of highbinder weapons: double-bladed and two-edged knives, pistols, and slung shots (blackjacks).

Helen Hunt, the Helen Hunt Jackson who later wrote *Ramona,* was another who tiptoed through Chinatown with great foreboding. She chose to make her safari in broad daylight but even on a noonday expedition she thought it wise to ask a local policeman whether danger lurked in the alleys. "Not at all, m'am, not at all," answered the officer. "At *this* hour of the day you can go with perfect safety through all these streets." Charles Nordhoff advised tourists that even ladies and children could walk safely in the main streets of the Chinese Quarter by day. But he urged those who wished to investigate farther after dark to get a policeman—one of the Chinatown specials—as combined guide and guard.

The sinister and mysterious aspects of Chinatown have always fascinated people. When the smoke of chimneys and braziers mixed with the night fogs to make the Quarter into an eerie Limehouse tourists huddled together in shuddering delight. A small army of Chinatown guides—a species now entirely vanished—did nothing to diminish the mystery.

It was a fearful correspondent who covered the Quarter for the English publication *The Gentleman's Magazine.* He wrote that "there are certain parts which, at his own risk, the white man is free to traverse, though in no case is it prudent to visit even these without the escort of a properly armed police officer well-known on the Chinatown beat." Another Britisher who toured Chinatown before the quake, W. H. Gleadhill, was horrified by an entire street occupied by what he termed delicately *"merchandeuses* [sic] *d'amour,"* underground gambling hells which he called *"tripots,"* and opium dens filled with "white, sickly faces and glassy eyes." Probably his guide escorted him to the labyrinth under the trap doors of Bartlett Alley. This subterranean haunt was so noisome with mold and seeping sewage that it was dubbed the Dog Kennel by the press. Gleadhill returned from Chinatown almost in a state of shock.

The problem of Chinatown crime was complicated by the fact that for most of the nineteenth century, San Francisco was badly underpoliced. In 1863 there were still only 54 men in uniform. (They were outnumbered by the *mignons Chinoises de nuit* alone.) Yet the force made 5,422 (citywide) arrests. In 1871, Chief Crowley complained to the Board of Supervisors that New York had 3 times as many policemen per capita as San Francisco; that London had 3 1/2 times as many; and that Dublin had (and doubtless needed) 5 times as many. Pat Crowley had to make do with 4 captains and only 100 men. The combination of tong troubles, continuing hoodlumism and anti-coolieism taxed the law-and-order power of the city to the breaking point.

The colorful Crowley cast about for alternatives when he was not given the extra men he needed for Chinatown details. He strongly urged more drastic methods, even to the abolition of firecrackers and the prohibition of shooting galleries near Chinatown. He felt that the latter were too attractive to the tong hatchet men. "Nearly every Chinaman in the city," he said, "is the owner of a pistol, and we all know how handy he is in its use."

In 1874, when the strength of the force was brought into line with a realistic policy, it was Theodore Cockrill who was chief of police. Cockrill was a Kentuckian who had not really sought the office, but had allowed friends to place his name in nomination. As a Democrat he had not had the slightest hope of winning, but though the general Republican ticket swept the field Cockrill won the office of Chief by a 4,000-vote margin. He proved to be an effective leader but the problems of Chinatown were too much for him and persuaded him to flatly refuse renomination for a second term. Cockrill felt the growing tension in the air as the anti-coolie agitators voiced loud threats. He was determined that no harm would come to the 25,000 Chinese for whose safety he was responsible; he promised them full protection and he gave it to them.

Chief Cockrill struck out at Chinatown crime, as so many of his predecessors had done, with an attack on the bagnios. An ordinance was passed which made it unlawful to sell any human being, such as a slave girl, or even to be in, enter into, remain in or dwell in any brothel. But Benjamin Brooks, attorney for the San Francisco Chinese, told Congressmen that this ordinance was used by San Francisco police strictly for blackmail purposes. One wonders how many of the 13,007 arrests of 1873-1874 can be chalked up to this practice. In any case, Cockrill was proud that, thanks to his energetic activity, no Chinese brothels remained on main thoroughfares.

The chief had less success with gambling, since fan-tan players switched from brass "cash" (Chinese coins) and American silver to beans or buttons to fool his raiders. Either Cockrill was of excellent character or he was an able politician. Since he served only one term as chief, deliberately, the former is the more likely. His flowery pronouncement in regard to fan-tan was laudable enough. In his opinion it was far better for a few fan-tan operators to go unpunished for a misdemeanor than to have the police assuming unauthorized and arbitrary powers. A decade or so later this policy would be exactly reversed. City hall, in desperation at the number of tong killings, adopted a "get-tough" policy in Chinatown which infringed on many honest Chinese people's rights but which paid off in terms of affecting the tongs.

Tense as the situation was in the mid-'70s, it would have been much worse but for the restraining influence of men like Cockrill and Governor William Irwin. The latter, when he addressed a great anti-Chinese meeting in 1876, cautioned his listeners against violence. Of course to Cockrill an order was an order and an ordinance was an ordinance. While he stood ready to protect the Chinese from violence he also continued the enforcing of hazing legislation, such as the Cubic Air Ordinance. He arrested 518 Chinese for this offense in April, 1876, alone. Ambivalence came to be an occupational disease with police patrolling Chinatown eighty and ninety years ago.

In the spring of 1876, the new chief of police, Henry H. Ellis, had his hands full with the anti-coolie crowd and was also presented with one of the first major tong outbursts. Several Chinese witnesses against murderer Muck Son were violently assaulted in St. Louis Alley by 15 to 20 highbinders. The intimidation attempt failed because of prompt police action. The officers seized 4 or 5 of the hatchet men and locked them up. In all probability the attack was Muck Son's idea; he had learned how to deal with witnesses in the past. He had committed burglaries in Spanishtown, San Mateo County, in 1866, but incredibly the local authorities had locked him up with the sole witness against him. Not only did Muck Son make his escape but he closed the mouth of the witness forever by killing him.

So grave was the situation in 1876, that General John W. McComb notified the chief of police that the militia was ready to turn out to help him to preserve order on the shortest notice should the anti-coolie men resort to mob violence. Luckily the police department's strength had again been raised and the chief could now rely on a force of 325 without calling on the state troops. Ellis was a firm and resolute man. He neither panicked nor hid behind the militia's skirts. This New Englander was a veteran of the vigilance committee and had served as Deputy United States Marshall during the Civil War. (He would eventually spend twenty-two years on the force.) He was a professional peace officer.

Despite all of Ellis's watchfulness the Centennial Year and the one which followed it were the highwater marks of the shameful period of anti-Chinese agitation in San Francisco. Prejudice, selfishness, ignorance and bigotry were handmaidens of the sand-lot demagogues. In March, 1876, Mayor A. J. Bryant appointed a committee of twelve to report on Chinese immigration. The Anti-Chinese Union was formed that year and the eventually discredited but then widely read document, "Chinese Immigration, its Social, Moral and Political Effect," was sent to the United States Congress from San Francisco. Reverend Gibson accused Mayor Bryant of being an out-and-out sand lotter himself, probably for his allowing the Board of Supervisors to revive the despicable Queue Ordinance. The uneasy presidents of the Six Companies again requested the Government of China to stop further emigration to America of its nationals, fearing mob violence on the Embarcadero when so-called coolie ships arrived. The officials also wrote Bryant: they listed the abuses the Chinese had suffered, including unprovoked and unpunished acts of violence, and asked him for protection. And they called his attention to the widespread rumors of an imminent attack upon Chinatown—rumors which were causing much anxiety among the Chinese people.

In 1876 and 1877 there were times when Chinatown looked like a ghost town. A reporter described a walk through the Quarter on one such occasion:

> At nine o'clock last night the streets in the Chinese quarter were almost deserted and nearly all the stores closed. Special policemen were stationed at each corner and the place had decidedly the appearance of a town under martial law... The dozen Chinamen stationed on Dupont and Jackson Streets were probably members of the noble Highbinder Association or pickets ready to warn their countrymen of any approaching danger. The hoodlumistic element was lightly represented but restrained from acts and even words of violence by the presence of the police who were stationed at nearly every corner and who guarded the entrance of every alley. Never in the last fifteen years have the streets of this great part of San Francisco been so free of

Chinamen as they were last evening.

Mass meetings still peddled the myth sociologists called the "coolie fiction"—that the immigrants were all enslaved coolies kept in debt bondage to the Six Companies. The latter continued to be confused with tongs and were described as "secret organizations, more powerful than the courts." At first the speakers urged full protection and the guarantee of rights to the Chinese already settled in California. What was wanted, they said, was an immediate cessation of the immigration of coolies. But the listeners were of neither the mentality nor temperament to draw fine distinctions. In any case, the Anti-Chinese Union was soon openly boasting that it would not only secure a complete stop to Chinese immigration but would also obtain the forced repatriation of every Chinese on the Coast. Little wonder the board of presidents was a worried body of men.

The Six Companies sent a "Memorial" to President Grant at this time, having President Lee Tong Hay of the Chinese Y.M.C.A. sign it. The document reminded the President of how industrious and law abiding the Chinese people had always been in America—never interfering with the established order of politics or religion. It proudly stated that the Chinese had opened "no whiskey saloons for the purpose of dealing out poison and degrading their fellow men."

In their manifesto the Six Companies actually put themselves on record as supporting the prohibition of further Chinese immigration. They did this so that troubled American minds would be relieved of worry over excess labor and resultant depression. They also suggested the repeal of the Burlingame treaty but reminded the American people that it was the white capitalists who were calling for cheap Chinese labor, and getting it.

Whether true or not, stories began to appear in the press at this time to indicate that Chinatown was preparing for a siege by becoming an armed camp. The newspapers reported a run on pawnbrokers' shops for revolvers and bowie knives. One dealer alone was said to have sold sixty pistols to Chinese in one day.

On April 1 the Six Companies sent a letter to Chief Ellis accusing him of setting up a double standard of justice—of making few arrests when the victims of assaults were Chinese. This was published in the daily *Aha California*. The *American Missionary* then attacked the police force and "the policeman who, for a consideration, has known how to shut his eyes or be somewhere else when Chinese gambling and prostitution come too clearly into view on his beat." Partly as a result of such attacks as these, Chinatown's special force of police was discontinued in 1877. These watchmen and auxiliary police had won a reputation, probably well deserved, of being bribetakers and bribegivers rather than law officers. For "protection" service some of these specials earned up to $1,000 a month. They were not related to the police department's regular Chinatown squad.

On April 5, 1876, a riot seemed imminent and the Six Companies' presidents again appealed to Mayor Bryant. He gave orders to the police to protect the Chinese Quarter at all costs. He swore in 200 extra men, but there was no riot. On May 17 the Six Companies received a threatening letter purportedly from an organization calling itself the San Francisco Anti-Coolie Secret Society. If they did not clear San Francisco of coolies within twenty-one days the society would clear them out by force of arms. It was all bluff, or a hoax. One of the Six Companies' presidents turned the letter over to the chief of police but nothing more was heard from the society, if it actually existed in fact.

During April and May the police closed down Chinatown's gambling houses as potential trouble spots during that riotous period. They were booming again by August—probably after a June or July payoff to politicians.

The hearings of the State Senate's investigating committee on the Chinese question did not help matters any. The committee heard mostly biased, anti-Chinese witnesses, some of whose testimony was so wild it had to be stricken from the record. F. L. Gordon was one such muted star witness. He claimed that a Protestant missionary (Reverend Gibson?) was engaged in the business of selling Chinese women for the purpose of prostitution.

Civic leader Sam Brannan, the apostate Mormon Saint turned millionaire and a man who should have known better, advocated violence against the Chinese in May while the State Sunday school convention, perhaps eager for a crack at heathen souls, rose up in support of the

Chinese against their persecutors. The Marin *Journal* did its bit to keep trouble brewing by crying out that the Chinese of San Francisco, "by a secret machinery of their own, defy the law and keep up the manners and customs of China and utterly disregard all the laws...." Police Judge Davis Louderback made a public statement that he thought the Chinese mendacious, but doubted very much that they had secret tribunals in the city.

Gotham was viewing the San Francisco crisis with rapt attention. The New York *World* deplored the deterioration of the social climate in San Francisco, and in its editorial columns observed that the holy crusade against coolies was being run by brawlers, hoodlums, small politicians eager to curry favor with labor during a depression, and by newspaper sensation mongers. The *World* was sure that the overwhelming majority of Californians were against the nonsensical crusade. Perhaps the *World* was right. But it was also right when it observed that the voice of common sense could not be heard in the midst of the turmoil raised by the agitators.

If 1876 was a bad year, 1877 was even worse. Ill feeling mounted among the sand-lot crusaders as news of strikes in the East reached them. On July 23, 1877—to be known in police annals as Riot Night—a three-day reign of terror began.

A mass meeting of perhaps 10,000 was held in the sand lots fronting the city hall that night. The most rabid anti-coolie men seized control of the meeting and the mob began to march on Chinatown. Suddenly shots were fired into the crowd from nearby buildings and two men fell wounded. This attack angered the hoodlums all the more. As the first windows of Chinese establishments—outside of Chinatown—were smashed by young hoodlums 1,500 soldiers of the National Guard were put on an alert in the city's armories. But the enormous crowd broke up and only a splinter group plunged on toward the Quarter. They were turned away from a Chinese washhouse just off Leavenworth by a courageous and defiant policeman, Officer Charles A. Blakslee, who stationed himself with drawn pistol in front of the building. Officer John Sneider, on horseback, drove them away from another washhouse at Pacific and Taylor Street, but they wrecked a Chinese laundry at Leavenworth and Turk Streets, still far from Chinatown, and then set it afire. When firemen tried to put out the blaze the young ruffians impeded them and cut their hose. A white woman upstairs in the building was almost killed by the flames.

The mob of from 500 to 600 men surged down Geary Street to Dupont. There they started up the hill to Chinatown, but at Pine Street they found their way barred by Captain William Y. Douglass and a solid line of police stretching from one side of Dupont Street to the other. The ranting rioters charged the police in an attempt to break through by swamping them with sheer force of numbers. Officer James Pugh, in arresting a hoodlum who had assaulted a Chinese, was roughly handled by the mob and had his revolver taken away from him. But the police swung and chopped with their batons, sending clubbed and bleeding ruffians staggering to the pavement. Timely police reinforcements arrived from city hall and the line held firm. Sergeant John W. Shields and Sergeant Abraham Sharp led charges which forced the rioters back. But the maddened crowd pressed its siege, shouting a monotonous but ominous "To Chinatown! To Chinatown!" An overexcited special reporter for the Sacramento *Record-Union,* flashed the word to the State Capital.

"The police hold Dupont Street at the corner of Pine," he began, "against the main body of the mob while strong squads are posted at the intersections of cross streets west of Dupont, the main object being to keep the mob from Chinatown." By the time the reporter had filed his third dispatch to the capital at 12:50 A.M. the police were in complete control and had even arrested the man who had fired into the crowd out of wanton mischief. No other shots were fired. The militia was not called out. It was a proud moment for the tired but only slightly battered cordon of police.

A second mob of from 500 to 600 tried to outflank the picket line of policemen and to overrun the upper end of Dupont Gai by approaching from the Broadway, or North Beach, side. But here, too, a police line held fast. The Chinese stayed off the streets and locked themselves in their homes, shuttering their windows tightly. Only one small party of attackers broke through the police lines. This handful penetrated to Washington Street, above Stockton, where they stoned the windows of the Chinese Mission before they were arrested.

The correspondent of the *Record-Union* paid the police a well-earned compliment as the mob began to melt away: "The prompt and coura-geous action of the police barely prevented a bloody riot, for had the mob gained the heart of the Chinese quarter, it would have been impos-sible to foretell the result."

Another anti-Chinese meeting on the 24th kept the crowd's momen-tum up. Again the hordes gathered in front of the city hall, as if to defy the municipal government itself. Handbills had mysteriously appeared during the day to announce a great rally. Notices had been left at news-paper offices by anonymous callers who bought space, paid in cash, and hurried out.

The prescient but anonymous Sacramento reporter predicted: "It is quite probable that in view of the present and possible future distur-bances, efforts will be made to effect some organization among the bet-ter class of citizens looking to the maintenance of law and order." He was right. Chief of Police Ellis, fearing that a mob might wield itself together in such numbers as to overwhelm his police force, welcomed the formation of what amounted to a third vigilance committee, although it was not so designated. William T. Coleman, the old "Lion of the Vigi-lantes," came out of retirement to head up an executive committee and an informal army which grew within a day or so from 150 to 5,000 citi-zens. The formation was called the Committee of Public Safety, rather than a committee of vigilance, but it was soon dubbed "the Pick Handle Brigade"—for the armament it relied upon most. The committee issued a stern statement to the public, stating that it recognized there was a Chi-nese problem, but that "the public peace and security to life and property in this city shall be maintained and protected at all hazards." This was followed at noon on the 29th by Mayor Bryant's proclamation summon-ing *all* law-abiding people in San Francisco to assist in the preserving of peace from "a large class of desperate men and women." All he asked them to do, however, was to remain quietly at home and not to form crowds in the streets. General H. A. Cobb suggested that military help be summoned, but Chief Ellis declined to call in the militia except as a last resort. Nevertheless, Governor Irwin asked the Secretary of the Navy for United States naval vessels from Mare Island. Wide-eyed children and adults alike saw the U.S.S. *Pensacola, Lackawanna* and *Monterey,* with a force of marines aboard, steam up to the Embarcadero in battle array. The *Pensacola* anchored within cannon range of the Pacific Mail Steamship Company docks—a prime target of the rioters because of the company's policy of hiring Chinese to man its ships. The *Lackawanna's* guns covered the Ferry Building. On Alcatraz two companies of troops were readied for action. Admiral Murray was prepared to land marines and blue jackets—armed with rifles and Gatling guns—from his small flotilla at a moment's notice.

Mayor Bryant did his best to quiet a nervous city. He stated, "There is no cause for individual excitement. The city has a force of ten thousand men ready for an emergency… Any attempt to excite a riot will be crushed at the commencement… The law is supreme and shall be maintained at all hazards."

The ranks of the Pick Handle Brigade were swollen by more and more volunteers. Whole posses of special police were sworn in. Even the grand Army of the Republic mustered for action. These veterans were still young men in 1877 and were sworn in as law officers to help sustain the peace. Four rifle companies of thirty of them—and some Confederate veterans as well—were formed np and headquartered at Dashaway Hall under Colonel James H. Withington. All gun stores in the city and all fire alarms were placed under guard. The better-class citizens—even those not accepted for active duty—laid up stores of arms and ammunition.

The mob quickly began to realize the magnitude of its plans. The Peoples' Reform party and the Anti-Chinese party suddenly repudiated any connection with the rioters. P. J. Healy of the Workingmen's party took exception to the speeches of the rabble rousers, and the Brotherhood of Locomotive Engineers stated publicly that it had no sympathy with the hoodlum demonstrators. Archbishop Joseph Sadoc Alemany asked all Catholics to enforce law and order. (Firebrand Dennis Kearney, a member of the Pick Handle Brigade who later became the greatest coolie hater of them all, eventually accused His Grace of becoming a tool of the "coolie protectors.")

"Fire! Fire on the Pacific Mail docks!" The cry swept through the crowded streets and the mob stampeded toward the Embarcadero. The word also reached the citizens' committee, 3,000 strong, in Horticultural Hall at Stockton and Post, at 7 P.M. One hundred men, armed with the ubiquitous pick handles, were sent to the scene as an advance guard. Then another 100 marched to the waterfront. The remainder formed up into companies by city wards and tramped to city hall to await the orders of the chief of police. The chief sent 60 men to Sixth and Howard Streets to dislodge and disperse a mob there. Muskets were readied but the skirmishers moved out with only pick handles and pocket firearms. They found that the mob had stoned houses South of the Slot and had fired four lumberyards. Ships at the Pacific Mail docks were towed to safety, but the mob—awed by the cannon guarding the Embarcadero's wharves from the bellicose ships offshore—vented its anger on the innocent lumberyard owners of the area of First and Brannan Streets. More than one hundred shots were fired either into the mob or over the rioters' heads. Several were killed and a number wounded. The mob loosened showers of stones at the police and Coleman's neo-Vigilantes, but many were arrested and quickly manacled to the long chain stretched in front of the Pacific Mail property. The Pick Handle Brigade closed off all streets leading to the lumberyards but a mobster sneaked through the lines and cut a fire hose at one burning yard. He was shot down in his tracks.

The anti-coolie meeting of the 25th, in keeping with the blazing piles of lumber, featured incendiary speeches, but the mob which gathered was a dwindling one. No more than 800 men congregated that day. But the tension did not let up. Threatening letters were received by prominent members of the Committee of Public Safety. William T. Coleman himself received word that both his San Francisco and San Rafael homes would be burned to the ground. As late as August 5, an arson attempt (the second) was made on his Washington and Taylor Streets home. An incendiary got inside the house and set it afire with boxes of tar but the servants put out the blaze. When the attempt was made to ring in an alarm from the nearby fire-alarm box they found that the arsonist had put it out of order. However, Coleman's house was connected with the American district telegraph and the police were summoned by wire.

The prompt action of the police and the Pick Handle Brigade crushed the riot by the third day. On the 27th James Smith was arrested for starting the lumberyard blazes. On the 30th the Committee of Public Safety disbanded. When the crisis was over, Patrick Crowley, who would earn the title of Riot Chief for his participation in this affair as well as the

Potrero riots and other mob actions, fainted. The strain and fatigue of the long days of vigilance had proved too much for even his tough system.

By August 1, 1877, the worst was over. American-Chinese relations in San Francisco would never again sink so low, even in the depths of the tong wars. Of course the mob was not through yet. The turncoat Pick Handler, Dennis Kearney, would soon be the darling of the sand lotters.

Kearneyism eventually grew so strong that politicians began to court Kearney. On August 22, 1877, the Workingmen's Trade and Labor Union was formed with Kearney as secretary. His power and influence grew until Kearneyism elected a mayor of San Francisco, and framed a California State Constitution in 1879. Crowley arrested Kearney for inciting a riot and was on the verge of arresting Mayor Isaac Kalloch himself when Chief Ellis dissuaded him. Kalloch was another philosophical turncoat like Kearney. He had led the largest Chinese Sunday school in the city, then turned on the Chinese as a violently anti-coolie politician. Earlier, when the *Chronicle* attacked him in print, he made scurrilous remarks about the mother of the De Young brothers, publishers of the *Chronicle*. Thereupon, Charles De Young shot Kalloch and wounded him badly. (Many feel it was this qualified martyrdom which won him the election.) In April 1880, Kalloch's son shot De Young in his office, and was acquitted. Far reaching indeed were the effects of Chinatown's troubles.

Sand-lotism hit its peak quickly, and then crumbled away as a political force. The one good result of the anti-Chinese riots was that they caused the city to increase the police force to a total of 400 men. For crime in Chinatown-- no more than in the rest of the city—had not disappeared with the emergence of Kearneyism. On the contrary the police had to look in both directions at once.

A particularly shocking incident took place on June 12, 1878. Substitute Officer John Coots was patrolling Pike Street, the narrow thoroughfare lined with houses of ill repute. He spotted two hoodlums, John Runk and Charles Wilson, the latter a jailbird, coming into the street at about 1:30 A.M. They began to abuse the inmates of the cribs by shouting obscenities and threats through the grilled windows of the girls' quarters. Coots warned them to stop, but they laughed at him and began to abuse him too. They defied him to arrest them. This was too much as far as Coots was concerned. He placed Wilson under arrest, and as Runk followed them by a few feet marched him toward the police station in the old city hall at Merchant and Kearney streets. They reached Clay and Dupont, in the very heart of Chinatown, where Joe Kelly was stationed. "Need any help?" he asked Coots. "No," the other patrolman answered. "This fellow thought I couldn't take him down."

Kelly watched Coots and his prisoner go on. He saw them reach Clay and Brenham, then heard a shot, and saw his brother officer fall. The two ruffians ran through Brenham Place, through Washington Alley and Bartlett Alley, and into the arms of Officers Tom Price and Edward R. Eaton. These two policemen had been summoned from their Barbary Coast beat on Pacific Street by Kelly's frantic whistling. Runk still held the pistol with which he had killed Coots. He had shot the unsuspecting officer in the back of the head. There was no proof that Wilson had helped him in the murder, so he was released. Runk was tried, convicted, and hanged on November 12, 1879.

Ironically, although criminals of both races now prowled Chinatown fattening on blackmail, prostitution, murder and gambling (on July 7 one Chinese stabbed another to death in Stout's Alley), and anti-coolie agitators circled the Quarter like cowardly coyotes, the tide slowly began to turn in favor of the Chinese.

Symptomatic of the easing off of tension was the return of a sense of humor to San Francisco. Lecturer George Francis Train, for example, found himself defending the Chinese to an audience loaded with Fenians. He harangued them with: "Twelve hundred Chinamen arrived this afternoon upon a single ship. You cannot send them back. Will you shoot them? What will you do with them?" A wag in the gallery shouted back, "Vaccinate them!"

One of the men who helped turned the civil-rights tide was Judge Stephen Field. Though not widely remembered today, he is recalled by many for his role in the shooting at Lathrop. His bodyguard killed the fiery ex-judge, Davis S. Terry, at this town in the culmination of one of San Francisco's many feuds. It was Field who found that Ho Ah Kow had been disgraced by having his head shaved under the Queue Ordinance. His action ended the Bobtail Order for all time.

Judge Field's opinion included some language and some thinking which were ahead of his era, but which began to clear the air in San Francisco. It would take a long time for complete civil rights to come to the American-Chinese, but Field's decision was a milepost along the way. The judge stated: "When we take our seats on the bench we are not struck with blindness and forbidden to know as judges what we see as men. When an ordinance though general in its terms only operates upon a special race, sect or class, it being universally understood that it is to be enforced only against that sect, race or class, we must justly conclude that it was the intention of the body adopting it that it should only have such operation, and treat it accordingly... Nothing can be accomplished by hostile and spiteful legislation on the part of municipal bodies, like the ordinance in question—legislation which is unworthy of a brave and manly people."

Unfortunately for Chinatown, Judge Field still represented a minority, although a steadily growing minority. The temper of the times was more accurately portrayed by a series of McCarthy-like hearings on Chinatown vice and crime conducted by self-appointed muckrakers and crusaders. These men lumped all Chinese, good or bad, into one category which bore their label of *Undesirable*. But almost accidentally in their probing of the subsurface of Chinatown these investigators performed a service for the community in that they threw light on the highly secret (so far) activities of the fighting tongs which were growing like a cancer in the midst of Chinatown.

# CHAPTER SIX

# THE INQUISITION

*"They [the hatchet men] are a class of*
*men who go around and black' mail both the*
*Chinese merchants and the prostitutes... if*
*they do not get it they will raise a fight... I*
*arrested one of the men and sent him to the*
*County Jail for, I think it was, some kind of*
*misdemeanor, either assault and battery or*
*carrying concealed weapons, or something*
*of the kind. Shortly thereafter, the same house*
*was visited by three of those highbinders. One*
*of them, when he got to the door, pulled a*
*pistol out and shot the woman in the head...."*

—Testimony of Officer Michael Smith
before a joint Congressional committee, 1876

AT THE SAME time that sand lotters were taking the law into their
own hands, men of no less anti-Chinese bias but of more respect for law
were making the hundredth anniversary of America's independence the
shameful year of the great inquisition in San Francisco.

While the city's Chinese businessmen were collecting a donation of
$500 to send to the Centennial Fund, a parade of witnesses was filing
into governmental hearings. All had their minds neatly made up a priori.
Their answers were ready long before the grand inquisitors began their
probing of the so-called Chinese problem. The roots of the auto-da-fé
went back to at least 1852, when the California State Senate first appointed a committee to investigate the exotic newcomers. This commit-

tee had dourly predicted that disputes would take place and that blood would flow as the result of the growing community of Chinese in the midst of—yet separate from—San Francisco.

Early in April, 1876, the resolution of State Senator Creed Haymond was adopted. It called for the appointment of a committee to investigate the problem of Chinese immigration with all its ramifications. The committee was empowered to publish its findings in a formal report. The timely creation of the highly publicized investigating committee in the midst of the anti-coolie furor and hysteria was a Democratic ploy, although Haymond—the appointed chairman—happened to be a Republican. The Democrats had an eye on the November elections. They wanted to see to it that the Chinese Question was kept alive as the one issue most likely to appeal to a voting population of whom one half were foreign born. It was sure fire; the great mass of people whom they would offend (the Chinese) were disenfranchised anyway.

The committee was weighted toward the city, with four of its members being San Franciscans, one (Haymond), a Sacramentan, and only two from the country. It was stacked in favor of the Democrats by a ratio of 5 to 2. The San Francisco quartet—Frank McCoppin, W. M. Pierson, M. J. Donovan, and George H. Rogers—were all Democrats, as was one of the pair of hinterlanders, E. J. Lewis of Tehama County. Only Chairman Haymond and George S. Evans, of San Joaquin County, were Republicans.

The end result of this probing investigating committee was a three-hundred-page document titled "Chinese Immigration; its Social, Moral and Political Effect." Published in August, 1877, it was a modest bestseller. It was rushed to members of Congress, State governors and newspaper editors. Probably 10,000 copies were printed and distributed. Among its effects was the impressing of the Kearneyites with the idea that their voices were being heard in high places—-far from the sand lots.

Of the 42 Americans called as witnesses, 4 were clergymen and one was a lawyer. There were 5 "experts" on the Chinese, rendered so by having resided in the Middle Flowery Kingdom for varying lengths of stay. Although The committee was supposedly dealing with the problem of Chinese immigrants and labor, it actually spent much of its time on

Chinese crime and collected a wealth of information. Whether this information was slanted or not, many facts came to light which otherwise would have been lost. Witnesses who detailed the inroads of crime in the Chinese community included one police judge, 5 regular police officers and 5 special Chinatown police. The remainder of the witnesses was made up of 11 public officials from San Francisco or the State Capital, 2 journalists, one farmer, 2 manufacturers, an expressman, a gentleman in the marble business, and the captain and the mate of a British ship engaged in the coolie trade.

In evaluating the testimony of the hearings it must be kept in mind that more than one half of all witnesses called were officials or public servants of one stripe or another. (One fourth were law officers.) Therefore it is obvious that at least one half of the testimony rendered was by men dependent on political favor.

Of the Chinese witnesses called, 6 were company presidents, 2 were interpreters, one was a genealogist, and 8 were workingmen. Of the 23 public officials called, all but 2 were decidedly anti-Chinese. But to the great surprise of Senator Creed Haymond, of the 19 witnesses who were not actively connected with politics, 7 were pro-Chinese, 5 could be considered as moderate in their opposition, one was noncommittal, and only 6 were vociferously "anti."

The three-hundred-page document contained, in addition to a transcript of the testimony itself, a "Memorial" to Congress and "An Address to the People of the United States upon the Evils of Chinese Immigration." About four pages of the latter were devoted to what was ostensibly the *raison d'etre* of the hearings—the effect of the Chinese on white labor. Seven pages were wasted on an irrelevant discussion of the failure of the Chinese to Christianize. A full fifteen pages, however, were concerned with crime in Chinatown, ten of them dealing with prostitution alone. The address stated categorically that of 100,000 to 125,000 Chinese in California, at least 3,000 were slave girls. But Gibson and historian Theodore H. Hittell bluntly disputed these figures by taking San Francisco *Evening Post* and Customhouse statistics to show that there were only 78,000 Chinese in California. If the second figure of the committee was as far off as the first, it was in grave error indeed.

The handling of the perfectly respectable Six Companies' presidents was bungling and embarrassing. They were naturally insulted by the preponderance of questions on prostitution and gambling. They were asked few questions on occupations, wages, or social integration of their people—supposedly the issues of greatest importance. In the published document their information occupied fewer than 10 of the 300 pages.

Obviously all of the findings of this committee must be taken with deep reservations. Nevertheless, as an opened window on the law-and-order situation in Chinatown, the document is valuable and revealing. And even Dr. Mary Coolidge, with her distaste for the drumhead board of inquiry, and to admit that "on this particular charge [Chinatown crime] the report appears to have represented the testimony accurately."

Hittell labeled the committee's report as strictly grist for the political mills grinding away in San Francisco's sand lots. Dr. Coolidge, for her part, found it difficult to imagine that it was taken seriously by anyone. Yet, State Senator Frank McCoppin presented it to the subsequent United States Congressional Joint Committee on Chinese Immigration as the official opinion of the entire California State Senate.

The Senate committee's hearings opened at 11 A.M. April 11, 1876, in the San Francisco city hall. The first person called to testify was Frederick F. Low, an old China hand and a former governor of California. He volunteered information about conditions in the Empire and in the Big City of the Golden Mountains: 'The Chinese come here solely to make money. When they get that," he said, "they return to China. They come under contract to repay amounts advanced just the same as Eastern [United States] people came to California in 1849, the only difference being that a Chinaman keeps his contract where a white man fails it."

Perhaps because this was hardly the damning testimony expected of the State's ex-chief executive, he was quizzed about the attitude of the Chinese toward the American system of justice. Low replied, 'The guilds in China have absolute power... [Here] they don't know the law other than as the company prescribes. It is this absolute power which governs their affairs." This was more acceptable. Ex-Governor Low was excused.

The second witness was ex-Senator W. J. Shaw. He was one of the first to describe the tong troubles which lay ahead. He did not use the still unfamiliar word tong, but his testimony was prophetic. "Where our laws come into conflict with theirs, ours are disregarded. In Singapore, India [sic], there are 80,000 Chinese inhabiting a distant quarter of the town. They have frequent quarrels among the companies [the tongs] or sets of men, and then they rush about like Wild beasts, stabbing and killing whoever they may."

The next day saw Reverend Gibson defending the Six Companies by making a strong rebuttal to Shaw's testimony, although Shaw had really been criticizing the tong organizations of the Malay States. Gibson insisted that the Six Companies had no judicial or criminal power over Chinatown; their only control being the exit-ticket agreement with the Pacific Mail Steamship Company to prevent debtors fleeing from San Francisco. He acknowledged that the Chinese were great arbitrators and that the Six Companies often intervened in cases to settle a debt.

Actually, said Gibson, "The Chinese companies are for mutual protection, to see to their countrymen arriving here and leaving, to arrange business matters, and to settle differences among themselves. The Chinese companies at the present time and since I have been in this country, so far as I know, have no criminal power and do not exercise any. The Six Companies so far as the people are concerned, are arbiters. When they cannot arbitrate a case, they go into courts."

Questioned about their reputation for criminality, Gibson said of the Chinese: "Gambling is a mere matter of buying the managers and purchasing the privilege to violate the law. Regarding the women brought here for purposes of prostitution, a percentage of the profit goes to persons other than Chinese, in order to secure freedom from interruption. A part of it goes to men around city hall. Regarding interference with justice in criminal cases, I will say that the Chinese are exceedingly clannish. When a man of one clan kills a man of another clan, his comrades do all they can to protect him from justice."

Concerning the tongs running the red-light district, Gibson had this to say: "The company [tong] collects a tax of forty cents for every prostitute imported and afterward collects two bits a week, part of which goes to the Chinese company and part to certain white men in this city. I do not know who the whites are, and I am under a pledge of secrecy not to tell the name of the person who informed me of the fact. Chinese gambling houses have paid five dollars a week to policemen to secure freedom from molestation. Last year as high as thirteen dollars was paid per month, part going to someone about the city hall."

Charles Wolcott Brooks, ex-Minister to Japan, followed Gibson to the stand. He stated: "The Six Companies, I think, have their own code of laws, and the existence of this hostile force within the laws of the United States is bad." He thought the Chinese already in the city were a definite asset to San Francisco business but was opposed to further immigration.

A subcommittee consisting of Lewis, Donovan and Evans made a safari through Chinatown on April 13 with the Reverend Gibson as guide and beater. They first explored filthy Spofford Alley, replete with whorehouses and some twenty gambling halls. Gibson translated the signs over the doorways of the latter—EVERY DAY AND EVERY NIGHT THE TABLE IS SPREAD and RICHS AND PEACE and so on. Most doors were shut to them, as the proprietors had long before learned, through the Chinese grapevine, of their coming. But they were able to enter one den to watch a game of fan-tan.

Next, Gibson took them to a religious meeting in his own Methodist Episcopal Church; one which he had probably staged carefully for the Senators' benefit. After listening to a Chinese expound the gospel to two hundred apparently enthralled countrymen, the impressed legislators were led by their guide to the rookery which was the old Globe Hotel. Here the stench forced them to clasp handkerchiefs over their noses. After dropping in at one of the Chinese theatres the little band of hardy committeemen trooped into the office of the Sam Yup Company to meet some of the leaders of the "natives." Greeting them were the chiefs of the Sam Yup, Yeung Wo, Kong Chow, Ning Yeung and Yan Wo Companies. They informed the Senators that their societies took up and arbitrated only mercantile matters and never meddled in criminal affairs. They told them that they knew of gambling payoffs but they could not (or would not) identify the city hall grafters. They insisted that they wanted the gambling houses and bagnios of the Quarter closed. But they felt that they could be suppressed only if honest police officers were appointed.

After E. J. Lewis reported on the subcommittee's tour, George W. Duffield, a Chinatown special policeman, was called. The questions were put to him thick and fast, and information on Chinatown crime began to build up. After reporting that there were between 40 and 50 houses of prostitution, Duffield was asked by George Evans, "How many gambling houses are there?"

"Very few," the special answered. "There used to be a great many. I don't think I can find one now."

"How many were there six weeks ago?" asked Evans.

"Forty, fifty or sixty."

"As many gambling houses as houses of prostitution?" queried Evans.

"Yes, sir," responded the officer. "They have the reputation of being gambling houses, but the police could never catch them. I have not seen a game of *tan* played in three years. In the early days there used to be tables for white men. As many white men played as Chinamen. There are no gambling houses running now."

Donovan then took over the questioning: "The heads of the companies told us that the gambling houses had been in the habit of raising and paying money to men at the city hall to secure themselves from interference, and the same thing regarding the houses of prostitution. They said that if we could get honest American officers there would be no more gambling and prostitution in Chinatown, but until that time they will continue to exist. This was told to us by the heads of the companies, the six presidents present."

Duffield said, "In answer to that, I will state that all those men talking to you were interested in those gambling houses—"

Senator Haymond cut in. "How is this population as to criminal propensities?"

Duffield's answer was, "They are a nation of thieves. I have never seen one that would not steal."

Haymond went on. "Do you know anything of the spiriting away of witnesses and compounding crimes?"

"Yes, sir. They will do it all the time—from the presidents down."

When asked if they settled cases outside of court Duffield answered, "They all do it."

"And they settle crimes whenever they can do so?" asked Haymond.

"Sometimes one company will prosecute another, but where they can settle for money they will do it."

"Have they any regard for justice here?"

"No, sir, not a bit."

"How does their testimony stand in the courts?"

"They think no more of taking an oath than they do of eating rice," stated the opinionated officer. "They have no regard for oaths at all. Their own oaths they regard as sacred and the only way you can get them to tell the truth is to cut off a rooster's head and burn Chinese paper."

Haymond continued the questioning. "Is it not often the case that on a preliminary examination there is testimony enough to convict a man, but when you come to the trial these same witnesses testify exactly the reverse, or else will not testify at all?"

"Yes, sir."

Senator Pierson interjected a question. "Do you know of the existence of any Chinese opium dens?"

"Yes, sir." The cocksure officer smiled.

"Every house is one. Ninety-nine Chinese out of one hundred smoke opium."

"Do you know of any white people being interested in the business of Chinese prostitution—receiving any part of the profits?"

"No, sir," answered Duffield with a straight face.

Pierson turned the questioning back to the chairman, and Haymond asked, "'Why are the gambling houses closed now?"

"Because the police officers made raids on them. This excitement has had a great deal to do with it. How long it will last, I can't tell."

"Have you had any instructions from the head of the department as to your duty in closing them up?"

"No, sir."

"Have you had any instructions in regard to closing up houses of prostitution?"

"Since Mayor Bryant has been in office he has given me instructions. I never received any before."

Senator Evans had another try at Duffield. "How are you special officers paid?" he asked.

"By the Chinese. We draw nothing from the city treasury. We have no regular salary but we depend on the voluntary contributions from the storekeepers."

On April 15 another lawman was called, but this time a regular police officer, James R. Rogers. He was asked about Chinatown's grubby alleys—"To what purpose are the alleys devoted?"

"Partly devoted to prostitution," responded Rogers, "and there is a part which are [sic] the rendezvous of thieves—Cooper's Alley, for instance."

Rogers turned out to be a font of information. He was particularly knowing on gambling: "The number [of gambling dens] has decreased lately. I should judge that before this excitement, there were from one hundred and fifty to one hundred and seventy-five, and including lottery ticket houses, fully five hundred. They draw the lotteries twice a day—at 4 o'clock in the afternoon and at 11 o'clock at night—and are patronized by many white people. Eight hundred people would be a fair estimate of the number engaged in and about houses of prostitution. There is not a Chinaman but what gambles. I believe there are very few Chinamen but what are thieves. I know some six or eight Chinamen in this town that are reliable but they are, as a nation, thieves... In court we cannot believe their testimony. They will swear to anything. I have had them come to me to ask how many witnesses would be required to convict men. They will produce enough witnesses to either convict or acquit, as the case may be."

Asked about secret courts in Chinatown, Rogers answered, "I do not know of my own knowledge that such a tribunal exists. I only know that when a Chinaman swears differently from what they want him to, his life is in danger. A Chinaman has just returned here after an absence of three years. A man was killed by accident and he was notified that he must pay twelve hundred dollars. His partner had a knife stuck in his back on Jackson Street, and he was told that he must pay twelve hundred dollars. He asked me what he should do and I said not to pay it. He said they would kill him or get Chinamen to swear him into State prison...."

After Rogers defended the Chinatown specials as fine police officers, he was asked by Pierson, "Do you know of the Chinese paying money to persons other than special policemen for the purpose of protecting themselves in their business?"

"I have been told so by Chinamen," replied Rogers. "Chinese who collected the money told me of its payment. The Chinaman was Ah You, a keeper of a store and gambling house."

"To whom did he pay the money?"

"Five hundred dollars, one month, to_____ _____. [The name of the party was stricken from the public record by the committee.] He said he paid it from the gambling houses to secure freedom from interruption. He said so much money was paid per month to allow gambling houses to run."

Asked about another quasi-legal law-and-order agency in Chinatown, the system of Chinese intelligence officers or informers, Rogers said that there were eight or ten. "They are rather independent of the companies. There is one on Bush Street, kept by Sam Kee. He has been letting out a lot of thieves lately but I told him he would have to quit or find the thieves. He did find them. I took steps to have his license revoked and he then found the thieves."

The clerk of the police department, Alfred Clarke, was heard on the 17th of April, and produced a bill of sale for a Chinese trollop, Ah Ho, and testified about the singsong girls. Clarke was followed by President Leung Cook of the Ning Yeung Company, who testified through interpreter Charles Jamison. He elicited laughter from his audience when he was asked "Do you know that there are Chinese prostitutes in this city?" His answer was, "There are Chinese prostitutes here. How many I don't know because I am not in that line of business. You can find that out by inquiring of the officers on the beat."

Clarke, recalled, was asked, "Have you heard of the bribery of officers by the Chinese?"

"I have heard of such things, but investigation always has failed to fasten the crime on anybody. The special-police system has its evils, but it does much good. It would be impossible to keep down crime and secure the partial administration of justice in the Chinese quarter if we had to depend upon our regular force… The specials make a great many arrests, but our best reliance would be on regulars if we could spare them from other parts of the city…" He finished by saying, "The effect of this large criminal population is very injurious to the morals of the community. There is ten percent of the Chinese population that makes up the gamblers, prostitutes and thieves."

President Lee Ming Hown of the Sam Yup Company was asked by Frank McCoppin, "What does the Sam Yup Company do with one of its members that commits a crime?"

"If they found it out, they would deliver him to the authorities at the city hall. We don't deliver him up ourselves, but get an officer to take possession of him."

McCoppin followed up with another question, "If one of that company steals from another, or whips another, don't they settle it with money—make him pay for the injury?"

"No, sir."

"Do any gamblers belong to your company?"

"I don't know. Very likely there may be some."

"Do you know of Chinamen paying anything to Americans to be allowed to gamble?"

"I don't know. That kind of gambling business the people don't dare to let the company know anything about. They belong to the inferior classes and will not let the company know. If they told us, we would advise them to discontinue."

When Ah You was called, he—like Lee Ming Hown—made use of Jamison's interpretation. McCoppin quizzed him closely on Rogers' claim that he made payoffs. "Did you tell Rogers that you paid _____ five hundred dollars a month?" (The name was again deleted.)

"No, sir. I told Mr. Rogers that if I had any trouble I would get Mr_____to attend to it."

Haymond took over. "What did you expect to have trouble about?"

"Gambling houses."

"What would the Sam Yup Company do if they found a Sam Yup man conducting gambling?"

"Tell him to quit."

"Suppose that he wouldn't quit?"

"The company has no power to stop it. But the company has posted notices on the street, telling gamblers to stop, and it was stopped."

Creed Haymond returned to the matter of bribes. "Did you ever tell Officer [Thomas] Kennedy that you were paying Officer Duffield money for guarding his house and could not pay him any?"

"No, sir."

"You never told Officer Rogers that you paid somebody five hundred dollars, or any amount of money, to protect gambling houses?"

"No, sir. Sometimes Mr. Rogers was collecting money for this kind of business, but he was not going to attend to it. Some parties paid him three hundred dollars. Three Chinese persons gave it to him. Two gave it and three were present—Ah Hung, Ah Chune and myself... It was given to him in the rear of Gum Wo's store. I was not there as owner of gambling houses or whorehouses, but as a witness to see that money paid. Mr. Rogers himself came to me and wanted me to be a witness that the money was paid. He told me to tell the Chinamen to subscribe a few dollars for his benefit and he would stop arresting."

The committee had inadvertently cracked the shell of Chinatown, in asking the Chinese about the protection racket which the specials as well as the highbinders had organized. The festering rottenness below the surface was beginning to show.

Senator Donovan asked Ah You, "Do you know Mr. _____?"

"Yes, he is my counsel." "Did you ever give him five hundred dollars?" "Yes, to work up murder cases for the Yu Chuy Lung. They employed him to convict the murderers. Four men are under arrest for murdering one man, and these men are the ones they want convicted. Deceased belonged to the Kwo Yee tong, or shoemakers. Three of the murderers are .bailed out on fifteen thousand dollars, but one is in jail."

Special Thomas Kennedy was next sworn in. "Do you know the Chinaman who last testified?" he was asked.

"Yes, sir. I always took him to be the boss of a house of prostitution... There was a small house of prostitution started on the north side of the Globe Hotel. I went there to secure my pay and met this man. He told me he paid George Duffield and could not pay me. He claimed to be the proprietor of this house. He was always around there. There were three women in that house."

Donovan asked, "He claimed he was not running that house; did you hear him? Is that a specimen of Chinese swearing?"

"Yes, sir. When it is to his interest a Chinaman will swear to anything."

When Rogers was recalled, he testified under oath, "Ah You offered

90

me three hundred dollars as he says, but I refused to accept it. I pronounce his statements an utter falsity."

David Supple, who had been defending Chinese from hoodlums a few years earlier, proved to be anything but friendly to them on the stand. Asked, "How do the people live?" he replied, "They live in small places, more like hogs than human beings."

"What proportion of the people belong to the criminal classes—engaged in prostitution, gambling, violating city ordinances and laws relating to health?" (Haymond was casting as big a net as he could.)

"About all of them," said Supple. "I have never seen a decent, respectable Chinawoman in my life."

Ex-District Attorney D. J. Murphy testified also on the 18th of April, noting that of 700 cases before the Grand Jury one year, 120 involved Chinese—usually burglaries. 'They are very adroit thieves," he said. "In capital cases, particularly, we were met with perjury. I have no doubt but that they act under the direction of superiors and swear as ordered. In many cases witnesses are spirited away or alibis are proven. They can produce so many witnesses as to create a doubt in the minds of jurymen and thus escape justice. In cases where I have four or five witnesses for the prosecution, they will bring in ten or fifteen on the part of the defense. They seem to think that numbers must succeed, and it very frequently so happens. It frequently occurs that before the Grand Jury, or on some preliminary examination, witnesses swear as to convict, but on the trial they turn square around and swear the other way. I have heard it said that they have secret tribunals where they settle all these things but I know nothing of that... I have had to appeal to executive clemency for pardon for Chinamen sent to the State prison by false swearing, under circumstances which led me to believe them to have been the victims of some organization of that kind."

"Innocent men can be convinced?"

"Yes, and I have no doubt innocent men *are* convicted through the medium of perjury and 'jobs' fixed up on them...."

Special Officer Andrew McKenzie was interrogated by Pierson. He was a veteran of 24 years as a peace officer, including 4 1/2 years as a Chinatown local. "We have never entirely suppressed gambling," he volunteered, "but generally manage to keep it under some restraint. We have driven it and prostitution to the backstreets and off the street itself."

McKenzie was not as loud and sure in his criticism of the Chinese as his brother officers. "There is a great deal of dishonesty [among them] but I think there are some honest men. I don't look upon them as being as honest as white persons. The Chinese look upon us as rascals and we look upon them in the same way."

"Would you believe them under oath?"

"A great many I would not believe. That is the rule. There are exceptions, of course."

McKenzie appeared to be a little more honest and straightforward than his mates. Asked, "You are paid by the Chinese, are you not?" he answered in the affirmative and admitted that a large part of his pay came from gamblers and prostitutes.

"Does the closing of these houses affect your salary to any great extent?"

"Yes, sir. We do not make such big collections. There is a dark hour in all kinds of business, and this is our dark hour just now."

After Judge Davis Louderback of the police court testified to the low degree of veracity of Chinese witnesses in general and to the facility with which some of them used American law to revenge themselves on their enemies by malicious prosecutions, Yung Ty testified. He was president of the 24,000-member Hop Wo Company. He was followed to the stand by Sing How, President of the Kong Chow Company. They said pretty much the same thing through an interpreter. Their companies had neither gambling nor prostitution interests. Si Quon, President of the Yeung Wo Company, said he did not even know any gamblers. Chin Fong Chow, President of the Yan Wo Company, also testified but most of his answers were translated as "I don't know."

An interesting Chinese, and a lusty type in general, was called next. Wong Ben, once an interpreter in the police court and county court, opened the eighth day of testimony on April 20. He really woke up the courtroom when he was asked, "Were you a witness in the police court yesterday, where some Chinese prostitutes were tried?"

"Yes," said Wong Ben. "Last year I had two boys with me, and we tried to break up the gambling houses and houses of prostitution. We tried to have the policemen arrest keepers, but Charley Duffield kicked the boy in the head and told him to go away. He would not let us go into the gambling houses to see who were there so that we could have them arrested."

As Duffield squirmed uneasily, the nervy Chinese was asked, "Are you helping the police?"

"Yes, sir, but Charley Duffield told us we had no reason to go against the keepers of those houses."

"Who are these keepers?"

Wong Ben thought a moment. "Wong Woon," he said, "a big fellow who keeps a house of prostitution. An Geo, another big fellow. Every time a woman gets into trouble he gets her out. He goes and collects commissions from women and makes them pay so much a month. He gets lawyers for the gamblers, too, and collects five dollars a week and ten dollars a month. They keep gambling houses and houses of prostitution. They buy women in China and bring them here to be prostitutes. And they sell them again here."

"What do they say if you testify?"

"They put up one thousand, five hundred dollars to put my life out," Wong Ben told the astonished audience. "They tell me if that don't do it they will put up two thousand and then three thousand. He told me last night he would give me a hundred and fifty dollars if I would not say anything, and that I must take it or 1 would have my life put out. Wong Woon and An Geo collect thirteen dollars each month from gambling houses, eight dollars a month from lottery houses, then five dollars a week more from gamblers. They tell me I must not go against them, and they would give me money. If I would not take it they would put my life out. I won't take it because young boys come here and spend all their money in gambling houses and houses of prostitution, and by and by he hasn't got a cent. .."

"Who brings the Chinese women here?"

"Wong Fook Soi, Bi Chee, An Geo and Wong [Woon]," he answered.

"What do these men do?"

"They keep gambling houses and houses of prostitution."

"To what company do these men belong?"

"An Geo belongs to the See Yup Company. Wong Woon to the Sam Yup Company. That fellow has got lots of money. He buys women in

*Richard H. Dillon*

China for two or three hundred dollars and brings them out here and sells them for eight or nine hundred to be prostitutes."

"How do they get these women in China?" the committee asked.

"In Tartary. They are 'big-feet' women, and are sometimes bought for ninety dollars. When they bring them out here they sell them for nine hundred. They make them be prostitutes... They don't treat them well at all... Chinawomen in China are treated first rate, but in California these 'big-feet' women are treated worse than dogs."

"How many Chinese prostitutes are there in this city?"

"Take in the high-toned prostitutes—those that live upstairs—and I guess there are about eight hundred."

"How many gambling houses?" Wong Ben was asked.

"An Geo, Wong [Woon] and those big fellows have got six big houses and seventy-five or seventy-six smaller ones. Last year I got two boys and we counted eighty-two gambling houses in this city. Duffield said if we didn't stop he would break our heads."

"Who is Duffield?" angrily asked the chairman, forgetting that the local had earlier been a witness.

"He is a policeman who watches houses of prostitution and gambling houses. He gets lots of money."

"How much?"

"Five dollars a week from the gambling houses and four bits a week from each prostitute."

"Do you know of any Chinaman being killed for taking away women from these houses?"

"One boy got killed up in Ross Alley nearly four years ago. Those big fellows hired men to kill him. Three men ran up and shot him and ran a knife into him. And that is the reason other boys are afraid to help women..."

"How many gambling houses were there two months ago?"

"Over eighty."

"And how much a month do they pay the police?"

Wong Ben, who was becoming the star of the whole proceedings, gave full details again. "Five dollars a week, each one. These four big fellows, besides that, collect thirteen dollars a month to pay a white man to get them out of trouble. The lottery houses pay eight dollars a month.

94

There are two or three hundred lottery houses. When I tried to get into gambling houses to see who were there—so I could arrest them—they wouldn't let me in. The bosses tell them and when they see me coming they shut the door. I get a green boy from the mountains to go into a house of prostitution so he can talk and see what kind of a house it is, so I can make him swear. The boys working in this city here get twenty or twenty-five dollars a month and they spend this in the houses of prostitution or gamble it off. They come to me and say, 'You get the gambling houses and houses of prostitution shut up and you will be a great man.'"

Wong Ben went on. "Charley Duffield put one man in jail one hundred and ten days for nothing, because he was helping me. Yesterday I had ten or twelve boys ready to swear in court against the gamblers and whorehouse fellows. I told them not to be afraid, that nothing would happen to them. When they found out that they would get hurt if they swore, they all run away. They put up a notice on a wall to put out my life for one thousand and five hundred dollars. But when I went to get it, they tore it down."

"Did you ever see any other notices offering a reward for killing Chinamen?"

"Plenty of them," answered Wong Ben. "On a five-story house on Jackson Street. These big fellows had a place where they kept their books and money and a list of all the men interested in gambling houses and houses of prostitution. I knew I could not get in there so I told Ying Low to go there and see if he saw any books on their table. The first time he saw plenty of books, and I went and got policemen to go there but those big fellows had all cleared out. I think they will have another meeting in two weeks or ten days, and I guess I can catch them then."

The little Chinese caught his breath, then continued. "Last month Wong Woon put up eighteen hundred dollars that he got from gamblers to fight the law. Yesterday 1 had fifteen witnesses to swear against those fellows, but when Wong Woon saw that he asked for a continuance and this morning I have got only two witnesses. My company tells me to break up these houses, and the Six Companies have put up a notice saying that if any more notices of reward are put up they will fight."

Ah Chung, when called, verified Wong Ben's statements that An Geo, Bi Chee, Wong Fook Soi and Wong Woon were the procurers.

He was asked, "What do the Chinamen do with anybody who testifies in court against the women?"

"An Geo, Wong Woon and Ah Fook put up money to kill them."

Cigarmaker Ah Gow also said his life was threatened by An Geo, Bi Chee and Wong Woon. He was asked, "What were you put in jail for lately?"

"George Duffleld said I bothered the women and the gamblers by coming into court against them."

"Are you afraid?"

"Sometimes. I do not go out at night but stay in house and lock my door."

Chief of Police Ellis, when he was called, estimated the criminal population of Chinatown to run to 2,000 persons. He was asked, "What is the greatest difficulty in the way of suppressing prostitution and gambling?"

"To suppress these vices," said the chief, "would require a police force so great that the city could not stand the expense... It is generally believed to be true that the Chinese have a court of arbitration where they settle differences... If in secret they determine to convict a Chinaman or acquit him, that judgment is carried out. In a great many cases I believe they have convicted innocent men through prejudiced evidence."

Haymond asked Ellis, "Do you know anything about offers of rewards being posted up in the city for the murder of Chinamen?"

"Yes, sir. I have had such notices taken down and interpreted."

"Do you know anything about money being collected for the purpose of paying men around here to see that they were not molested in their criminal pursuits?"

"I have heard rumors of such things, but I have never known anything definitely."

The committee met in Sacramento for three days, where they heard similar testimony including information on the tong murder of interpreters Ah Quong and Ah Gow; then reconvened in San Francisco. The first witness called on the thirteenth day of the hearings was F. L. Gordon, an ex-publisher of a Chinese newspaper.

Gordon said he knew of several men assassinated by hatchet men. "The first case I know of is that of Ah Suey, a member of the Wah Ting

San Fong society. He did something contrary to their rules in regard to the collection of money. I was in Ah Suey's house the very day that he was killed. He knew there was a reward offered for his death and he had not gone out for some days. He told me he was going to collect some money and would go to China in a sailing vessel. I told him I heard there was a reward for his death and he had better look out. During the day he went into Washington Alley, thirty or forty feet, when he was shot in the back and instantly killed."

"Who offered the reward?"

"I heard that the society offered it. I think the amount was eight hundred dollars."

"Have you seen rewards of that kind posted up?"

"Yes, sir. They are written on red paper."

Senator Donovan asked Gordon to mention other highbinder cases.

"A Chinaman on Jackson Street was sent for by Chinamen to whom he had loaned money, and was told that if he would go to a certain room on Jackson Street they would pay him. Two men waited for him there, and they killed him."

"Was there any evidence of a reward having been offered for his death?"

"I heard it spoken of in this way, before it happened, that there would be money paid for his death. I was in a house two days before the killing and there heard the matter spoken of. I am perfectly satisfied that his death was the result of a reward."

"Do you know of any other cases?"

"There was a priest in Spofford Alley who was told that if he gave any testimony against other Chinamen he would be killed. He was badly cut soon after, but I think he recovered. Mr. Locke [Chinese interpreter for the police court] and myself waited two or three hours for the man to come to do the cutting, in order to arrest him. We knew the fellow who had threatened to do it. After we left, the attack was made."

"What was the date of these two murders?"

"I think one was a year ago in February, and the other a month or two later."

Gordon went on. "I know of a case where a woman was cut because she would not consent to be blackmailed. A Chinaman, Ah Chuck, went into a house of prostitution and Chin Cook, a prostitute, borrowed his pocketknife and after using it laid it on the table. In a few minutes he said he was going and wanted his knife. It had disappeared from the table, and he said she would have to return the knife or pay him for it. He said it cost him one dollar and twenty-five cents, and he would come the next night for the money. Mr. Locke was sent for, and he told her to pay no attention to it; that the Chinaman was trying to blackmail her. She gave Locke two dollars and fifty cents and told him to buy as good a knife as he could for the money. He did so and she offered the man the knife. He refused to take it, saying his knife was a broken one and he didn't want a new one. She pawned some of her clothing for twelve dollars, but he would not take that. He then said his knife was worth eighty dollars and told her he would slash her if she did not pay it. He afterward cut her with a knife. She screamed and tried to get under the bed when he cut her again. Mr. Locke and myself found him on Clay Street and arrested him. The next day he was bailed out; when he went up there and cut her again with a hatchet. Another woman, Chin Woey, was cut in the head and arm and face for refusing to pay thirty dollars blackmail to two Chinamen, one of whom kept a gambling house and the other a washhouse. Locke and myself arrested the gambler, and he was bailed out. The next day he and two others laid in wait for me with iron bars. My revolver, however, frightened them and they retreated."

"Was there a reward offered for your death?" Donovan asked Gordon.

"Yes, sir. There was a reward of six hundred dollars offered for me and one of two hundred and fifty dollars offered for a Chinaman in my employ. In March of this year I was told not to go to a certain house on Clay Street or I would be killed. One day I went there and was asked into a room where several Chinamen were—two with iron bars, one of whom threatened to kill me. The door was locked after me and these men advanced. I sprang to the door, drew a pistol, and kept the Chinamen off while I unlocked the door from behind and ran into the street and escaped. I saw a notice offering a reward for my death posted up in Chinatown. I cut it down and have the translation. It says that any man who wants to get rich suddenly can do so by killing me, for six hundred dollars will be paid for my death. It was authorized by the 'Washhouse

Society.' I had threatened to sue them and recover three thousand, four hundred dollars on a contract for printing and they thought they could escape payment by murdering me. My Chinese servant knew of this arrangement and was my friend, so they offered two hundred and fifty dollars for his death."

"What are 'hatchet men'?" asked Donovan.

"Fighting men; a class of men in Chinatown that can be hired to defend any house or store that is threatened, and will cut and kill indiscriminately. About a year and a half ago a store at number 907 or 908 Dupont Street was threatened. A riot took place, and hired 'hatchet men' broke into the store, shooting, cutting and destroying. Some months ago a riot occurred at number 810 Dupont Street regarding the employment of Chinese in shoe factories and the retention of wages. Storekeepers hired 'hatchet men,' and they fought the strikers. Nine were wounded, and fifteen or twenty arrests made. None were convicted. I know a large number of professional fighters here."

"Do you know of any regular system of blackmail among the Chinese?"

"Yes, sir. About three months ago three Chinamen went around to do their regular collecting. They belong to a society having its headquarters on Ross Alley. They went around among Chinese prostitutes and told them that a new chief of police had come in, and unless he received a handsome present would shut up the houses. They collected from one and a half to five dollars from each one, and it was divided among the members of that society."

Lem Schaum, a character of the '70s—a Christian Chinese—contributed a little more information on the advertising for hatchet men via posters. He said, "That is a Chinese custom. When members of a company do anything against the rules of that company they are punished. Suppose one member of a company comes to me and says, 'Go and steal a woman from a Chinaman,' and I do so for him. Because I favor him his enemies prove I stole the woman, and put up a reward of five hundred or one thousand dollars to have me killed. That is the way they do."

"Do they post those rewards up publicly?"

"I think not. I think they do that in secret."

"Has it been your experience that those secret judgments are carried into execution?"

"Every time."

The committee met in Haymond's office in Sacramento on its 15th day of hearings. For all its anti-Chinese bias and political angling, the investigation had laid bare the corruption and crime in the Chinese Quarter. Thanks to the information offered by witnesses like Wong Ben and F. L. Gordon the truth was out, and the truth—in the committee's words—was that "the Pacific Coast has become a Botany Bay to which the criminal classes of China are brought in in large numbers."

The State's investigation of Chinatown affairs was quickly followed by a Federal inquiry. Pacific Coast Congressmen had a Joint Special Committee to Investigate Chinese Immigration appointed. Through illness and withdrawal this sixman group was in a short time practically reduced to a three-man junta composed of Senator Aaron A. Sargent and Representative William A. Piper of California and Senator Henry Cooper of Tennessee. It would soon be enlarged by an ex-officio member and a rabid anti-coolie Californian, Frank M. Pixley.

The committee heard 129 witnesses in 18 days of hearings in both San Francisco and Sacramento. Some 1,200 printed pages of testimony resulted, representing a formidable reading stint for the members, if nothing else. To" everyone's surprise, about half of the testimony could be considered friendly to the Chinese. Even more of a shock to Sargent, Piper and Cooper were ailing Chairman Oliver P. Morton's notes. When published they formed a veritable minority report strongly favorable to the Chinese of California. Morton suggested that the Chinese be allowed to become citizens. He also stated, "Their difference in color, dress, manners and religion have, in my judgment, more to do with this hostility than their alleged vices or any actual injury to the white people of California."

Thus the skeleton committee had to lean heavily on the testimony of their cadre of carefully primed witnesses plus a superwitness and aide in vociferous Frank Pixley. A pioneer California counselor and San Francisco city attorney, Pixley later became a journalist and editor of the *Argonaut*. In 1876, however, he set himself up as *the* representative of the entire city of San Francisco to the joint committee and acted more like a prosecuting attorney in collusion with a judge—in this case, Senator Sargent.

One of Pixley's favorite witnesses was Thomas H. King of San Francisco whom he introduced as a merchant with experience in China. According to Dr. Mary Coolidge this claim was true enough—the experience had consisted of King's helping Consul Bailey to embezzle immigration funds at Hong Kong. Dr. Coolidge, a close if critical student of the investigation, found King's testimony particularly fascinating, not only because of the occasional untruths which spiced the transcript, but also because of his language which was illiterate to the point of unintelligibility.

Star witness No. 2 was Dr. Charles C. O'Donnell who solemnly stated that there were at least 150 Chinese lepers running loose in the streets of San Francisco. Dr. O'Donnell was shortly to achieve much local fame as the first great anti-coolie sand-lot orator. He was, in fact, Dennis Kearney's mentor. O'Donnell was not new to the limelight; many remembered (and doubted the credibility of his testimony for this reason) that he had been charged with an abortion murder in February, 1871, but discharged on insufficient evidence.

Representative Piper liked to bully witnesses when he was not contradicting them. But he could not compete with Senator Sargent. The latter had a marvelous facility for expanding what he wanted to hear and compressing (down to nothing) what he did not find to his liking.

Although this rigged and costly legislative circus did not clear up a single disputable point, like the State investigation it did result in hundreds of pages of testimony including some startling information on Chinatown crime. Much of this was unearthed by Pixley's determined digging away at witnesses. The document as a whole served to extend bigotry and to haze over the issues. The only real light it cast was on the subject of Chinatown crime and nascent tong troubles. Senator Morton tended to minimize the evils of gambling and opium addiction in Chinatown, and Professor S. E. W. Becker, in publishing a criticism of the committee's report in *The Catholic World,* agreed with Morton. But the others involved with the investigation were not of this mind.

At one point Pixley asked Police Clerk Alfred Clarke for his estimate of the number of Chinese criminals in the city. Clarke, by now an old hand at this sort of work, said, "There is a big number of Chinese prostitutes and gamblers, but it varies a good deal in proportion to the energy of the police in prosecuting them or breaking them up."

Pixley asked Chief Ellis to take the stand. Morton put the question to him, "Will you state why these dens of prostitution are not broken up?"

"We can only break them up according to law. We cannot go into these houses and force these women out of the country, to go somewhere else... We can only abate them by convicting the persons guilty of the offense and putting them in jail. If they pay the fine there is nothing to prevent them from committing the same acts over again, except the fear of the law."

In regard to Chinese "bondsmen" seeking to return to the homeland, Thomas H. King had this to say: "When breaking his contract, the companies' spies hound him to prevent his return to China, by arranging with the steamship company or through Chinese in the steam ship company's employ to prevent his getting a ticket, and if obtained by others for him, he will be forcibly stopped on the day of sailing by a large force of the Six Companies' highbinders who can always be seen guarding them."

Senator Sargent asked, "What do you mean by 'highbinders'?"

"I mean men who are employed by these companies here to hound and spy upon these Chinese and pursue them if they do not comply with their contract as they see fit to judge it."

"It' is a term used to express Chinese persons who act in that capacity?"

"I have often heard the term applied to designate bad men..."

Piper tried again. "Are they not men who could be hired to assassinate a man?"

"I think they are," said King, "and that they frequently do assassinate about this town. I am told they frequently assassinate Chinese in this town..."

"You have seen these men?" asked the persistent Piper.

"Yes, sir. I have."

"Is there any distinguishing mark upon them?"

"No, sir. Only that they are better dressed than coolies and other Chinese found in the state."

Alfred Clarke, the clerk of the police department, reported that Chinese had even hired whites to pose as policemen, complete with uniform and badge, and to "raid" houses of prostitution and "arrest" the girls and then carry them off to a rival house.

The tongs were mentioned for the first time by Clarke. "Mr. Gibson made a complaint at the police office that a certain Chinaman whom he had married to a Chinawoman had been invited to appear before the Hip Yee tong and there to give an account for the purchase money or otherwise conform to the customs of his countrymen. Mr. Gibson thought that an important case, and we took means to try to bring it to light. Officers were sent to make inquiries. They did so, and I think watched the place. The result of it, at any rate, was that eight Chinamen were arrested in the rooms where this tribunal held their sessions. They were tried in the police court on a charge, I think, of conspiracy. But the statement which Lup Sam Yung—I think that was his name—gave was to the effect that having married this woman he was called before the Hip Yee tong and told he would have to pay the price for her.

Sargent asked, "What do you mean by the Hip Yee tong?"

Clarke explained, "That is the name which this tribunal, I am speaking of, had. This case was tried in the police court. This Chinaman testified that he was threatened before that tribunal and that weapons were drawn. He was told in substance that if he did not pay for the woman he would be killed... But the result of the trial was that the parties were acquitted or discharged, because the evidence was insufficient to obtain a conviction."

Chairman Morton asked, "Where was this tribunal held? Where did it sit?"

"On Jackson Street, between Dupont and Stockton, if I remember rightly. We brought down the safe, and after some difficulty got the thing open and found some books, and among the books was one which contained a list of women. I think about one hundred and fifty women, and some accounts. I cannot now state from memory, but it was understood at the time that these papers related to the transactions of this society or company called the Hip Yee tong."

"Were there any convictions growing out of those prosecutions?"

"No, sir. On account of insufficient proof."

Mayor Bryant then asked, "Does not your knowledge lead you to believe that this organization [the Hip Yee tong] goes outside of prostitution?"

Clarke, after some rambling—for he was confused over the several tongs and the half-dozen companies—answered, "I think they try to settle other affairs among themselves. But this Hip Yee tong we were speaking of was, I think, limited to affairs connected with prostitution."

Bryant persisted, "Do you think there is another tribunal to try cases where Chinamen get into difficulty or have disputes about money matters, such as have existed in this city for the last ten years?"

"The clearest statement I can make," began Clarke, "about that is that the police have been occasionally called to suppress riots and disorders which have occurred at assemblies of Chinamen."

"Secret assemblies?" asked Pixley.

"I suppose they were. Of course, we could never find out what it was about. But sometimes there would be half-a-dozen Chinamen badly hurt, and a number would be arrested."

When Frederick A. Bee was allowed to testify in defense of the Chinese he was immediately put on the spot by Senator Sargent. "I wish to understand whether any member of the Chinese Six Companies has ever said to you, to your recollection, that there was a tribunal among the Chinese which settled matters, criminal or civil?"

"No, not in such words as that. But a man would say that the thing had been arranged or settled among themselves—fixed up."

"Does that relate to criminal as well as civil matters, in your observation?"

Bee conceded the point. "Yes, it is my observation that it relates to criminal matters, to some extent—to a considerable extent."

Triumphantly, Sargent trumpeted, "Do you know of any benevolent secret society, Masons, Odd Fellows, Sons of Temperance, among white people where they compromise the crimes committed among themselves or assume the jurisdiction of crimes committed by their members?"

Bee could only answer, "No, I do not."

Chief of Police Ellis, when interrogated, revealed that he had personally seen posted assassination notices in Chinatown. Benjamin S. Brooks questioned him to show that the Barbary Coast and Tar Flat were more aggravated police problems than the Oriental Quarter. He pretty effectively destroyed the image of Chinatown as a festering sector of lawlessness.

Brooks first asked, "How many police officers of the regular police force [150] are detailed to this quarter for these thirty thousand Chinese?"

"We have seven or eight officers engaged in that locality." 'Those have charge of these thirty thousand Chinese?" "We have a lot of special police for the Chinese." "These are all the regular officers for that people?" asked Brooks, tapping home his point. "Yes, sir."

"And sometimes, you say, the number of Chinese rises as high as sixty thousand in the wet season?" "I think so."

"Do you increase your number of *regular*"—again he stressed the departmental force, as opposed to the watchmen specials—"police officers there at that time?" "No, sir."

"How many police officers does that give you there on duty at a time?"

"Five or six regular officers, and there is always a lot of special police."

Bee took up where Brooks left off, hounding Chief Ellis toward conceding that the hoodlums of the city were far more of a problem to law enforcement than the Chinese. Then Congressman Meade asked Ellis about the help given the police by Chinese. "You mention having received some assistance in the administration of your office from the Chinese?"

"From the more respectable members of the Chinese companies, societies, and merchants. We have had their assistance, from time to time, in apprehending criminals and sometimes in giving evidence, and sometimes in the recovery of property. For instance, lately there was a police officer shot in Chinatown. I sent for some of the heads of the Chinese companies. Three or four of them. They came down. I told them they must get the man. They said that they would, and they did. They brought him down and delivered him up. That is the most notable case I recollect of late."

Meade inadvertently touched on the casual attitude of the police toward Chinatown troubles when he asked Ellis, "When these difficulties occur in Chinatown, are you in the habit of sending for these men?"

"It has not been common to do so. In this case we did it, and in cases of importance we do it."

"When you call on them, are they reluctant?"

"No. They always promise fair, and occasionally we succeed. I have not any reason to disbelieve in their good faith."

"It is simply a question of their ability to perform?"

"Yes, sir," answered the chief.

But the hearing was placed back on Pixley's track when Chief Ellis described a Chinese shoemakers' riot on Dupont Gai in which hatchets and ironbars were used. When Brooks asked him, "They are generally pretty sanguinary in their fights?" he answered, "Yes, sir, they are desperate fighters."

Bryant, who thought tribunals no longer existed in Chinatown, at least got into the record the fact that he had been told by Six Companies officials that city hall had long thought it was a good idea for the Chinese to settle their own quarrels.

Brooks quizzed Police Judge Louderback on crimes not usually committed by Chinese—drugging and robbing, confidence games, rolling drunks, and forgery, although the Orientals had been adept at forgery and con games as early as the '50s.

"Yes, sir," answered Louderback, "but there are some robberies and forgeries and 'rolling drunks,' as you call it. I think we have had Chinamen up for that thing... but as a general thing that is done by white men."

"Is garroting done by whites?"

"Garroting is done by whites."

When Brooks pointedly asked him if a great number of Chinese arrests were not the result of ordinances aimed especially at them, the judge tried to wriggle out by proclaiming the great importance of the Cubic Air Ordinance "to secure pure air and promote public health."

Pixley interrogated Officer Michael Smith on "filthy" Chinatown, the Globe Hotel, gambling, brothels and secret tribunals.

"There is also a society of men here called highbinders or hatchet men," volunteered Smith.

"Explain that more particularly," suggested Pixley. "That is something the commission has not heard about."

"They are a class of men who go around and blackmail both the Chinese merchants and the prostitutes. They go around sometimes and go into a house and demand money. If they do not get it, they will raise a fight." "Do these highbinders blackmail gamblers too?" "They, I believe, do every kind of idle business. I suppose they are gamblers, blackmailers and thieves of all kinds..."

"Why are they called hatchet men?"

Officer Smith explained. "A great many of them carry a hatchet with the handle cut off. It may be about six inches long, with a handle and a hole cut in it. They have the handle sawed off a little, leaving just enough to keep a good hold..."

Pixley asked Smith about police raids on the transient headquarters of the hatchet men.

Smith described how he operated. "Very often I go up there with two or three officers and get inside of the room and search each Chinaman as he comes in, and sometimes arrest quite a number of these Chinamen for carrying concealed weapons such as hatchets, knives and pistols—"

Pixley interrupted, "You say these people are the terror of the Chinamen?"

"Oh yes. Business Chinese come to me very often and tell me where they [the highbinders] are. And sometimes new men get among them and point them out. They are the terror of Chinatown."

George Duffield was called and reported his pay came to $25 or $50 a week. He stated that six or seven other specials were on duty in Chinatown besides himself.

Bee asked him, "If the Chinese did not support them [the special police] voluntarily, would they be there at all?" "No, sir, they would not."

Meade then asked him, "You collect what you please?" "Yes, sir," answered Duffield. Then Sargent had his turn. The Senator asked Duffield, "Have you not received as high as five hundred dollars some months?"

"No, sir, I think not."

At this time Chairman Morton asked, "Would it not be in the power of a [special] policeman to oppress the people? That is, to make exactions upon them by threats, and otherwise make large contributions?"

"No, sir. I do not think it would."

"Is it not a position capable of being greatly abused?"

"It might be," Duffield finally admitted, "if the party saw fit to do it."

Later James R. Rogers, a regular officer, began his statement. "Some two or three years ago, we had an institution—whether it exists today, or not, I do not know—called the Hip Yee tong. We used every means and exertion to break it and tried to find out the bottom of it, but we failed... I think the same institution exists today but under another name."

Many witnesses now began to be called, representing agriculture, the railroads, trades, the anti-coolie associations and even evangelists.

A most interesting exchange ensued when Benjamin S. Brooks testified that many of the anti-coolie men were bummers. Asked what a bummer was, he answered, "A bummer is a man who pretends to want something to do and does not want anything to do. He never begs, but borrows with no intention of repaying. He hangs around saloons with the expectation of somebody inviting him to take a drink. These are his principal characteristics. If there is a building being erected, or a dog fight, or a man falls down in a fit, or a drunken man is carried off, it is necessary for him to be there to see that it is done right."

Pixley was no easy antagonist. He was a fanatic and he had marshaled a good deal of evidence to support his views. In the "Memorial" which he prepared with Eugene Casserly and Philip A. Roach, he used it to claim that the Chinese criminal classes were growing rapidly and breaking away from the restraint of the Six Companies. In this respect Pixley showed remarkable clarity of vision. Because of the wild accusations he was accustomed to make, this quite accurate evaluation of the Chinatown situation was either ignored or disparaged. This was so even though he cited the testimony of intelligent and law-abiding Chinese who also denounced these "most abandoned and dangerous of criminals." He quoted them as saying, 'This class is dangerous and a constant source of terror to their own people, embracing as it does gamblers, opium eaters, hangers-on upon dens of prostitution, men of abandoned and violent character who live upon their countrymen by levying blackmail and exacting tribute from all classes of Chinese society."

Brooks answered Pixley partially by blaming the squalor of Chinatown on city authorities who made no attempt to clean the Quarter's streets. (The corrupt Chinatown special police were supposed to have men to keep the streets clean but few of these dollars ever went to the street cleaners.)

Brooks cited the poll tax as primarily a harassment of the Chinese. He might as well have suggested the queue and laundry ordinances or the old (1861) ordinance which raised the taxes on street peddlers from $10 a quarter to $100 a quarter. This hit hard at the poor Chinese hucksters who hawked tea through San Francisco's streets.

The attorney took Pixley's figures apart. "There are no ten thousand criminals nor two thousand prostitutes nor anything like it. The proportion of criminals is not greater, if as great, as among other people. There are not over five hundred prostitutes—about the same proportion to the population as whites." He then contrasted bitterly the treatment of white and Chinese trollops. Of the former he said, "No laws oppress *them*—they live in sumptuous luxury."

Finally, Brooks did not think there was an alarming increase in the number and power of Chinese criminals in Chinatown. But the tragedy of the tong decades ahead would show how wrong the counselor was and how right journalist Pixley was when he intoned:

"This criminal [highbinder] class is beyond the control of the Six Companies, and by their number and desperation are becoming equally dangerous to the better Chinese as to the whites; [they] live off their countrymen by blackmailing, enforced by threats and violence, supplementing their indiscriminate thieving and pillaging."

# CHAPTER SEVEN

# SALARIED SOLDIERS OF THE TONGS

*"The highbinder tongs hold secret
sessions, the business of which is to arrange
for the collection of tribute. Each long has
its regularly appointed 'soldiers' who are
commonly known as 'Hatchet Men.' It is the
sworn duty of these Hatchet Men to murder all
those who have invoked the displeasure of the
tong."*

—Thomas F. Turner, Investigator, United
States, Industrial Commission 1901

MARRIED men were a rarity in San Francisco's Chinatown in the nine-teenth century. There were only 1,385 Chinese women there in 1884, as compared to 30,360 males. Of the female population, perhaps 50 percent or more at that time were "singing girls," as the brothel dwellers of the Quarter were euphemistically called.

The rootless young men of Chinatown, some with criminal records and all without families, became great joiners. They tended to form not only clan and provincial groupings, but also tongs. These were fraternal and mutual-aid societies supposedly patterned after the secret patriotic societies of the old country. The word tong, from the Mandarin or Pe-kinese *t'ang,* signified nothing more mysterious or notorious than asso-ciation, hall, lodge or chamber, much as *ui kun* meant lodge or asylum.

There were, technically, laundry tongs or washermen's guilds, medi-cine tongs (drugstores) and even "Sunday tongs"—churches. But there was no mistaking the direction which the so-called fraternal tongs took in the '70s and '80s, although they skilfully shielded their operations from the police, and indeed, from all whites. These highbinder or fighting tongs had no clan or birthplace requirements for admission. Members were drawn from all ranks and walks of Chinatown life. Reverend Frederic Masters aptly described the typical San Francisco tong as "a resort for all who are in distress, or in debt, or discontented." Theoretically at least, anyone could join a tong, and they included in their ranks Caucasians, Japanese and Filipinos, though certainly not in large numbers. Some San Francisco Chinese tried to play it safe by joining more than one tong. Some were members of as many as six of the organizations, hoping thus to secure immunity from the street warfare of the roaming bands of or killers.

The tongs started out in life with a show of good intentions, like the similar patriotic societies of old China. They may have meant what they said at first. The *Call* thought so, describing the politically oriented Chee Kong tong as a benevolent society at its start, although "gradually hard characters crept in, absorbed the office, and for years past have used it as a weapon for the purpose of levying war." It was difficult for a tong to turn down an appeal for help from a member; just being asked brought the tong prestige. Winning the appellant's battle against an individual or a rival tong raised its stock in the community enormously. There was plenty of room for them to expand their power. They existed in what was, governmentally (the Six Companies notwithstanding) a near vacuum.

Perhaps the first recruits for these fighting tongs were men of small and weak clan associations who were either jealous or fearful of the power and prestige of such clans as the Wongs, Chins, Lees, Yees and the Four Brothers, all of whom tended to dominate Six Companies' affairs. (The Four Brothers Clan was a multifamily association of long and close ties which acted like a single family unit.) According to New York tongman, Eng Ying (Eddie) Gong, the tongs were organized primarily by See Yup district men.

There was crime and murder in Chinatown before, during and after the heyday of the tongs—crime which was quite independent of their activities. The murders of Captain Charles Barbcouch, of the prostitute Celina Boudet, or of Officer John Coots, were crimes which could have occurred in any sector of the city. The murders in which both attacker and victim were Chinese were usually lumped, out of slovenly journalism, as "tong killings," whereas a number were nothing of the sort. Thus the 1896 killing of Ah Foo by Sing Lin was done in the heat of a personal quarrel. The hatcheting of a Stockton Street Chinese woman in 1899, was done by her paramour, a professional thief, when she refused him money. The stalking and killing of young Jue Do Hong by Jue Lin Ong in 1901 was the culmination of a family feud which had begun in China but which was in no sense a tong vendetta.

But increasingly the tongs tended to corner the market on crime—at least crime that yielded any considerable profit—in the Quarter. And by the 1890s, the fighting tongs had secured a near monopoly on murder in Chinatown.

The tongs as militantly organized bands of criminals and killers are far from unique in the record of mankind. Among their historical antecedents the earliest were probably the Assassins of Persia. Their name was carried to Europe by the Crusaders as a new synonym for "murderers." These hashish addicts of the Ismaili sect were terrorists who were convinced that their sacred duty lay in the murder of their enemies. They were wiped out by the Mamelukes in the thirteenth century. The Thugs of India were similar professional killers and they, too, contributed a new word to the dictionary. Like the Assassins of Persia—and the tongs of San Francisco—they were addicted to religious ritual, secret language and signs. Their weapon differed from that of the highbinders in that it was a pickax. The Thugs were crushed by the British in the mid-nineteenth century.

Most familiar to Americans of all the societies which resembled the deadly tongs was the Mafia. This brotherhood of evil erupted in Sicily in Napoleonic times to exercise despotic, criminal power. Much like the original tongs in China, the Mafia and the similar Camorra began as patriotic resistance movements against invaders and conquerors. Like the tongs, the Mafia emigrated to America, and long before entering into Chicago gangsterdom, murdered the New Orleans chief of police, David Hennessy (1890), and terrorized a jury into the acquittal of the killers. The people of New Orleans were not terrified, however. They stole a leaf from San Francisco's book. A vigilance committee was formed, the jail was stormed, and all eleven Mafiusi lynched.

It did not take long for the tongs to show their true colors, although the public was slow to realize how deadly they were becoming. The Belgian forty-niner, Dr. Jean Joseph Francois Haine, sized them up accurately. He said, "Among the Chinese is to be found a body of assassins called Highbinders or Bravos which is always ready, for the sum of a few hundred piasters, to exterminate the poor wretches who are pointed out to them."

Perhaps no more desperate breed of fighting men were developed in the Old West than the 20 percent or so of the tong membership who were "salaried soldiers" or *boo how doy.* These were the real highbinders—the professional hatchet men. Unlike the anarchical road agents, cattle thieves and brigands of the Hispano-American and Anglo-American frontier, the killers of this Sino-American frontier were fanatical and militarily disciplined. It was not mere bravado or vanity which led them to call themselves salaried soldiers; that is just the role they played. Their battlegrounds were the alleys off Jackson and Sacramento streets, and their enemy the rival tongs.

These hatchet men were not all of a kind, however. When the correspondent for *Blackwood's Magazine* toured the San Francisco city jail before the earthquake he was shown two cells containing tong "soldiers" all of whom were likely to pay the extreme penalty of the law. The first cell contained 6 men; 4 were stoically playing cards while the other 2 kibitzed over their shoulders. The Englishman had never seen men who appeared more callous or indifferent to their fate. On the other hand, the second cell was part of Solitary. The lone man in it, a tong murderer, paced back and forth like a caged animal. To the correspondent his face reflected cunning, cruelty and ruthless brutality.

The hatchet men were usually fearless and were often fair to good shots. They frequently ate wildcat meat before a battle or an assassination in hopes of acquiring the keen vision of the bobcat. When Jack London was in grammar school in Oakland he heard of the large sums of money the San Francisco tong men paid for wildcat meat. He and a friend periodically armed themselves with slingshots to go trekking over the hills of Piedmont to try to make a fortune out of the demands created by tong troubles.

Before the tongs took root on the West Coast a journal like the *Sci-*

*entific American* (1850) could write: "This [Chinese] population is the most orderly, industrious and prudent of any class in the city. You never catch any of the long queues in any of the haunts of dissipation, and per consequence, none of them in the police books." By 1875, the *Scientific American*, thanks to the malevolence of the *boo how day*, was ready to eat its words; by 1885 it was thoroughly sickened by tong warfare.

The origins of Chinatown's tongs are clearly discernible in China. There, the opposition of Chinese to the Tartar or Manchu Empire established in 1644 was solidified through the creation of patriotic and secret organizations. These tongs, for such they really were, dedicated themselves to the overthrow of the haughty Manchus who had humbled Ming Dynasty China and forced the Chinese to wear queues as a sign of servility. The queue resembled a horse's tail and the Chinese, like horses, were slaves to the conquering northerners. The pigtails also made it easier for the always mounted Manchus to seize the Chinese.

The beginnings of the tong-like organizations in China are somewhat hazy but definitely predate the Manchu conquest. In the era of the Han Dynasty, about the time of Christ, there were such organizations as the Red Eyebrows (or the Carnation-Eyebrowed Rebels), the Copper Horses, the Yellow Turbans, and later the powerful White Lotus Society. The Red Spears started out as a farmers' protective association, the White Lily and White Cloud Societies with religious, connotations, having been founded by Buddhist monks. But even the quasi-religious groups later went in for violence and plunder, imitating such organizations as the Ko Lao Hui, or Society of Brothers and Elders, which was not only responsible for anti-Tartar riots—its motto being Overthrow the Manchus, restore the Mings!—but also for personal revenge and banditry. This association and its close relative, the San Ho Hui or Triad Society, were formed after the massacre of Shui Lum monks by Tartar troops.

San Francisco tongs were founded by political refugees from such organizations as the Triad Society. This society was so called because its members venerated a trinity composed of Heaven, Earth and Man. Other names for this secret organization included the Heaven and Earth Society, the Hung Family, the Dagger Society and the Hung League. These refugees, mixed with some out-and-out criminals, entered San Francisco unnoticed among the hordes of coolie laborers. Members who fled to other parts of the world also set up tongs, and in Penang, Singapore and Malacca the British Government had to pass special legislation to protect the people of the Straits Settlements from the exactions of these secret societies. Membership alone was considered a penal offense for Chinese-British colonial subjects.

First to throw light on the tongs was a Reverend Dr. Milne of Malacca whose report of 1825 was read to the Royal Asiatic Society. It was titled "Some Account of the Secret Society in China called 'the Triad Society.'" Milne accused the secret organizations of only posing as mutual-aid societies while they were really responsible for the many dead men found floating in the harbor with their arms and legs tied together in a peculiar way and their ears lopped off. Little more was known about them until 1840, when two British Army officers, Major General Wilson and Lieutenant Newbold, read another paper on the Triad Society to the Royal Asiatic Society. In 1863, Gustave Schlegel, a Dutch official, obtained documents seized in a police raid on a tong member's house in Padang, Sumatra. The result was a book—the first work to compare the Triads with European Freemasons. Finally in 1900, a British detective in Hong Kong published another work which reported that the Triad Society "in California, where it is known by the name of Highbinders, has made itself notorious in consequence of numerous daring murders and other criminal offenses."

In 1891, an Englishman named Charles Mason tried to make himself Emperor of China with the help of the Ko Lao Hui Society, of which he became a member. But Mason bungled his very first filibustering action—the attempted piracy of a river boat—and ended up in prison. Meanwhile in San Francisco the Triad Society had metamorphosed into a secret fraternal order, the Chee Kong tong, or the Chamber of High Justice. In the East, on Doyers Street and thereabouts in New York, it came to be known as the Yee Hung Oey or Society of Righteous Brothers.

The power of the tongs in San Francisco was dramatically demonstrated in March, 1888, with the funeral parade of Low Yet, one of the greatest processions in the city's history—almost rivaling that of Little Pete, later the King of Chinatown. The streets of the Quarter were crowded with highbinders and curious, fearful or impressed Chinese townspeople. The former swaggered about in ceremonial dress of helmets and bucklers. Fully a thousand tong members marched in the parade or took part otherwise in the funeral ceremonies. Starting at noon from the Chee Kong tong headquarters on Spofford Alley, the long procession wound its way through Chinatown. Those on foot soon climbed into waiting vehicles to accompany those already mounted for the long haul to the Chinese cemetery. The line of march extended for a full mile when the head of the procession entered the cemetery's gates.

The men of the advance guard bore gaudy banners. After them came distinguished Chinese in carriages; next the Chee Kong tong members. Following them was the hearse, drawn by four black horses. Behind the hearse marched the professional mourners hired for the occasion. They wore what looked like linen dusters and had strips of red-and-white cloth wound around their heads. All the way to the cemetery they kept up an energetic (and doubtless well-rewarded) wailing of artfully simulated grief. Bringing up the rear of the parade was a company of Chinese "soldiers" armed with rifles and another equipped with cutlasses and shields. In the afterguard straggled a motley fleet of battered buggies, express wagons and vehicles of all kinds in all states of decrepitude. These were literally swarming with the common people of the Quarter. Here and there in the long queue were bands dispensing what to Western ears sounded like unremitting discord and cacophony but which were apparently Celestial dirges.

The chief feature of the procession was the dead man's horse. The animal was saddled and bridled and led by an equerry. Although white, not black, is the color of mourning to the Chinese, the mount was covered with a mantle of black thoughtfully provided by a Caucasian undertaker.

At the cemetery the coffin, covered with a red pall edged in white, was placed on a catafalque in back of a shrine. The family of the deceased and the professional grievers approached the casket and knelt around it. Joss sticks and joss paper were lit, and offerings of roast fowl, tea and *sam shu* (Chinese brandy) were placed before the shrine. The Americans who watched the scene were amused when a flageolet squeaked out a flimsy fanfare. A priest, mounting a parapet to the right of the altar, wore gold vestments and a gilded head cover. He embarked on a monotonous chant which lasted for nearly an hour. From time to time he would punctuate his prayer with a clashing of the cymbals he carried. At intervals, too, an acolyte rang a bell, much as in the Catholic Mass, but it appeared to be merely a signal for the flute player to loose a series of ear-piercing blasts.

While all this was going on others were placing, just to the left of the shrine, a large model house of tinsel-covered bamboo. This symbolized the deceased's worldly possessions. It was set on fire and bushels of joss paper and punk were thrown on it. Toward the end of the priestly incantations in the background the mourners stripped off their colorful ribbons and threw them into the pyre.

When the priest was finished the coffin was borne to the open grave and lowered unceremoniously into it. Each mourner then walked past the grave and tossed a handful of popcorn and a handful of sand on the coffin. The grave was quickly filled in and the people began to disperse. That is, all dispersed but certain Caucasian tramps who hung back to feast upon the offerings left at the shrine—but not before they got their "lucky money." At the gate an attendant, hefting a bag of five-cent pieces, gave a shiny nickel to each person as he or she filed out.

Who was this man, that the whole of Chinatown would feel obligated to turn out for his funeral ceremonies? (Or was it that they feared the consequences of failure to put in an appearance?)

Low Yet was the founder and first president of the Chee Kong tong. He was therefore the founder of all tongs in America, and rightly or wrongly, on his shoulders must be placed much of the blame for the bloody tong wars of Chinatown. He was a leader in the Tai Ping Rebellion, which lasted from 1850 to 1864. But Low Yet was forced to flee China long before the soldiers of fortune, Frederick Townsend Ward and Chinese Gordon, with their ever-victorious army, finally crushed the rebels. When Low Yet arrived in San Francisco he broadcast the seeds of the Triad Society and soon harvested a hybrid society—the Chee Kong tong. It was not a secret revolutionary movement, though it was secret, but it was sufficiently warlike even for an erstwhile "long-haired rebel" of Hung Siu Tsuen's, like Low Yet.

Soon the Chee Kong tong prospered enough to slough off dissatisfied portions of its large membership. These dissidents created their own rival tongs and the San Francisco press was faced with the problem

117

of sorting out a multitude of more-or-less secret organizations whose names proved thoroughly bewildering. A reporter had to keep track of Suey Sings, Suey Ons, Hop Sings, Hip Sings and Hip Yings, Bo Ons, Bo Leongs and Bing Kongs, while not forgetting Bo Sin Seers, Gee Sin Seers, Sai Sin Seers, plus a dozen more tongs and a host of variant spellings, mispronunciations and bad translations.

As surprising as the number of tong progeny spawned by the Chee Kong tong was the manner of Low Yet's passing. The founder of all of San Francisco's fighting tongs died, aged eighty-seven years, of natural causes. Most would have laid bets that he would die "in action," for through him such scenes as that described by Senator Aaron Sargent came to pass: "I have seen a hundred or two Chinese lining each side of a narrow street, violently gesticulating at each other and apparently casting insults as if each party sought to provoke the other to the first blow. Then, like a flash, the clashing of swords and knives and half-a-dozen men were in the dust with mortal stabs."

The true intentions of the tong members were well-kept secrets, guarded from both police and press for years. But, piece by piece, the force and the reporters began to put the story of the tongs together. The San Francisco *Call* on December 5, 1887, ran a long article on the highbinders. The most startling fact, perhaps, was the wide variety of members. The membership was not confined to professional toughs by any means. Sam Ah Chung, killed by a rival highbinder a week before the article appeared, was revealed to be a tong man though he was employed as a servant in a private home where he was considered to be extremely meek.

The sweet-sounding names affected by the tongs fooled neither police nor press. One of the most notorious was the Progressive Pure Hearted Brotherhood. Signs outside other tong headquarters proclaimed, in translation, their associations to be: the Society of Pure Upright Spirits, the Perfect Harmony of Heaven Society, the Society as Peaceful as the Placid Sea, the Peace and Benevolence Society, and the Society of Secured and Beautiful Light. But the inner workings of the organizations remained well-kept secrets until they were broken by the San Francisco police in the late '80s and early '90s.

Each tong had two or three English-speaking members who scanned the newspapers to keep their societies posted, and dealt with American lawyers and other English-speaking people when necessary. But they passed on no secrets to the "foreign devils." Many Six Companies' men were beginning to feel the pressure and joined one or another of the tongs, which varied from 50 to 1,500 members in 1887. The Chee Kong tong was the largest. Merchants often joined it or another tong out of pure fear of the consequences of nonaffiliation. But the surface of Chinatown remained serene.

Frederick A. Bee, Chinese Consul in San Francisco for a time, noted that the tongs preserved at least vestigial traces of rebel underground units. One tong in particular, which he did not identify but which was probably the Chee Kong tong, deliberately refused to observe Chinese holidays or to recognize Imperial authority in any fashion. This tong even flew a black flag over its headquarters rather than the white and yellow of the Chinese Empire. And when the flag did fly from the staff it indicated one of two things: it was a tong holiday or a crime or tong war was due.

It is not known how extensive was anti-(Chinese) governmental activity by the highbinders, nor how adept at anti-Manchu espionage they became. But it is unlikely that they had much time for such diversions. The day of the typical salaried soldier was a full one of loafing, wenching, gambling, blackmailing, and now and again murder. However, there was no denying that in June, 1885, the Chee Kongs welcomed an unknown eighteen-year-old Chinese to their Spofford Alley headquarters and befriended and protected him during his initial three months' stay on the Coast, as well as later. The lad was Sun Tai Cheon, later Sun Yat Sen, founder of the Chinese Republic. His dream, the overthrow of the Manchus, seemed as remote as the moon in 1885. But Sun was in the United States long enough to become impressed with American democracy and republicanism, and he determined to introduce these systems into China. Therefore he would only accept the first part of the slogan of the Triad Society and its San Francisco kin, the Chee Kong tong—Overthrow the Manchus, restore the Mings! He saw no reason to rid China of one emperor only to replace him with another. The Chee Kongs were dubious about Sun's democratic ideas but they supported him. For 211 years they had fought the Manchus, and before Sun's successful revolution of 1911

119

they would have participated in five unsuccessful revolts against China's Tartar overlords.

The tongs did not fool Sinophile Masters for one moment. He hated them and labeled them publicly "bands of conspirators, assassins and blackmailers." He was irked by what he saw as public gullibility in accepting the brief of the tongs that they were Chinese Masonic societies. Masters quoted J. S. Hopper on this score: "There is no more resemblance between Freemasons in this country and the Yee Hing [Triad] Society than there is between the Grand Army of the Republic and the Chicago Anarchists." Masters added: "These hatchet societies believe themselves invincible and have defied every effort of the authorities to reach them by constitutional means."

A letter from a highbinder (Lew Yuet) in the interior to officials of San Francisco's Chee Kong tong was intercepted and translated by Jonathan Endicott Gardner, a Customs interpreter, in January, 1889. It suggested a type of conspiracy in which the tongs indulged:

> On the 5th instant Lee Shan came by stage to our store and said that the Chee Kong Tong had deputed him to come here and collect from Chan Tsung, Lieu Ming Chew, and Chew Keuk Min. He passed the night in our store. The next day he started out. He then stopped with Szlo Kam until the night of the 10th. Soon after it had turned 1 o'clock, Chew Keuk Min died. On the 12th there were certain townsmen of ours who reported that Chew Keuk Min was killed by Lee Shan. Now they are going to arrest Lee Shan. Today Szlo Kam was taken into custody. The trial, however, is not yet commenced. Today the different brethren held a conisulation and decided they would require Lee Shan to make up the sum of $200 for funeral expenses; that they would not be satisfied unless he did make up that amount. How this affair is going to end I do not know. It evidently is going to be quite serious. We hope in some way you brethren will contrive to eave him, somehow. This is the most important thing to do just now. Furthermore, we have no able person here to attend to the matter. The authorities [took him] into custody and yet no trial has taken place. The young woman, when pressed by the

authorities, positively identified Lee Shan as the guilty man. We
hope you will soon send us word.

But it was a police raid on Chee Kong tong headquarters in 1891
which smashed the secrecy around the tongs. A book of ritual was captured. This was passed on to Masters for translation and he found his
long-held suspicions to have been correct. The book detailed the oaths
of initiation, the secret signs, the passwords, and the military-like rules
of the tong. Masters discovered that the neophyte had been escorted to
Chee Kong tong headquarters by an Introducer. At the first portal the
recruit was challenged by a guard and threatened with death. But having
been given the password by his escort, the candidate would be allowed
to enter. Inside he was told to get out of his Manchu costume and unplait
his queue. These, of course, were signs of his renunciation of allegiance
to the Manchu Emperor. He was then dressed in clothing of the Ming
Dynasty, a five-colored gown with a white girdle around the waist, and
a red turban such as those which figured in the Tai Ping Rebellion. Entering another portal, the Chee Kong convert was forced to drop on his
hands and knees and to crawl under an archway of sword blades held
by Lectors and the Chief Swordsman. He then had to bow to the Grand
Master of the secret society, called the Ah Mah, or Mother. He too was
dressed in Ming-style robes, with long but unbound hair.

The hatchet man-to-be, after declaring his acceptance of the tong's
twenty-one regulations, was given a potion of wine and blood (including some of his own) to symbolize the blood relationship with his tong
brothers. He was next ordered to swear an oath:

> By this red drop of blood on finger tip, I swear
> The secrets of this tong I never will declare,
> Seven gaping wounds shall drain my blood away,
> Should I to alien ears my sacred trust betray.

The candidate then crawled under the bench or chair on which the
Ah Mah was seated, symbolizing his "rebirth" as a tong member. After
renouncing all allegiance to Emperor, family and clan, the young man
was led to a third portal which opened into an area where he was intro-

duced to the secret signs of worship of Heaven and Earth and the spirits of the monks slaughtered so long before by the Tartar soldiery. Incense and gilded paper were lighted, and wine and tea poured to propitiate the gods.

Newcomers who were guilty of past transgressions against the tong were forced to run a gantlet in which they were given a severe beating. However, this thrashing absolved them of any sins they had committed.

The final act of the initiation ceremony saw the newcomer joining the members in rhythmically chanting thirty-six oaths before the high altar as a rooster's head was chopped off: a pointed reminder of the fate of any tong man who might break his oath. The chant was:

> From rooster's head, from rooster's head,
> See how the fresh blood flows,
> If loyal and brave my course shall be,
> My heir immortal renown shall see,
> But when base traitor and coward turn I,
> Slain in the road my body shall lie.

Many if not most of the other tongs had less impressive ceremonies than the tradition-conscious Chee Kongs. Candidates for membership in these other societies knelt in the tong's joss room before a war god like Kwan Kong—also known as Kwan Ti or Kwan Yii—the military hero of the Three Kingdoms and originator of the Chinese blood-brother oath. Then, on the floor, before crossed swords and with another blade held over his head, the new highbinder swore fidelity and obedience to his tong.

The Chee Kongs had borrowed heavily from the ritual of the Triad Society in China. They kept a multiplicity of secret symbols and signs, even to the arrangement of a teapot and cups on a table top. The familiar Willow pattern of Chinese plates was actually a secret symbol for the Triad Society. Objects were also laid out to form the character "Hung," for the secret name of the old Triad Society—the Hung League. A tripod was on hand, too, as a symbol of the Triad. Another secret sign was the peculiar way in which members wore their queues, winding them from left to right around the head rather than vice versa, and letting the ends

122

hang down over the right shoulder instead of the left.

Masters found that the Chee Kongs even had a secret code of ludicrous but deadly euphemisms. To kill a person was rendered "to wash his body" (i.e., with his own blood). A rifle was called a "big dog," a pistol was a "puppy." Powder and bullets were actually called "dog feed" and the command to kill was "Let the dogs bark!"

Another crack in the tong's armor of secrecy had developed about 1889, when the police seized a Chee Kong hatchet man in Victoria, British Columbia. On his person they found not only the usual weapons and coat of mail but also a document dated July 2, 1887. It was decorated with the seal of the Victoria branch of San Francisco's own Chee Kong tong and was addressed to the bearer. It read:

> To Lum Hip, Salaried Soldier. It is well-known that plans and schemes of government are the work of the learned holders of the seal, while to oppose foes, to fight battles and to plant firm government is the work of the military. This agreement is made with the above-named salaried soldier on account of sedition from within and derision and contempt from without. You, Lum Hip, together with all other salaried soldiers shall act only when orders are given; and without orders you shall not act. But in case of emergency when our members, for instance, are suddenly attacked, you shall act according to the expediency of the case and enter the arena, if necessary. When orders are given, you shall advance valiantly to your assigned duty, striving to be the first and only fearing to be found laggard. Never shrink or turn your back upon the battlefield.
>
> You shall go under orders from our directors to all the vessels arriving in port with prostitutes on board and shall be on hand to receive them. Always be punctual; work for the good of the society and serve us with all your ability. If, in the discharge of your duties, you are slain, this tong undertakes to pay $500 sympathy money to your friends. If you are wounded, a surgeon will be engaged to heal your wounds, and if you are laid up for any length of time, you shall receive $10 per month. If you are maimed for life and incapacitated for service, you shall receive

the additional sum of $250 and a subscription shall be opened to defray the expenses of your passage home.

This document is given as proof, as an oral promise may not be credited. It is further stipulated that you, in common with your comrades, shall exert yourself to kill, or wound, anyone at the direction of this tong. If, in so doing, you are arrested and have to endure the miseries of imprisonment, this society undertakes to send $100 every year to your family during the term of your incarceration.

Masters blamed the terrifyingly quick growth of tongs and highbinderism upon what he thought was shameful laxity and corruption in the courts. Law-abiding Chinese were also "locked out" of American courts, of course, by the prevailing climate of prejudice and misunderstanding. A California Chinese bitterly explained this feeling of isolation from law and order to Interpreter James Hanley: "In China, money can suborn witnesses sometimes when there is no positive proof and acquit a man of the crime of murder. But in this country money can acquit a man no matter how positive the proof. Several hundred persons witnessed two of my brethren cut to pieces like hogs, and because the murderers had plenty of money they were turned at large. If you call that law," he snorted, "what ideas can you have of justice?"

Masters was convinced that most Chinese tong members in California would abandon the tongs for the side of the law and order *if* they had any confidence at all in the administration of justice in San Francisco. "Rightly or wrongly," he mused, "they believe that criminals never get their just deserts." He once described a shooting fray of October, 1890, which was witnessed by a large number of Chinese. When they were questioned, all the police could get from them was silence or a *"no sabe,"* and looks of stolid indifference. Masters explained the situation. "This taciturnity of the Chinese witnesses to highbinder crimes is very provoking, but the terror of the tongs is upon them. They dare not tell."

As early as 1854, there were three tongs flourishing in San Francisco: the original Chee Kong, the Hip Yee and the Kwong Duck. To the dismay of the helpless district associations and family clans, these antisocial fraternities preferred to arbitrate their differences, real or imaginary,

124

with an ax. Some say the Kwong Duck tong was organized by decent folk to fight the warlike Hip Yees. For a time the Kwong Ducks worked with Customs, identifying incognito slave girls as they disembarked from Pacific Mail steamers. The Hip Yee tong, too, was said to have started out honestly by protecting unwilling slave girls. But both ended up deep in criminal activities.

The Kwong Duck tong was apparently formed by Mock Tan who patterned it after San Francisco's vigilance committees and who used terror and violence to force large family clans to quiet down. The Hip Sing tong, the only coast-to-coast tong, was begun with fifty members and a lot of fireworks, by Num Sing. The Hip Sings were then set up, and Yee Low Dai formed the Suey Sing tong. The Bing Kong tong, another secret society whose members liked to pose as "Chinese Masons" was started in Los Angeles. It failed there and was moved to "Big Town" (San Francisco) and "Second Town" (Sacramento) where it flourished in the hothouse climate for crime of those two cities. Eventually a Los Angeles branch was established. The tong's head was Wong Du King, and although he was a fierce fighter he was liked by the singsong girls, who called him *Kai Yee,* or Godfather.

The Suey Sing tong got so big that its right wingers split off to form the Suey On tong while the far left deserted to form the Sen Suey Ying tong. But the great mass of Suey Sings were held together by such leaders as Hong Ah Kay, the poet, scholar, calligrapher and highbinder. Hong went wrong after his father was robbed by his associates and the Six Companies refused to help him. He was also in love with a slave girl named Kum Yong. When Kum Yong, fearful of the wrath of Hong's rival, committed suicide, Hong was frenzied with rage and grief. He kicked the brothel's madame down the stairs, wrecked the place, and started on a binge which may have been a record for an Oriental. It was at this time that he became a tong gunman, practicing his marksmanship in the fields outside Fresno. According to Eddie Gong, he was the man who changed the *modus operandi* of the hatchet man from cleaver, or ax, to revolver. When the Suey Sings took on the powerful Wong clan, Hong Ah Kay personally killed seven Wongs, or so the legend goes. The story is that his last victim was a prisoner in a cell next to Hong's in the city jail. The clansman taunted and insulted Hong, so he stole a piece of barrel hoop, got a sharp point on it by honing it patiently on the stone floor, and stabbed the man to death. Hong Ah Kay escaped in the confusion and his tong shortly got him on a China-bound steamer. The Wongs were not asleep however. They tipped off the police and the vessel was searched. Hong was found in a tub under a coil of rope. He was convicted of murder and hanged. The Suey Sings and the Wongs finally called a truce. But the tongs were firmly in power now.

The Hop Sings hired Sing Dock, originally a Hip Ying but by then a member of eight tongs. He was believed to have been entitled to eight notches on the handle of his hatchet before he was killed in 1911, on the Bowery by Yee Toy—nicknamed Hangman's Noose because whenever he appeared someone died. Sing Dock, called the Scientific Killer, and his seven cronies took on both the Bing Kongs and the Suey Sings. The Hip Sings were cautious, taking no part in the Suey Sing-Hop Sing-Bing Kong war. They did bestir themselves to wipe out the weak Hip Ying tong, however, and managed to take over the Chinatown in San Jose fairly well. But no one tong could be said to have been the sole master of San Francisco's Chinatown.

One of the very first Americans to understand the tongs and the whys of their existence in Chinese-American society was the interpreter James Hanley. He warned the city, as early as 1856, of the tong men among the personnel of the Six Companies: "These institutions are without blemish if their members would only act in accordance with the established rules. But, unfortunately, they not only assist each other benevolently, but often in deeds of darkness, as we have witnessed here in California. For the last two hundred years they have been much oppressed by the Tartars and the venality of the magistrates, which has caused them to combine themselves into secret associations sometimes defying all law and order and carrying out their views just as they want them. Vigilance committees are of very old date in China...."

Not many years later, in September 1862, the Sacramento *Union* was already reporting such items as the following: "By telegraph from San Francisco we are informed that the war between the See Yup and Hop Wo companies of Chinese has commenced in that city. Two Johns were fatally wounded yesterday and sanguinary work is anticipated."

The company men involved were undoubtedly tong members as

well, though the Union did not realize this. In another twenty years reports of guerrilla warfare by these malevolent societies called tongs would be much more common and certainly no matter for levity. By that time tongs advertised brazenly on posters for the heads of their enemies. Hatchet men toured the bill-covered walls of Chinatown much as sailors congregated at a hiring hall. Possibly the first "advertised" tong killing in San Francisco was caused by an attack on Low Sing of the Suey Sing tong on a spring evening of 1875. He refused to tell police his attacker's name but he told his fraternity mates. It was Ming Long, a Kwong Duck *boo how doy* and a rival for the hand of the slave girl Kum How. A poet named Mon Fung read aloud to the Quarter's illiterati from the *chun hung,* or reward poster, on the wall at the corner of Clay and Dupont streets. It was a challenge to the Kwong Ducks to either send their best fighting men to Waverly Place at midnight of the following day or admit their error, compensate the Suey Sings, and apologize. The battle took place and the Suey Sings, crying *"Loy gee, hai dai!"* (Come on, you cowards!) scattered the Kwong Ducks. The small Chinatown squad had to call for reserves to break up the melee but there was not a single arrest made. All the combatants "evaporated," save for three dead Kwong Ducks and one Suey Sing. (Six more men of both sides were on the wounded list.) The Kwong Ducks had to take up a collection among the merchants and turn it over to the victors with their apologies before they were invited to drink rice wine together again like brothers. According to highbinder Fish Duck, Low Sing recovered from his hatchet wounds and married the cause of all the trouble, frail Kum Ho. His rival, Ming Long, fled to China.

*Scribner's Magazine,* in October, 1876, published a translation of one of the *chun hungs* of Chinatown which had been captured and used as evidence in a "chopping" case in which one man was murdered and 6 wounded. The magazine stated that 50 highbinders had invaded the merchandise store of Yee Chuy Lung & Company at 810 Dupont Street, and attacked 12 men eating there. The diners dropped their chopsticks, abandoned their meal, and came up swinging meat axes and hatchets. Police officers A. J. Houghtaling and David A. Peckinpah broke through the crowd and forced the riot to a halt. A few Chinese carrying bloody hatchets were chased onto the roof and captured, but most of them melted away as usual in the crowded alleyways of the Quarter. Left behind as souvenirs of the scuffle were three iron bars, a club, a meat ax, a revolver, and four new hatchets, their blades ground razor sharp. The head-hunting poster featured by *Scribners* was not connected with this particular tong raid but was typical of the whole school of *chun hungs*. It read:

> WING YEE TONO PROCLAMATION. THE MEMBERS OF THE WING YEE TONG OFFER A REWARD ON AC-COUNT OF CHEUNG SAM'S SHOE FACTORY VIOLAT-ING OUR RULE. CONSEQUENTLY, OUR SOCIETY DIS-CONTINUED WORK. UNLESS THEY COMPLY WITH OUR RULES AGAIN, WE WILL NOT WORK. SOME OF OUR WORKERS SECRETLY COMMENCED TO WORK FOR THEM AGAIN. WE WILL OFFER $300 TO ANY ABLE MAN FOR TAKING THE LIFE OF ONE OF THESE MEN WHO SECRETELY COMMENCED THE WORK, AND $500 IN FULL FOR THE KILLING OF SAM LEE [Cheung Sam], WE WRITE THIS NOTICE AND SEAL BY US FOR CER-TAINTY. THE REIGN OF QUON CHUE IN THE SECOND YEAR. THE FOURTH OF CHINESE FEBRUARY.

In November of 1894, yet another crack appeared in the tough shell of secrecy overlying tong activities. Sergeant J. W. Gillin captured secret documents from Mar Tan. The latter was known to Gillin as a capper for attorneys. He would follow Gillin and the Chinatown squad around and notify white lawyers of arrests made, and therefore of customers for bail. On Friday night, November 2, Officer John Lynch arrested a Chinese and marched him to city prison. Mar Tan, alias Ah Chung, followed at a discreet distance. But Lynch spotted him, and as he left the scene the officer tailed him. He shadowed the capper until he saw him engage At-torney N. S. Wirt in conversation, apparently making arrangements for the new prisoner's release. Lynch arrested the capper on the spot and was surprised when Mar Tan tried violently to escape. Sergeant Gillin had to run up to help Lynch subdue him.

The reason for Mar Tan's energetic attempt at flight was soon evident when the officers searched him. Besides the cards of six attorneys, they found two small Chinese documents in his pockets. One was on red paper, one on white.

They were taken from him over his howls of protest and given to Chinese scholars to translate. The red document turned out to be his San Francisco tong membership card, the white one his Sacramento card. The documents had a great deal of secret code which the experts were unable to translate.

The *Call* hoped in print that Mar Tan would be deported, but was crushed when the Chee Kong highbinder was released on only $20 bail. This was shocking to the *Call;* even a routine vagrancy charge normally required $150 cash or a $300 bond. The paper contrasted this bit of legal leniency with the case of an earlier Chee Kong highbinder, Tom Fun, who had also been a capper for attorneys. Caught with similar documents on his person during a visit to China in 1887, he was beheaded. The Chinese Consul General in San Francisco, perhaps in hopes of securing some of the same attention for Mar Tan, got the two certificates from the police and opened diplomatic correspondence with the authorities in Hong Kong, urging them to turn over to the Chinese Government all Chinese deportees from San Francisco. While all this excitement was going on Mar Tan calmly sought a change of pace. He found a new job as a lookout for a lottery parlor at 633 Pacific Street.

Near the turn of the century either a San Francisco *Call* reporter successfully became a hatchet man, or else—well primed with information cribbed from Reverend Masters and others—he pulled off a first-rate hoax. According to his own feature story, B. Church Williams joined the Chee Kong tong in either late 1897 or early 1898. The *Calls* Sunday section for January 9, 1898, carried an almost full-page drawing of Williams by the eventually famous artist, Maynard Dixon. It depicted the reporter, stripped to the waist, taking the blood-brother oath of the secret society whose watchwords were Death to all Tartar rulers!

Williams said that his sponsor was an old-time Chinese criminal who deposited his entrance fee, or "rice money," and told him to wait developments. One day the reporter, who had lived in China as a boy and who spoke Cantonese fluently, was told that a rendezvous was arranged for midnight of the next full moon. Two *boo how doy* showed up right on schedule. One was to be his father and the other his mother in the secret society's ritual. Passwords got the trio through an iron door and into a low-ceilinged room whose walls reeked of dampness. An assembly of men squatted on their heels, unsmiling, facing an improvised altar at one end of the room.

Williams was led to a corner and asked to strip off all his clothes. He did so, and his body was scrutinized carefully for birth marks—but just why he did not learn. Allowed to pull on his trousers, he was ordered forward to meet the Grand Master of Ceremonies. This man looked like a pirate. A saber scar disfigured even more a face already made ugly by smallpox; the cicatrice ran from his forehead to the end of his nose.

Williams had memorized the traditional responses, and when he was asked "Have you carefully considered the step which you are about to take?" he answered correctly, "Yes, Reverend Scribe."

"Are you ready to storm the Great Wall?"

"Quite ready, Reverend Scribe."

"Have you been prepared with weapons?"

"Not as yet."

"How can a child be born without a mother?"

"My revered mother accompanies me, Reverend Scribe," said Williams, gesturing toward the tough at 'his side. "She stands upon my left, and my godfather stands upon my right."

"Are you ready to become a blood brother?"

"All ready, Reverend Scribe."

"Then let thy mother proceed to shed the blood of maternity."

The reporter was led to the altar. Upon it lay the insigne and symbols of the Chee Kong tong. These included dishes of sugar to remove all bitterness from hearts; ears of corn to symbolize plenty; a dish of oil so all could have light in the future; and a bowl of vinegar into which the blood of the neophytes would be mixed.

Williams' "godfather" pricked the reporter's finger with a needle. As it dripped blood he plunged it into the vessel of vinegar, stirring it. Others in the assemblage did likewise. Then each man placed his finger in his mouth and sucked it dry before exclaiming loudly, "Thou art my blood brother!"

130

When it was the journalist's turn to take part in the ceremony he surrendered to his fastidiousness and surreptitiously dipped his finger into the bowl of oil first, covering his finger with the viscous fluid, and only then performed what he called the "disgusting operation" with the bowl of blood and vinegar. But he shouted as loudly as the rest, "I am thy blood brother!" and he was greeted with a loud "Ho!" (Good!) from his new tong brothers.

Led before the Grand Master, Williams was ordered to kowtow three times. This he did. Next, his personal courage was tested. He was made to walk between two lines of sword-bearing men. As he walked they dropped the sharp-bladed swords onto his shoulders. But as each blade fell it was skillfully turned at the last moment so that it was the flat of the blade which fell on his naked flesh.

The Grand Master then outlined the objects of the tong and prescribed on diet and deportment. He finished by saying:

> Should a brother fall by the wayside, either through sickness or violence, it shall be your duty to assist him, both with your purse and your right hand. The sign of distress is clapping your hands three times above your head. Upon this manifestation you will hesitate and bold yourself in readiness to do battle with the coming enemy. Should the brother exclaim *"Ah ga la!"* [Strike him] do *not* proceed. Should he exclaim "Um ah!" [Do not strike] you must assist him in every means at your disposal. You must interpret each expression as the reverse of its actual meaning.
>
> Know you that our Society is most potent and its brothers inhabit every corner of the globe. Where ever your steps may carry you, there you will also find the true heart and the strong arm of the Chee Kong tong. Bear also in mind that while the Chee Kong tong protects it also punishes, and should you prove traitorous to our cause your blood shall pollute the soil of the land. Be you where you may, the Chee Kong tong will find you out.

After hearing this warning, Williams and the other neophytes took oaths to observe these instructions, and in a grand finale swore, "Should I prove untrue to my promise, may my life be dashed out of my body as I now dash the blood from this bowl." With that they raised bowls of chicken blood and hurled them to the floor where they shattered in hundreds of pieces. The ceremony was over as his prey collapsed without a sound on the landing Big Queue coolly walked down the stairs past the lazing bodyguards to disappear into the street crowd. This murder was followed by the Sam Yups boycotting all See Yup stores and products. Commerce in Chinatown was virtually paralyzed for a time, but eventually the embargo was lifted and the feud forgotten. It would be revived when Little Pete came to power in Chinatown.

When the Six Companies campaign in opposition to the Geary Exclusion Act went down in defeat the tongs quickly tried to capitalize on a situation made to order for them. The leader of the opposition to the Chinese Registration Act was none other than their old antagonist Chun Ti Chu. He had lost face in the defeat of the Six Companies' campaign of passive resistance to the Geary Act. The tongs put a price on his head and "published" (posted) the fact widely. Described as a friend of the police and an enemy of the tongs (true enough), he was worth $300 to them dead. But Chun was not worried, and Detective Christopher C. Cox explained why he was not. "Chun Ti Chu is one of the ablest and smartest Chinese here. He can fight as well as talk. He is a fine shot, and the highbinders fear him as much as they hate him. He is brave enough to stand off three or four highbinders."

Chun Ti Chu was one of the men responsible for the new policy of forbidding membership in the Chinese Native Sons or office in the Six Companies and Chinese Chamber of Commerce to any member of a fighting tong. But success would not crown his efforts until the Americanized *ki di* (short hair) portion of Chinatown's population grew larger in both numbers and strength. Already the handwriting was literally on the wall, however, as a legend was placed over the door of the fine Kwan Kong Temple on Waverly—HIGHBINDERS, KEEP AWAY!

Chun Ti Chu escaped tong vengeance, but less brave and powerful opponents were not always so lucky. In 1900, the Consul General of China, shamed by the fact that since December, 1899, a Chinese had been either killed or wounded in Chinatown by hatchet men at a rate of two a week, posted a proclamation outside the gate of the consulate general on Stockton Street. He began it with an appeal and the recruits were now literally hatchet sons.

Opposition formed against the tongs, but it was sporadic and not unified. Chun Ti Chu, president of the Sam Yup Company, tried to turn back the tongs in the '90s by forming a sort of vigilance committee of Six Companies men. But Richard H. Drayton proved himself recklessly overoptimistic when he exulted that "since the establishment of that committee the fertile fields of plunder have been fenced in against the highbinders, and hard times [for them] have followed." It took the earthquake of 1906, plus the formation of the Wo Ping Woey Peace Association in Waverly Place in 1913—not Chun Ti Chu's Vigilantes—to create a condition of (lingering) tong moribundity.

Another who fought the tongs was Loke Tung. He was also the head of the Sam Yups for a time. According to Eddie Gong, he changed his stripes however. After tipping off police to gambling dens and brothels he is said to have moved in to start them up again after they were raided and closed. If we can believe Gong, he was a hijacker rather than a reformer. Gong also claimed he harassed his rivals by forming a real-estate syndicate, and was soon boasting he could smash the See Yups like eggs at any time he chose. Loke was able to get a murderous restaurateur off when he shot a young See Yup, by claiming that the man was a robber. The boy's family association, Chin, demanded justice at the same time that the See Yups were out to get Loke and his partner Mark Kem Wing. The latter fled to China but Loke Tung stood his ground. He simply took the precaution of securing a bulletproof vest and a pair of bodyguards. The Chins are said to have gone to a small mining town in the interior for a hatchet man unknown to the people of Chinatown. A killer named Big Queue was their choice. He methodically stalked Loke while in the guise of a beggar. Big Queue scorned firearms, being a *boo how doy* of the old school. But he knew that an ordinary thin-bladed dirk might not penetrate the coat of mail which Loke Tung wore under his clothing. So the assassin filed a knife steel to a needle point and finally caught Loke unprotected on a staircase. His two bodyguards were waiting in the street below. The hatchet man grabbed him by his coat, stabbed him

133

in the neck just above the armor, and ended it with a threat. "I implore my people to keep the peace. In a country so far from our native land, a colony such as exists in San Francisco should be in continuous peace. We should be as one brother to another. There should be no more quarreling. It is shameful in the eyes of other nations. Only two tongs are engaged in the present war and this is not their first quarrel. These men must change their ways and not be like wild beasts of the jungle. If this trouble is not settled without further blood I will invoke the aid of the Six Companies and the Merchants' Association and bring the offenders to American justice."

This particular war between the Hop Sing and Suey Sing tongs started, as usual, over a woman. She was a resident of Marysville but the feud spread to San Francisco. It is said that the valley town's Chinese section was depopulated by 200 of its 300 inhabitants going to San Francisco to go to war. The maze of alleys and yards and rooftops of Chinatown was much more suited to guerrilla warfare than the Yuba County town. After 4 Hop Sings were killed and 4 wounded a truce was patched up. The Suey Sings were not so badly battered, but they had lost 2 men and had had another wounded. The armistice was quickly and dramatically broken by the murder of a Suey Sing by a Hop Sing determined to even up the score. A big battle was arranged. The Hop Sings, although theirs was the Tough Brick tong and their leader was the able Wong Yem Yen, were hopelessly outnumbered. Many of their fighters were in the interior, working in fruit-packing houses or in Alaska canneries. They chose to "no show." The police were tipped too—possibly by the Hop Sings. The battle did not take place. Luckily for the Hop Sings and all Chinatown, the Chinese New Year was coming. This was not only a time of good feeling and the forgiving of quarrels; it was the busiest and most prosperous season for the Chinese section. The merchants were able to secure peace so that business as usual could be maintained. But together with the Hop Sings, the storekeepers had to buy this peace with cold cash from the Suey Sings.

The truce was broken in 1900, and soon *chun hung* posters were offering rewards totaling $17,000 for various tong leaders. Some of the reward bills pasted on the blind walls of Chinatown were of a high degree of literacy, if not decency. All manner of insult was heaped upon the projected victim, much of it quite "unprintable" but not unpostable in Chinatown. The Consul General repeated his 1887 action of hiring a force of private detectives. The chief of police added twenty men to the Chinatown squad and closed all bagnios and gambling dens. Federal officers searched the Quarter for Chinese without Geary Act certificates, and managed to deport a few illegal entrants. These vigorous actions scared the thirty or more tongs into a brief period of quiet, but tong troubles soon resumed. They would continue as long as a residuum of legislative and social restrictions furnished them with a socioeconomic base and as long as strong Chinese tradition supplied them with members.

Efforts of the Six Companies to arrange for an extradition treaty between the United States and China so that they could clean house in Chinatown and drive out the tong blackguards went down in defeat three times. Each time the victor was the American missionary lobby. These do-gooders preferred to have hatchet men fatten on the innocent San Francisco Chinese than to have these highbinders suffer the cruel punishment of the Chinese Government which would be their sure fate if they were sent home as outlaws. Probably the greater portion of the criminals (estimated to run from 500 to 3,000) among Chinatown's more than 30,000 people would have lost their heads had they been extradited. Instead, San Francisco became a haven for the criminal classes of China, and they clung to their new home. The Six Companies could only screen, or at least keep tab on, new arrivals by steamer. But more and more Chinese were being smuggled in from British Columbia to Baja California. This traffic would eventually become as important an operation as the opium racket.

So the tongs flourished. In Richard H. Drayton's words, "They did not have to work, other than preying upon merchants and brothel keepers and their inmates." And their play was a murderous game with their toys being sharp-edged hatchets and mushrooming pistol balls. As more and more tong troubles erupted, such as the annihilation of the Hip Yings in one night by the Hip Sings, the public's attention was focused on the phenomenon by various periodicals. In an article in the *Wave*, for example, titled "Highbinders and Tong Wars," a writer who used the initials W.I. and who was almost certainly Will Irwin, explained the strife in Chinatown. He blamed it on the fact that there were no nonjoiners in the Quarter:

> The difficulties which lead up to highbinder wars are in-
> finitely complex and not easily understood by the Occidental
> mind. China is a fabric of close associations, for there the club
> idea is carried to the furthest possible extent. The poorest coolie
> in the Empire belongs to a labor union, a social club, a politi-
> cal club—all these are not merely easy associations, as among
> us, but close fraternities bound by the strongest oaths... Certain
> fraternities have lost their hold in California while certain others
> have grown to an importance out of all proportion to that which
> they had in China. To this class belong the highbinder tongs...
> Before many years they became absolutely dominant in
> Chinatown. It has been supposed that the Six Companies were
> the ruling influence among the Oriental population. On the con-
> trary, their power is nothing beside that of this sinister asso-
> ciation [the Chee Kong tong] and the others which followed in
> its path. Removed from the rigid suppression of the merciless
> Chinese laws, these thugs have pursued their work unmolested
> by our justice. No Chinaman, however wronged, ever appeals to
> our tribunals. It is the old law of private vengeance with them.
> Consequently, a number of opposition societies arose in San
> Francisco. Chinese who had suffered at the hands of the Chee
> Kongs would bind themselves into a rival tong for mutual pro-
> tection and vengeance.

Chinese secrecy, fear and fatalism were at fault. All these factors
made for the rapid breeding of crime in Chinatown.

Will Irwin felt that the crucial moment for Chinatown came in the
1890s, when the hired gunmen ran away with control of the tongs during
the boycott of Sam Yup establishments. A real reign of terror resulted.
Of arrested highbinders he said, "They thrived on the beans and stale
bread of prison fare and were worthless as chain-gang laborers." Irwin
approved of the police-state methods of the city's desperate authorities,
especially the flying squad which periodically raided and wrecked various tong headquarters. He also approved of the rousting of groups gath-

ered on corners. Even elders, congregating to chat over a pipe, were rudely told by police to "Move on!" These drastic measures, as Irwin pointed out, prevented more trouble, though they did not actually cure tong wars.

Two of the more notorious rivals to the Chee Kong tong were the Gee Sin Seer and the Bo Sin Seer. The first of these two hatchet societies was the Guild of Hereditary Virtue, the other was the Guild for the Protection of Virtue. As far as the press could determine, the Bo Sin Seer was controlled by men who kept legitimate grocery stores as well as illicit fan-tan and bawdy houses, while the Gee Sin Seer was under the rule of entrepreneur Little Pete. In 1887, the *Call* publicly declared that the business of the latter society was murder and the fixing of trials. These two societies together were able to raise $30,000 in just one meeting, to defend Little Pete's henchman, Lee Chuck after he murdered Yen Yuen on Washington Street. The tong men boasted he would never hang. They were right.

During the gray '90s the highbinder tongs were at the height of their power. Chief of Police Crowley supplied Reverend Masters with a rogue's gallery of nine representative salaried soldiers in 1892. Number One was Leong Yuen Gun, a blackmailer and a fighter of the Wah Ting San Fong tong. When Crowley told Masters about Leong the latter was serving a ten-year sentence at San Quentin for shooting Jare Hoy on Dupont Gai. Wong Fun Kim, a Chee Kong hatchet man, was also in state prison for a murder in Humboldt County and a kidnapping in Chinatown. Another Chee Kong brother was Tarm Poi, sentenced to death for chopping Fong Hoy to death on the corner of Dupont and Jackson. Lee Chuck of the Gee Sin Seer tong was listed, of course, and the mug shot of Lee Sam could also be admired. This Chee Kong highbinder had an original way of operating. He was a vitriol thrower. He had almost blinded Fong Lin, a denizen of Sullivan's Alley, on November 11, 1887, but was acquitted of charges in Superior Court when the terrified woman, intimidated by Chee Kong toughs, refused to identify him as her assailant. Yee Lock was a robber gunman of the Suey On tong who drew fifteen years in prison for robbing and garroting the wife of Mah You Lin. He and his accomplice Yee Hong Yuen were also in Crowley's gallery. Fong Ah Sing of the Tak Tung tong and Bing Kong tong was represented, too, for having shot Toy Gam, the inmate of a Cum Cook Alley parlorhouse, to death. He was hanged at the county jail though he thought somehow that he was immune to arrest after having secured the formal incorporation of his tongs. "Now I have power," he had mistakenly said as he sallied forth to carry out his grudge against the singsong girl. Lee Kay, the last of the chief's beauties, was not as deadly as his gallery mates. The Chee Kong highbinder had drawn twelve years for throwing pepper in the eyes of a white woman and robbing her.

It is difficult to say how many tongs were active during the bloody '80s and '90s, what with mergers and splinterings, and the perennial problem of translating their names into English. Some say there were 19; others that there were as many as 30. Among the important secret societies were the Bing Kong tong, founded by secessionist Chee Kongs; the Wah Ting San Fong tong and the On Yick tong, controlling brothels; the Kwong Duck and On Leong tongs which handled the actual trafficking in slave girls; and the Hip Sing tong which controlled much of the gambling in the Quarter.

Police Lieutenant William Price in 1898, made a long, detailed statement to Commissioner of Immigration Hart H. North about these societies which euphemistically called themselves the Hall of Far Reaching Virtue (Kwong Duck tong), the Hall of Glorious Conscientiousness (On Leong tong), the Hall of Victorious Union (Hip Sings); the Hall of Auspicious Victory (Suey Sings), the Hall of Associated Conquerors (Hop Sings), the Hall of Realized Repose (Suey On tong), and the Hall of the Flowery Mountain Arbor (the Wah Ting San Fong tong). Price said, "If a member has anything against another man he places his case before the society and offers so much money to have the man killed. After they have settled on the man to be killed, his head is as good as gone. The societies' rules are so binding that those who are chosen are bound to kill their victims even if there were twenty policemen standing about at the time."

Price thought that there were as many as 3,000 highbinders in San Francisco just before the end of the nineteenth century. More realistic was Consul General Ho Yow's figure of only 400-500 real whatever the total membership of the tongs might be. They were both agreed that they constituted "the worst class of people on the face of the earth." Price reminded North, "They do not molest the white people, as they fear an uprising against their race in the event that any white man was killed." Yet some Caucasians were marked for death by the tongs. Jonathan Endicott Gardner, Chinese interpreter for the Customs House, received a letter from a Leung Tsun warning him of a price set on his head by highbinders. Leung himself had been approached to do the job for a $100 reward by bad man Lo Tsun.

The hatchet man wrote Gardner: "You have done me no harm. How could I bring harm to you? What I am afraid of now is that, with me not willing to injure you, he would find someone else who would be willing. I shall just appear willing; in point of fact, I shall do nothing. I send you word early so that you may be cautious as you go in or out, in order that others may not harm you in some unexpected way. I have long known of your doing good all the time. That is the reason why I am so bold in speaking of this matter as I do. Be sure not to let this go out for fear Lo Tsun should have a design on me for it. It is hard to describe his wicked ways. Be careful; that is all."

In May, 1900, a number of prominent Chinese came to the hotel room of Thomas Turner, investigating the tongs for the United States Industrial Commission. They were fearful of tong reprisal but corroborated what Price and Gardner had said about the immigration frauds committed by the tongs. Price had said, "One of the by-laws in all the highbinder societies is to the effect that every highbinder is *obliged* to aid in the landing of cooly [sic] laborers and Chinese slave girls." Jonathan Endicott Gardner said about the same thing—"Fully seventy-five percent of all the frauds committed at the present time against the exclusion law can be traced directly to the highbinder organizations."

Asked for details on the organized smuggling of "slots" or illegal Chinese entrants, he said, "I know of some who are banded together for the purpose of aiding Chinese in illegal entrance into the United States. I know that they make that their business. These men are well known to the Chinese community, so well known, and their business so well known, that they actually had a word coined for themselves, which is Bahn Gar, which means a Chinaman, or Chinese, in the business of importing coolies or Chinese slaves—"

Before Gardner could continue he was interrupted by his questioner.

*Richard H. Dillon*

"What part, if any, do the highbinders take in promoting this evil immigration?"

Gardner answered matter of factly, "They furnish false witnesses and frighten off anyone who might feel justified in coming forth and telling the truth."

"What do you know in a general way about the highbinders, their organization and so forth?" Gardner was asked.

"In general," he replied, "they are organized societies for the purpose of committing crime. They exist on blackmail, on pay for protecting gambling houses and disreputable places in general. I know that they take it upon themselves to try cases, to review judgments of our courts with utter disregard for our laws. I know that they nullify our decisions. For instance, if an American court had rendered a decision, they would intimidate the witnesses so that when the cases go into a higher court everything would be changed. They defy our courts by ways and means of their own. I know that they impose their own sentences upon offenders from their own standpoint. They levy fines in some cases and death in others. I know they have in their service paid men to do their killing, and so long have they had this service that the men have a particular name; they are called 'hatchet men.' I know they control our judicial oaths. That they can say an oath shall or shall not be taken. I know them as organized societies of crime. They distribute revolvers to their members and send them out—"

Again Professor Gardner was interrupted. "It is a fact, Doctor, is it not, that your life has been threatened by these highbinders?"

Without emotion Gardner replied, "Yes."

After a pause he continued. "I know, too, they use our courts, if necessary, to enforce their decisions."

"In what manner?"

"By laying a charge against a certain Chinaman and having our judge pronounce the sentence. I know that these highbinders furnish witnesses for anything wanted, at so much a head. I have had cases in which men have come forward to testify and when the time came, they were spirited away..."

"Do you think deportation is practically the only remedy?" Gardner was asked.

140

"Yes."

"In a general way, will you state why the Federal and municipal authorities are unable to break up these organizations or to detect the offenders when a crime is committed?"

"Because the highbinders furnish witnesses and terrify witnesses that the State may rely upon."

"What would be the result if some honest Chinaman would take the stand and give testimony against them?"

"He would be liable to forfeit his life."

Thomas F. Turner therefore asked Congress to employ the strongest measures against the hatchet men. He reminded the legislators that 95 percent of them were either aliens or criminals of the worst type. According to Gardner, these 1,500 to 2,000 men constituted the entire criminal population of Chinatown and were responsible for at least 75 percent of all frauds against the Exclusion Act in addition to a whole catalogue of other crimes. "The thing which they fear above all others, holding it in greater dread than all of our laws, our courts and jails," said Turner, "is deportation to China. The purpose of the highbinder, of the highbinder organizations, is vicious and criminal. Therefore," he concluded, "they should be suppressed by law of Congress, and membership therein or in any society having for its purpose the commission of crime or the violation of our laws on the part of aliens residing in this country should render such aliens liable to deportation."

While Turner urged these strong measures to put an end to the fighting tongs he was not sanguine of success. "The power of the highbinder tongs among the Chinese population is almost absolute," he warned. "So great is the dread inspired among the Chinese by these societies that few have the courage to resist their criminal demands. The State and municipal authorities have been powerless to suppress the crimes of the highbinders for the reason that no Chinese witness has the courage to appear and give testimony against a highbinder. Every witness who should so appear and testify would be marked for death."

Since this was indeed the case, San Francisco had to fumble along, depending on rumor and white witnesses and "experts" to fill them in on Chinatown's underground tensions. However, there was still time for one more investigation—one more inquisition. This one was the most thorough job yet, and when it was over the police had a house-by-house map of Chinatown crime and vice to pore over and to base their raids upon. The last of the Chinatown crusaders was Willard B. Farwell. And it was he who became cartographer extraordinary to the San Francisco police department.

# CHAPTER EIGHT

# CRUSADER FARWELL

*"He has positive traits of character, with*
*the courage of his convictions, is independent*
*in thought, utterly free from bigotry and kindly*
*and charitable to all beliefs and creeds."*

—Pioneer Benjamin F. Swasey, describing
Willard B. Farwell

LIKE A DISTANT ECHO of the great inquisition of 1876, Willard B.
Farwell burst on the San Francisco scene in 1885 with a great crusade
against Chinatown crime. The biography of this almost forgotten San
Franciscan is the story of the city's progress toward a showdown with
the tongs. Farwell, a member of the San Francisco Board of Supervisors,
was one of the last of the long line of knights who tilted against Chinatown criminality. Included were Chiefs of Police Theodore Cockrill,
Isaiah Lees, Henry Hiram Ellis, and Patrick Crowley plus the redoubt-
able Sergeant (later Lieutenant) Price, the Police Department's ax-man
answer to the hatchet men. Price was the man who destroyed the headquarters of the tongs in a campaign of what might later have been called
massive retaliation. (Perhaps Price went too far. Like Officer Cullinane
and Sergeant Cook, he was accused of brutality by both the good and
bad people of Chinatown.) But before Price and his Chinatown squad
could turn tong headquarters to kindling the secret societies had to be
located and pin-pointed on a map. This is one chore which Willard Farwell accepted gladly, and it was he who produced the handy guide to
Chinatown vice and crime which made Price's raids possible.

For men like Crowley or Price it was part of their job as policemen to clean up Chinatown. Farwell was subject to no such requirement, but as an elected official he was not content simply to warm an alderman's seat while the tong wars shamed San Francisco before the world. He resembled the fiery, sideburned Frank Pixley of the 1876 hearings. Like Pixley, his friend, he was a newspaperman, and like him he had a burning fanaticism to cleanse Chinatown of its evil—literally by fire and sword if necessary.

Farwell was an oldtimer in California, a pioneer with an adventurous and successful career in the State already behind him when he became a supervisor. Of English descent, his family had arrived in America about 1635. Among his antecedents were doughty Indian fighters. Doubtless this lineage contributed something of the drive and pugnacity which characterized him. Farwell was born in Marlborough, Massachusetts, in 1829. Family financial conditions prevented his going to Harvard; instead he worked as a bookkeeper in Boston. But there he organized the first New England stock company of goldseekers after the California Gold Rush. He brought the members of the Boston and California Stock Mining and Trading Company to San Francisco on the *Edward Everett* in July, 1849, and tried his hand at mining, shipping, business and farming before going to San Francisco in 1852.

There he joined Frank Pixley and three other men in publishing the *Daily Whig.* While still in journalism he entered a career in politics by being elected an assemblyman on the Native American party ticket. His New England heritage was soon in evidence with his first crusade—a successful one—against gambling. In 1856, the Whig party nominated him for State Senator but he was defeated by the Democratic nominee. Farwell was bitter about this setback, claiming his Irish opponent had won solely because of "the foreign vote." He turned back to journalism, founding a paper called the *Citizen,* but was soon made editor of the powerful and respected San Francisco Daily *Alta California.* The trend of the *Alta* toward conservatism and an anti-Chinese policy picked up speed with Farwell in the editorial chair.

He reentered politics and his star began to rise again. He went to Washington, D. C. in 1860, as Colonel E. D. Baker's private secretary when Baker was elected senator from Oregon. In 1861, President Lincoln appointed him to the post of Naval Officer, United States Customs

House, San Francisco. In this post Farwell was so diligent and efficient in uncovering revenue frauds that the Government ordered him to Europe to represent the United States in condemnation suits. He proved to Washington that he could smell out corruption in these Customs cases, and all of them were prosecuted safely, thanks to him. When his term of office expired he was appointed Resident Agent of the United States Treasury Department in Europe.

After five years in Europe on this roving commission, Farwell returned to the United States. He plunged into business and did not reenter politics until the '80s when he was named chairman of the Republican County Committee in San Francisco and a member of the party's State Central Committee. He was elected to the Board of Supervisors in 1884 and quickly became the commonly acknowledged leader of that body of men both because of his drive and his wide and varied background in Government service. Although he was the most influential member of the board—particularly after his Chinatown report and map—he chose not to run again, but instead tried his hand at writing. He was successful in this and his articles appeared in *Forum, Overland Monthly, Century, Popular Science Monthly* and other major periodicals.

A serious, dedicated man, Farwell was generally liked. G. W. Sullivan described him as "cultured, and refined. His society is greatly enjoyed by his host of friends. Charming as a conversationalist, he nevertheless is unobtrusive both in speech and manner." The only jarring note in the estimations of this civic figure came from Frederick Marriott, editor of the San Francisco *Newsletter.* In describing what must be considered Farwell's masterpiece—the Board of Supervisor's report of 1885 on Chinatown, master minded by him—Marriott not only denounced it as sensational and misleading but called many of Farwell's charges "mastodon falsehoods."

Just what did Farwell turn up in his ruthless expose? What was this special report which ripped the lid off Chinatown; which made Farwell briefly famous; and which—with its remarkable crime map of Chinatown—is still remembered by local historians?

The attention of the supervisors had been called frequently to the unsanitary, lawless firetrap which was Chinatown. Under Farwell's rigorous prodding they determined to discover why the district's evils were permitted to exist. They would also seek a course of action to correct these evils. By a board resolution of February 2, 1885, introduced by Farwell and adopted on his motion, a three-man committee was set up, headed by him. He quickly turned the committee into a one-man show. He went far beyond the main concern of the board (rattled by frequent scare rumors of plague) which was to survey "the foul and filthy condition of the premises in that quarter." Farwell was more concerned with Chinese crime than with the Quarter's lack of sanitation, although he, too, felt it was a serious menace to the health of the community at large. The wording of his resolutions was as follows:

> *Resolved,* That a committee of three be appointed whose duty it shall be to visit, thoroughly inspect and report upon that portion of the city commonly known as "Chinatown," with a view of ascertaining so far as possible whether a condition of things exist in such quarter injurious to the public health or public morals, and what measures it may be necessary to adopt, if any, to correct abuses and abate public nuisances commonly supposed to exist in such district.
>
> *Resolved,* That the Chief of Police be, and hereby is, requested to aid and assist such committee in their labors to the utmost extent of his power, and to detail such officers as the committee may require to aid them in their labors.

Not all members of the Board of Supervisors were impressed with the importance and size of Farwell's investigatory task. They first made a motion to call the Special Chinatown Committee to report on progress or completion of the investigation at the board's May meeting. A second motion, to repeal the enabling or empowering resolutions, threatened to kill Farwell's crusade before it was begun. But the tenacious Yankee fought for his plan and had the new resolution postponed indefinitely. He worked feverishly, and to be on the safe side, had his progress report in for the May 11th meeting.

At that time the board learned that the committee had made several visits to Chinatown, and more important, with hired special assistants had made a building-by-building survey of the twelve blocks which constituted Chinatown in 1885. The information was translated into a map which is now a classic of California. By using different colored inks in the printing of it, Farwell was able to show the board and the chief of police the geography of crime in Chinatown. There, in black and white and color were diagrammed the complexes of white and Oriental brothels, gambling dens, opium hang-outs and other features of Chinatown *criminalis.*

Farwell and his colleagues first sought some way to reduce the much-protested health menace of the Quarter short of removing the people altogether, which was not deemed feasible by the chairman. Farwell may have been a fanatic but he was not bereft of common sense. He disclaimed any sympathy with the rabid portion of the populace which cried out against the Chinese and threatened physical force to eject them. The health threat was not entirely a straw bogy. In twelve years there were 72 cases of either leprosy or elephantiasis, most of whom were shipped home to China. But 9 of them died in the city's smallpox hospital on Twenty-sixth Street.

The population of Chinatown was already spilling over the old boundaries of Broadway, California, Kearny and Stockton Streets, but the heart of the Quarter was the same dozen blocks as of old. Every room of every floor of every building of every block in the heart of Chinatown was visited by Farwell, his two colleagues, or the surveyors he employed. (The finished map showed only the character of the first-floor occupants.)

One of the by-products of the tours of inspection was the cleaning up of the district. The first visit by Farwell was an over-all survey of houses and shops. He reported streets and buildings to be "filthy in the extreme" and he worried in print about the precipitation of virulent epidemics upon the city from the litter and rubbish which caked the alleys, streets and courtyards. On subsequent visits he was surprised and pleased to see that many of the Chinese had cleared up their areas of garbage and debris, probably on the theory of an ounce of prevention, a pound of city hall cure. Farwell's crusade had a salutatory effect on Chinatown immediately, but he predicted a speedy relapse. At the end of his crusade he described the area as still "the filthiest spot inhabited by men, women and children on the American continent." (More than a decade later,

147

with deputized wrecking crews, the Department of Health began to pull down the most rotten buildings of the area. The job was finished by the earthquake and fire in 1906.)

The squalor of Chinatown so depressed Farwell that he claimed officially in a municipal document that some humans—by which he meant San Francisco's Chinese—lived in such degradation that they were scarcely a degree above the level of the rats of the Embarcadero.

Chinatown's denizens proved far too slippery for an accurate census, so Farwell hit upon the expedient of counting every bunk in the district (beds were almost unknown) and multiplying them by two. He estimated that each pallet or bunk was occupied by at least two persons, sleeping in shifts. There is a good chance here that he underestimated, for there were probably frequent "relays" during the daylight hours. He was undoubtedly right when he ventured that there was not an hour of the day or night that all of crowded Chinatown's bunks were not occupied by someone. Based on a tally of 15,180 bunks, Farwell came up with a figure of 30,360 Chinese in Chinatown as of 1885. For such a strangely arrived at figure this has the ring of accuracy, although Farwell himself feared he might have underestimated by as much as 20 percent. For one thing, there were many uncounted bedrolls in the buildings. In any case, Farwell flatly stated, in regard to his 30,360 figure, "Your committee believes this is the lowest possible estimate that can fairly be made."

There was no shortage of prostitutes. Farwell came up with a figure of 567. With them were 87 unfortunate children. In one house alone, on Sullivan's Alley, he found 19 prostitutes jammed in with 16 children. It was one of the most wretched tenements he saw.

Farwell went back to the two investigating committees of 1876 for added ammunition, but his report—though sprinkled with quoted passages from the earlier documents—was largely the result of his own diligence and zeal.

A "disgusting and surprising feature" of his tours of the streets of the singsong girls was the discovery that Chinatown was ringed by white prostitution. He did not attempt to enumerate the number of degraded Caucasian women in this line of business, but he confessed his shock at finding that "their mode of life seems to be modeled after that of the Mongolians to a larger extent than after the manners and customs of the race to which they belong." (On the other hand, some. Oriental slave girls, as early as the '70s, affected the hoops and crinolines of their white co-workers, although few abandoned the traditional gown and trousers of silk, and none the elaborate Chinese chignon.) Farwell lumped mistresses, concubines and common-law wives with prostitutes—for convenience's sake and to doubly damn the handful of white women (11 in all) living permanently with Chinese, mostly on Commercial Street.

It never seemed to occur to Farwell that much of the Chinese community lived in constant violation of municipal laws because of ignorance of them and of the English language, rather than because of wilful disobedience. He never made the obvious point that ignorance was no excuse. He and his associates reported that one-seventh of the city's population (the Chinese) ignored and violated the law at every turn and were never chastized by its penalties. Of course he was referring to such ordinances as the cubicair requirement—not crimes of violence. But Farwell's report promised a wholesale enforcement of existing laws and a promise of new and needed laws.

He was absolutely astounded by how healthy the Chinese appeared to be despite their violation of every known concept and rule of hygiene. They actually appeared to flourish in the miasmatic jungle of open cesspools and urinals, damp alleys and leaking sewers. The supervisor's serious explanation for the lack of epidemics was that the pall of smoke which hung over Chinatown from its myriad stove pipes, braziers and open wood fires provided a constant fumigation from attics to subcellars. He even went so far as to credit the fumes from the ubiquitous cigars, pipes and opium pipes of the people as being contributory to the arresting of the spread of zymotic diseases, if not cholera itself. He described the atmosphere of Chinatown as being not only semiopaque but "tangible"—ever present not only to sight, taste and smell but also to touch. More than fifty years before Los Angeles discovered smog, Crusader Farwell accused the Chinese of San Francisco of "human defiance of chemical laws."

Wryly, Farwell suggested that should the fumigating haze ever disappear from Chinatown skies Nature would resume her course and effectively "adjust" the Chinese problem without intervention of Congress or a treaty of the United States Senate.

To Farwell the most shocking area of the district was the so-called Palace Hotel on Jackson Street where the sewage of 400 people was carried off into the center of a courtyard to run into a common open cesspool Almost as bad was the vile den called the Dog Kennel where, in a loathsome basement on the east side of Bartlett Alley, Blind Annie and her cats lived in degradation and misery.

A careful scrutiny of the zone turned up 26 opium dens boasting 319 bunks, on 5 streets and 7 alleyways including now-vanished Dunscombe Alley. In even more obvious defiance of State and municipal laws—including some which Farwell had prepared himself as a State assembly-man—were 150 gambling dens apparently immune to laws which had closed down Caucasian gaming establishments. He found almost every one to be protected by heavy plank-andiron doors, grated windows and trap doors for quick escape. Some even had ironclad interior walls or partitions. On many doors he found the scars of police sledges and axes, but he noticed that the doors had usually held long enough for the play-ers to flush the *tan* markers down the overworked, noisome toilets if there were not carefully kindled kitchen fires for just such an emergency.

The police response to this section of Farwell's report was that there were not enough men on the whole force to patrol Chinatown effectively and at the same time watch and raid the gambling hells. They accused white businessmen of being all too willing to allow their buildings to be turned into bastions for the gambling fraternity of Chinatown. Far-well knew they were justified in this complaint, and accused the white owner of 806 Dupont Street of erecting what amounted to a police-proof gambling fortress. It was a stout brick building with door and street wall reinforced with boiler iron. All, in Farwell's words, "to enable it to resist police attack and siege." He listed 72 such barricaded gambling dens in an appendix to his report. Stout's Alley (now Ross Alley, nicknamed the Street of the Gamblers) topped the list with 22 fortified fan-tan parlors.

The third building from Jackson Street on the west side of the Street of the Gamblers was perhaps typical. The first-floor gambling room was guarded by doors of stout planking covered with sheet iron; the hall partitions were of iron too. Escape was provided by a trap door leading to the upper first floor, a space above the ceiling, and then to the sec-ond floor. From there gamblers could flee through a plank-andiron door which led to a hall, and thence to the roof and other roofs, descending to the street farther down the block.

Farwell reported to his board that for weeks police had had to be stationed at each end of Chinatown's alleys at night to search all passers-by and relieve them of concealed weapons. Of the tongs themselves, Farwell repeated the charges of the two committees which had sat nine years earlier, ending: "They exercise a despotic sway over one-seventh of the population." He placed much of the earlier testimony back in the record.

For all his fanaticism, Farwell was wise enough to know that it would be difficult for much of the Chinese population to be strictly law abiding in the American sense. To some extent he excused them of deliberately superseding local and State authority, because the American system was alien to them. "The race is one which cannot readily throw off its habits and customs," he admitted. "The fact that these customs are so widely at variance with our own makes the enforcement of our laws and compulsory obedience of our laws necessarily obnoxious and revolting to the Chinese."

Farwell's report and map of crime and vice in Chinatown was indicative of a trend away from the laissez-faire policy of policing the Chinese districts, and symptomatic of a future get-tough policy. By the close of the '80s, the police would be fighting fire with fire, roughing up highbinders and suspected highbinders, breaking up crowds and smashing lodge halls. But before this drastic program was implemented the police found some new allies in a strange quarter. The women of the Protestant missionary societies made possible a two-pronged attack on one of the foundation stones of tong power—the institution of Chinese slave girls.

# CHAPTER NINE

# SLAVE GIRLS

*"Women are bought and sold in
Chinatown every day and we have not been
able to prevent it. Cannot anyone suggest a
plan to remedy the evil?"*

—Margaret Culbertson, Director,
Presbyterian Chinese Mission House, 1896

ONE OF THE numerous puritanical admonitions of the Hung League
ritual was "Drink clear and pure water; touch not the wine of brothels."
This decree fell into complete disuse among the tong inheritors of Hung
tradition in old San Francisco. Countless gallons of *sam shu* and *bok
jow* sluiced the throats of highbinders who were never loath to repair to
their neighborhood brothel. There was always a house just around the
corner. At the time of the Spanish-American war there were over 400
singsong girls in the Chinese Quarter. Yet they could not keep up with
the citywide demand for their services, much less fill the requirements of
the State at large. The disreputable houses, together with gambling dens,
constituted a firm economic base for the fighting tongs. There was such a
need for harlots in the hinterland that Chinatown's girls—on the rare oc-
casions when they were allowed to parade the streets in their slit-skirted
*cheongsams*—were sometimes kidnapped in broad daylight. They were
even hijacked from their cribs under the very noses of their masters, in
order to be rushed inland to womenless agricultural or mining Chinatowns. In just one week of February, 1898, eight such incidents took
place. Decent women, including wives of prominent businessmen, were
not exempt from the highbinders' forays. In one of the most terrifying

kidnappings, hatchet men who had taken a merchant's wife to Tracy, deliberately slashed her face and disfigured her for life as police closed in on them. Singsong girls who thought that they had reached safety in the Presbyterian or Methodist Missions were recaptured from these havens by force or legal chicanery. Sergeant William Price of the Chinatown squad said of the hatchet men, "They even fool the missions. They get a Chinaman to go up and marry a girl from the mission. Then they sell her to someone else." In the most daring raid of the age a girl was stolen from the upstairs window of the Presbyterian Mission.

Usually the highbinders preferred trickery to violence when up against their missionary foes. They became most adept at concocting charges which caused the arrest of fleeing girls. As soon as the singsong girls were "safe" in jail they were repossessed by their masters who simply posted their bail and marched them back to more years of slavery under lock and key.

A case of this nature which concluded differently from most occurred in the summer of 1896. Officer McGrayan was startled to see a handsome young girl in Oriental costume running down Clay Street, blowing a police whistle as she ran. He followed and managed to coax her from under a restaurant table where she had taken refuge. No sooner had he done so than he found himself surrounded by shouting and gesticulating highbinders who claimed that the girl was drunk. As they jabbered at him to hold his attention some of their companions surreptitiously seized the girl and began to drag her back to Fish Alley. Suddenly the prostitute broke away. She ran to the policeman, fell on her knees, and threw both arms around his legs. As she clung to the startled officer she piteously begged him to save her. McGrayan was quite touched by the girl's desperation, and tried to lead her away. But now the toughs changed their tactics and assaulted him while they tried to tear the girl from his grasp. In the scuffle the girl lost both shoes and had most of her clothes torn off. But the highbinders could not get her away from the Irishman. The crowd which formed around her protector demanded that the prostitute be taken to California Street station and booked as a drunk. The battle was becoming too much for the lone officer, so he made a pretense of agreeing. But instead of taking her to the precinct house for booking and the usual bailing out by her oppressors, McGrayan took her to Margaret

Culbertson at the Presbyterian Mission. For once, the highbinders were thwarted. But most girls were not that fortunate in finding a protector, even when they made their escapes to the streets.

When slave girls had safely reached either of the two missions, the hatchet men sent police with warrants for their arrest, charging them with the theft of the jewelry they wore, actually baubles given them by visitors or their owners—the very complainants. Attorneys were frequently duped into lending their services to distortion and corruption of the law. Patrick Mogan was one example. He was supposedly hired to defend two of the "maculate females" on theft charges. Actually the bagnio operators had no intention of letting the girls come to trial. Henry Monroe, attorney for the Presbyterian Mission, warned the court of this and explained the old, sure-fire, bail-posting scheme of the highbinders; and Mogan found himself with no clients to defend. The lawyer did not appreciate being used in this fashion and he told the judge, "When Mr. Monroe made that crack in court today, that's the first I knew about the story. If he'd come and told me that last Friday, I might have taken a different stand. All I can say is, if I'd known these things at first, I wouldn't have had anything to do with the case." But the eyes of Mogan and the judge were opened too late. The girls were gone, and for good.

An agent of the Society for the Prevention of Cruelty to Children uncovered one avenue of supply of prostitutes when he raided a bordello on Bartlett Alley. There he rescued Toy Gum, a pretty little fifteen year old. He learned that she had been brought to the United States supposedly to dance in the Chinese pavilion at the Atlanta Fair. (Donaldina Cameron found this same trick was worked during the Omaha Exposition of 1889.) Toy Gum's theatrical career had been brevity itself. She was quickly sold into slavery, and just before being saved she had been sold to Wong Fook third hand for a neat $2,000. This was very good money. The going rate was far less. Kem Ying, brought to San Francisco from Portland by a pair of chaperoning highbinders, went on the block that year for $500, and Don Sun Yet brought a mere $350.

The men and women who struggled to eliminate the nefarious trade in prostitutes fought the highbinders with some of their own tactics. Kem Ying's cousin had her arrested on a vagrancy charge in order to secure her escape. Minnie Brown smuggled Ah Yoke into the outbound steamer *Peru* as a stowaway to guarantee her getaway from the tong men watching the Embarcadero. But the chief weapon of the anti-vice crusaders was the raid. Violence often had to be met with violence. Police officers sometimes had to shoot their way into or out of a building in order to rescue slave girls kept prisoners by hatchet men.

The long crusade against Chinatown's slave traders was that part of the bigger general battle against the tongs which really seized the public's imagination. It was not just another vice drive. The prostitutes were of exotic dress and features. Many of them were frail, childlike creatures. Indeed, most of them were of very tender years. Most important was the fact that a great number of the girls were unwilling captives of brutal masters—they were slaves in a very real sense. These girls had been entrapped into the oldest profession and they wanted to get out of it. Many were tricked into sailing for San Francisco by promises of quick marriages to rich merchants. Others were kidnapped. Even those who came with their eyes open, under signed contracts, soon found that their owners did not intend to abide by the terms of the documents. There was no way out of the business for the girls but death unless they could somehow escape to the sanctuary of either the Presbyterian or Methodist Mission Asylum. An old Chinatown hand, Police Officer David Supple, testifying in one of the several Government investigations of the Quarter, was asked, "Is it possible for these women to escape that life?" His answer was, "Sometimes the chief of police can give some protection, but it is customary for the owners to charge them with crimes in order to get possession of them again. Sometimes they kidnap them, and even unscrupulous white men have been found to assist them." "Do you know what they do with them when they become sick or helpless?" Supple was asked. "Yes, they put them out on the street to die."

Often a real attachment would develop between a girl and one of her customers and she would run away with him. The brothel owners in some cases had the temerity to appeal to American courts for repossession of their property. More often they just turned the case over to the hatchet men of the tong. The flesh importers threw a lot of business to the *boo how doy* of the Temple of United Justice, the Hip Yee tong particularly. About $40 a head was paid on girls imported, and a small but steady weekly consideration was also bled from the earnings of the

155

girls and given to the hatchet men once they were set up in San Francisco. Part of this money went to line the pockets of friendly policemen. Some of these protectors of the law were obliging to the point of standing guard over newly arrived girls to see that they did not escape from the *barracoon* (the detention house or so-called Queen's Room) where they awaited bidders. Officer Andrew McKenzie testified that one such officer was James R. Rogers.

There was no Donaldina Cameron to rescue the white girls of Chinatown. The Caucasians were slaves in only the most poetic sense. They had matriculated into their lucrative calling voluntarily. The do-gooders realized this, and drives in this area were simply to banish the girls. Groups like the Society for the Suppression of Vice urged that the evil be eradicated, but they had no plans for rehabilitating the girls once Brooklyn Alley was transformed into an economically depressed area.

The prostitutes of such sinful thoroughfares as Stout's Alley or Ross Alley were a mixed lot. The problems caused by the Caucasian women were not intimately related to crime among the Chinese, but unfortunately they did much to help give the Quarter a bad name. Two of San Francisco's most notorious homicides took place in Chinatown and involved white girls—Celina Boudet and Jennie French. The former was murdered by her paramour, while the latter got her boy friend to shoot down a harmless German.

The singsong girls picked up American slang and customs from such denizens of Chinatown's back alleys as Jennie French. They even copied the decor in Caucasian parlor-houses, and visitors to Stout's Alley were surprised to find Chinese harlots' walls hung with Currier and Ives prints. The idea of escape and liberty was perhaps germinated for the poor Chinese girls by their free white co-professionals. This influence weakened their fatalistic acceptance of their lot. It would be wrong to make ministering angels of San Francisco's white prostitutes, but they did play some little part in the undoing of the strict system of harlotry-slavery, if only by opening the singsong girls' eyes to the possibility of escape and freedom.

The Protestant missionaries in Chinatown did a magnificent job. However, they accomplished more in sociology than in religion. Baptists and Congregationalists had led the way with early missions in Chinatown, and the Episcopalians called a Chinese minister back from Ohio and Pennsylvania to preach in the Quarter. But the two major Christian outposts of nineteenth-century Chinatown were the Methodist and Presbyterian Missions, each of which boasted an Asylum for Rescued Prostitutes. They built upon the work already done by the law-abiding majority of the Chinese community. In the very early days of statehood, representatives of the merchants and other respected people of Chinatown had protested against the importation of loose women of the so-called "boat-people" class. But the city and State each turned its good ear from them, and the lucrative business continued to prosper. Not until 1870 was satisfactory evidence required of female immigrants that they were of good character and morals and that they came to California of their own free will.

By the outbreak of the Civil War, prostitutes made up three-fourths of all arrests of Chinese in San Francisco. That year saw 160 girls actually convicted in police court. The great majority were not even caught. Some forfeited their bail and went right back to "business as usual." In the mid-'60s the city set up a "house" of its own, but without visiting privileges. This was called the Little Jail, which it was. It was a *calabozo* restricted to oriental prostitutes. In 1866 there were more in than out; almost 90 were locked up and a mere 50 were left at large. This little jail was part of an ambitious campaign of the city fathers to remove all bagnios and their occupants to the suburbs. The supervisors passed the ordinance but it was thwarted by the State Legislature's enactment of a Chinese House of Ill Fame Bill. This was a completely ineffectual piece of legislation but it did take the wind out of supervisorial sails. The resulting calm proved to be a lasting one, and Ross Alley never did move to Burlingame or Kent Woodlands.

When a committee of the California Legislature investigated Chinatown in 1862, in one of the first of several official safaris through the district, the body praised the action of the Six Companies in regard to organized prostitution. The committee commended them for their attempts to send abandoned women home to China but lamented that these efforts had been largely frustrated by the pleas of vested interests that America was a free country and that Chinese women could do as they pleased.

Actually the girls had no say in the matter. They were treated as chattels. A correspondent for *Blackwood's Magazine* in England was appalled by the slave-girl traffic in San Francisco. He could find nothing to parallel it, not even the worst features of Tokyo's Yoshiwara district. Perhaps he had been given a look at the *barracoon*. It was situated underneath the joss house which fronted on St. Louis Alley and which ran through to Dupont Street. Here girls were stripped of their clothing and put up for bid. Those who resisted could be identified easily by the black-and-blue marks on their bodies from bamboo staves wielded by their highbinder masters. The most recalcitrant sometimes bore the sears of hot irons. But few were ever killed; they were too valuable for that, being worth up to $3,000 each. When old they were turned into cooks. Once in a while a pimp might kill his girl in a rage if she refused him money. This is exactly why little Toy Gun was shot three times by her master. Other murders of prostitutes remained complete mysteries, though many of them were probably crimes of passion. There was the case of Quee Sing. A highbinder walked up the stairs of Wong Ah Gum's Dupont Street brothel, stopped at the head of the staircase, poked a pistol barrel through the wicket and shot Quee Sing in the mouth. Quickly but quietly the man slipped downstairs and melted into the crowd, although police officers were on the scene in two minutes. Quee Sing's companion had been blinded by the pistol flash. There were no other witnesses to the murder and no clues. The murderer was never found.

According to two influential Chinese who called on the editor of the San Francisco *Bulletin* in 1873, Hip Yee highbinders began the prostitution traffic in 1852. Two years later the Six Companies tried to stop it but failed. Another try was partially successful and a handful of singsong girls were turned around and sent back to Hong Kong without being able to land in San Francisco. But shortly after the Civil War the Hip Yees stepped up production from their headquarters in Choy "Poy's Jackson Street restaurant. Under new management, the tong membership jumped from 50 to 300. An elite corps of hatchet men was formed and equipped to fight a war against any Celestials who dared to interfere in the slave-girl traffic. Soon respectable Chinese, who at first had protested against the traffic, feared the terrible revenge of the slave dealers. Newspapers estimated that the Hip Yee tong imported 6,000 women between 1852 and 1873, and netted $200,000 from the illegitimate traffic.

Mayor-Bryant loudly condemned Chinese prostitution but his words rang a little hollow. One of the presidents of the Six Companies remarked pointedly to him, "Yes, yes, Chinese prostitution is bad. But what do you think of German prostitution, French prostitution and American prostitution? Do you think them very good?" Since San Francisco was a wide-open town, there was little the mayor could say in answer. Occasionally Bryant or some other occupant of city hall made a big show of clamping down on Chinese houses of ill fame. Police measures of the '70s were particularly ludicrous, however. To "check" prostitution, courtesans were forbidden to stand in the open doorways of their dens. One policeman was heard to scold a prostitute, "You must close your front door. You may invite as many people as you please through your window, but I can't let you stand in the door any more." But the girls were permitted eight- to ten-inch openings in their doors, with movable slides to allow them to maintain good public relations.

Such were the methods employed by authorities while Police Officer James R. Rogers bragged: "It is almost impossible to entirely suppress them, for they will naturally open. But they *can* be kept closed and the business made unprofitable. There is no ordinance that cannot be enforced, and I presume the ordinances we have are sufficient to keep these houses all closed. It don't require a large force to close these houses. I can do it in one night. Arrest the inmates of one, and it travels like electricity from one to another and in ten minutes every one will be shut up and the doors will be barricaded."

Thoroughly impatient with such farcical "control" of the red-light district in Chinatown, the decent people of the city—particularly the women—decided to take action themselves; and they took a constructive course. The ladies began a deliberate and well-planned campaign to rescue slave girls from their masters. (As early as 1857 the city was shocked by the desperate attempt of two girls to escape their lives of slavery by throwing themselves into a well in attempted suicides.) One of the first to become interested in the singsong girls' plight was Mrs. H. C. Cole. She helped set up the Methodist Misson, but the matron had no customers for almost a year. Then, late in 1871, a despairing girl, Jin Ho, escaped from her bagnio, fled to the Embarcadero, and threw herself into the bay. A Negro fished her out with a boat hook and turned her over to police, but she refused to talk to any Chinese, even police interpreters. She told Captain Clark that she would speak only with a "Jesus man." So the captain sent for Reverend Otis Gibson. As soon as Gibson appeared the distraught girl fell on her knees and begged him, "Don't take me back to Jackson Street." He reassured her and took her to the Methodist Mission. A year later she became a Christian and married. By 1874, Jin Ho had seventeen "classmates" in the mission, all under the supervision of Laura S. Templeton.

The Presbyterians were not far behind. They opened their mission in 1874. At first they had a hard time attracting any refugees. The highbinders had begun a program of what would today be called brainwashing. They filled the heads of their girls with horrible nonsense about mission brutality and torture to deter them from escape attempts. They also secured dishonest lawyers and those on the thin line between light and shade—like Three Fingered Leander Quint—to produce writs of *habeas corpus* in order to recapture legally the girls who did make good their escapes. To the two asylums also came Hip Yee tong emissaries who posed as relatives of the girls hiding inside. They promised to take them away to a new and good life. The brothel owners also got girls to enter the asylum as spies. Once inside the mission they would try to persuade the legitimate refugees to leave. (Sometimes this strategy backfired on the Hip Yee men and they lost another girl.)

All of the tongs' countermeasures were doomed to failure. More and more public support came for the missions when Reverend Gibson translated and had published the text of cold-blooded bills of sale of several of the unfortunate girls. Typical of them all was the contract of Ah Ho. The document read as follows:

> An agreement to assist the woman, Ah Ho, because in coining from China to San Francisco she became indebted to her mistress for passage. Ah Ho herself asks Mr. Yee Kwan to advance to her six hundred and thirty dollars, ,for which Ah Ho distinctly agrees to give her body to Mr. Yee for service as a prostitute for a term of four years. There shall be no interest on the money. Ah Ho shall receive no wages. At the expiration of four years, Ah Ho shall be her own master. Mr. Yee Kwan shall

not hinder nor trouble her. If Ah Ho runs away before her term is out, her mistress shall find her and return her. Whatever expense is incurred in finding her and returning her, Ah Ho shall pay. On this day of agreement, Ah Ho, with her own hands, has received from Mr. Yee Kwan six hundred and thirty dollars. If Ah Ho shall be sick at any time for more than ten days, she shall make up by an extra month of service for every ten days of sickness. Now this agreement has proof. This paper, received by Ah Ho, is witnessed by Tung Chee in the twelfth year, ninth month and fourteenth day.

There were reversals for Gibson and the missionary ladies during their running fight with the tongs. One such defeat was the Yat Sing case. Yat Sing was a young man who aided three Chinese slave girls to escape. He took them to the Methodist Mission where he proposed marriage to one of them and was promptly accepted. All seemed well. Yet only a few weeks later Yat Sing and his wife came to the mission house, terrified. The former owner of the girls had taken the case before the Hip Yee tong. One of that society's destroying angels had looked Yat Sing up and demanded the girl or $350. When the young husband answered that he could not pay he was dragged by force before a tribunal of the tong in their secret council chamber. He was given three weeks in which to return the girl, pay the money, or be assassinated. Reverend Gibson consulted with lawyers and aided Yat Sing. He had 8 Hip Yee agents arrested for conspiracy to extort money from his Chinese friend. Before the case came up in police court, more than 50 Chinese merchants called on Gibson to encourage him and to promise their help against the tong. They themselves hired the brilliant Ward McAllister, the best legal counsel in the city, to aid the prosecuting attorney. But the latter suddenly refused to allow McAllister to help him or to take part in the trial in any way. He further refused to bring into court the tong's seized records which showed that the defendants were officers of the society. Gibson angrily exclaimed, "His whole conduct showed that he did not wish a conviction, and would not have it if he could prevent it." The hatchet men blandly denied that they were even members of the Hip Yee tong. Each brought forward two Chinese witnesses who swore that the eight were good and true men. As even Gibson anticipated, the jury brought in a verdict of acquittal. It was now commonly reported that the prosecuting attorney had been "consulted" by agents of the secret society and that the affair had cost the Hip Yee tong treasury a neat $10,000. Because of the greed or lack of fortitude of one attorney, Gibson's big chance to smash the Hip Yee tong was thwarted.

Shortly after the disappointing trial of the eight highbinders, the forces of good scored a few points. Ten Chinese women who had just arrived found their way to the Methodist Mission and asked permission to be sent back to China. Gibson told Chinese merchants of his acquaintance about them. These businessmen furnished money for the women's passage and assured him that they would do so for all women or girls who called upon them for help. They prepared a huge placard announcing this policy and had it carried through Chinatown. But the merchants feared the tongs enough to hire a white man to carry the sign.

In the meanwhile Gibson translated and published widely the text of another slave-girl's contract. The plight of Chinatown's singsong girls became a national issue when this contract was read in the United States Senate. Aaron Sargent, Senator from California, quoted it in a speech of 1876.

The text of the document—"An agreement to assist a young girl named Loi Yau"—was almost identical to that of Ah Ho's and just as damning.

The tide of battle between the tongs and the missions ebbed and flowed. The Six Companies re-entered the fray as an ally of the missions in 1878, making another try to turn back the flood of slave girls. They sent two representatives to call on Assistant District Attorney Darwin. The men told him that the *City of Peking* was bringing in 60 prostitutes. Darwin referred them to the police, and 25 of the girls were taken to city hall upon landing. Here they all said that they had come of their own free will and they showed certificates from the United States Consul in Hong. Kong. They had to be set free, of course, although the police knew that the girls had been coached with a catechism of answers and provided with forged immigration certificates. They were set at liberty and quickly rounded up and packed off to the *barracoon* by the waiting highbinders.

Immigration Commissioner Hart H. North asked Lieutenant William Price of the Chinatown squad what proportion of Chinese women landed on the Embarcadero were destined for the immoral profession. "Ninety percent. I would not take one bit off that," answered Price. "They are sold as fast as they are brought over. For every girl who comes here they get about three thousand dollars."

But the tide really began to turn against the tongs and brothels in 1895, when Donaldina Cameron entered the fight. Within a few years she would become a living legend. Her name—or nickname Lo Mo—is still very important in Chinatown. In her the forces for good had finally found an inspired leader. This beloved, gentlewomanly missionary had the equivalent of carbon steel in her makeup. The hatchet men feared her. Donaldina mounted a counteroffensive which rolled the tong broth-elkeepers back on all fronts. Lo Mo—old Mother—to all Chinatown, must be considered a potent factor in the ultimate destruction of the fighting tongs. It was she who knew best how to strike hard and repeatedly at the very foundation stone of their existence—the slave trade. With the courage and toughness of spirit of her Scottish ancestors, she became overnight a sort of Carrie Nation of Chinatown. With the help of the police, law-abiding Chinese, immigration officials, Consul General Ho Yow, an aroused public, and eventually an earthquake and fire, she put the tongs into a retreat which became a rout.

In 1961, Miss Cameron recalled for reporters how she had led the police into the brothels and fought the highbinders in court because no else would do so. Actually she was not the first to engage the tongs in combat over the alley girls. Mrs. P. D. Browne got Donaldina interested in the first place, and Margaret Culbertson—Donaldina's boss—was no novice. But it was Miss Cameron who became the accepted commander in chief almost from the very day she came to work—the same day on which a cleaning girl found a stick of dynamite in the hall of the Sacramento Street Mission.

Donaldina was more energetic and daring than her predecessors. She willingly and proudly occupied the same cell as slave girl Kum Quai when the latter was jailed on one of the traditional trumped-up charges. She was said to know every roof in Chinatown. She had slipped into the Quarter through the tight quarantine set up by the city government during the bubonic plague scare by using roofs and skylights as knowingly as the highbinders themselves.

From the moment of her first raid on a tightly barred brothel in Spofford Alley, Donaldina Cameron was as single minded in purpose as even Andy Furuseth, who was fighting his great battle for civil rights for sailors at the same time. On her "calls" Miss Cameron usually took along a trio of brawny policemen armed with axes and sledge hammers. Only once did she make a raid without police protection and she had cause to regret it. It was on the City of Peking building on Jackson Street. There she discovered a secret panel which led to the hiding place of the girl she was after. The cornered highbinders showed fight and might have ended her crusade then and there with an ax had not her aide Kum Ching blown a police whistle. Luckily, an officer was just around the corner. He seized the girl from her captors at the same time that he shielded Lo Mo from the hatchet men.

It did not take Donaldina Cameron long to learn conditions in Chinatown. She found that not all prostitutes were of the lowly boat-people class. Some were of high caste, like Jean Ying. This girl, the daughter of a well-to-do Canton manufacturer, had been kidnapped and sent to San Francisco. Donaldina came to realize, too, why most of the girls feigned great reluctance toward being rescued. They were worried that raids might fail. Miss Cameron even learned to lie like her enemy to protect her charges, though it must have hurt her Scots conscience. Whenever a policeman came with a warrant for a girl on some faked charge, Lo Mo would insist, "She's not here," while praying that he would not look under the rice sacks in the dark space behind the basement gas meter. She accepted the fact that she often had to break the letter of the law in order to uphold the spirit of it. She was doubtless guilty of trespass and of breaking and entering; contempt-of-court proceedings were instigated against her. But she knew that she was in the right and never wavered in her single-minded purpose.

Donaldina had a nose for trap doors, hidden staircases, secret panels and hiding places. Even when brothel owners hired young children to play with blocks and toys in front of their establishments to give them the appearance of legitimate family residences, Miss Cameron found them out. Once Sin Kee asked her to rescue his beloved from a "boardinghouse" on Mah Fong Alley. She brought a posse to the building, but when they battered down the locked door they found only thirteen Chinese inside, quietly smoking their pipes as though oblivious to the din of axes chopping into stout oak. Donaldina paid no attention to this carefully staged tong meeting but went over the room like a bloodhound. She climbed out of a window onto a rickety fire escape. Across the way she saw a painter on a scaffold. She quizzed him and found out that the girl had been whisked up through the skylight to the roof and over to the next building via its roof. She found the girl there and rescued her.

For all her success, Miss Cameron's actions sometimes ended in frustration, failure and even tragedy. One rescue attempt which failed was that of Yep Shung in 1898. He came to San Francisco from San Jose to join Lo Mo's crusade. The ladies of the Presbyterian Mission sent their new volunteer to Sullivan's Alley with one of their number along as his guide. She waited outside a den as he entered. She waited and waited for a signal. None came. While she was waiting ten highbinders inside were stripping Lo Mo's green commando and thrashing him. They then tossed him out into the street, naked, to the consternation of the mission lady awaiting him.

Some cases did not end ludicrously, but tragically. When Foon Hing managed to bring his cousin to Donaldina for safekeeping, the girl was made secure enough, but Foon Hing was shot down by hatchet men as he left the mission. Lew Yick was another young man who rescued a girl and delivered her to 920 China Street (as Sacramento Street used to be called). He was captured by tong toughs who had owned the slave. They held him prisoner in a room on Clay Street and kept him awake for a full thirty hours by torturing him with hot irons. They demanded he raise $700 ransom—an impossible requirement. Lew Yick had lost all hope, but rescue came in the eleventh hour as an immigration officer and a police posse finally ferreted out where he was kept prisoner. In a third case, which ended badly for Miss Cameron, Lem You, a Christian Chinese who had given the mission people information on slave girls, had a price of $1,000 placed on his head by one of the tongs. He was shot in the back on Clay Street by Quon Ah You and another hatchet man.

During these years of battle Donaldina Cameron learned whom to trust. She found that she could not put all her faith in all policemen.

Some officers were anti-Chinese, others were bribe takers. Lawyers were subject to purchase, too, she found. Her friend Attorney Henry E. Monroe angrily rejected an offer of $250 per month just for tipping off the tong men in advance on Donaldina's raids. But not all of his colleagues were quite so upright.

The years rolled on and Lo Mo kept up her raids, hitting brothels in Chinatowns as far away as Monterey and Marysville. She kept the slaving tongs always on the defensive. Willard Farwell's map of 1885 must have been graven on her mind. She could find her way blindfolded to every hidden den. Chinatown squad officer Duncan Matheson always claimed that the great change for the better in Chinatown which transformed it from a bloody ghetto into the most orderly district in the city was due to two things: the gradual education of the Chinese people, and character-building institutions like Lo Mo's.

# CHAPTER TEN

# THE TERROR OF CHINATOWN

*"If a Chinaman is to be got rid of,
the highbinders, for a consideration, will
undertake the task of removing him. An officer
of the secret police, from whom I obtained
much information concerning the Chee Kongs,
was himself black-listed, a reward of $800 set
upon his head. Being a cool man and a good
shot, and always well armed, he has thus far
escaped although two or three night attacks
and broken bones have resulted in the attempts
of the highbinders to remove their enemy..."*

—Lee Meriwether, Special Agent, United
States Department of Labor, 1889

DURING the 1880s, though the slave girls were still thriving, the sand-lotters were going into a decline. The Workingmen's party lost badly in the elections and Dennis Kearney was soon out of politics and back in the drayage business. Before long he was forgotten. Although the Burlingame treaty was abrogated, the pressure on the Chinese community from the outside began to subside during this period. The anti-Chinese measures of the 1879 California Constitution were declared unconstitutional by the United States Supreme Court, and the horizon appeared to be brightening.

But it was a false dawn. The highbinders were not yet out in the open. But they were confident; their control over Chinatown already amounted to a strangle hold. In the four years from 1877-1880, when they were just warming to the task, 27 of a total of 81 homicides were of Chinese victims. Of these, 22 were actually killed in Chinatown, and all—save one—were murdered by other Chinese. And where 13 were shot, 12 were either chopped or stabbed to death. (One was clubbed, and one was suffocated.)

At the same time that the threat of the hatchet men increased, crime in general was growing in the city Chief Crowley again and again asked for enlargement of his force. He had 400 policemen and 5 captains under him in 1886, but he pleaded for a mounted striking force, for a policewagon system, and for prohibition of "fortified rooms"—the iron-doored Chinese gambling dens. His requests were turned down by economy-minded supervisors.

The reports of Coroner D. L. Dorr tended to bolster Chief Crowley's good but losing arguments. San Francisco during the decade was enjoying almost double the murder rate of other cities equal in size or larger. Dorr pointed out to the city fathers that San Francisco had one murder for every 11,190 inhabitants, as compared to New York's one to 25,000. In San Francisco's Chinatown there was a murder for every 2,222 people. Dorr placed the blame for this squarely on the hatchet men: "The system of professional murderers among this peculiar people is frequently recognized, and during the year several of the assassins have evaded detection. These murders are of the most cowardly and dastardly kind, not one having the semblance of manslaughter or justifiable homicide and generally being undertaken for purposes of revenge in money matters."

The evasion of detection which Dr. Dorr mentioned would plague the police force for the next two decades. Chinatown was swept by a conspiracy of silence—almost a dead ringer for the silence enforced by the mafia on the terrorized folk of Sicily. Many Chinese feared that they had unconsciously violated some tax, custom or immigration law. They refused to even be witnesses in court cases, giving American justice as wide a berth as possible. And no man had the nerve to denounce even the most brazen hatchet man lest the highbinder's bloody-handed tong brothers exact revenge on him or his family. The situation was as if the tong killers held the entire population of Chinatown as hostages.

Coroner Dorr was disturbed by some of the idiosyncrasies of Chinatown crime. First, he was convinced that a great number of homicide cases in the Quarter were never reported but were completely and successfully concealed from the authorities. Second, he was shocked that Chinese women were frequent victims of assassins. And finally and most frustratingly, he knew well that many Chinatown murderers had no fear of capture after their crime, and made clean, easy getaways, almost as if they enjoyed the connivance of their very victims.

People all over California and the West, and eventually in all corners of the United States, came to know the names of the squalid Chinatown alleys which were the scenes of murders or pitched tong battles. Whether the killers struck with stealth by night or with bravado by day, they liked to carry on their wars in the alleys which sheltered them from police and white witnesses. For although their pride and code might insist that they be seen in the act of hatcheting or shooting their victim, not one of them longed for the cells of city prison. Escape was easy in the alleyways, particularly by night. Waverly Place's stygian blackness was hardly cut at all by the feeble street lamp, a few strings of paper lanterns, the dim light leaking through dusty, curtained windows, and the glowing braziers of the curbside foodsellers. Waverly, old Pike Street, and earlier yet, calle de las Rosas, would become the most notorious of all of San Francisco's murderous alleys. It was near there that Little Pete, the King of Chinatown, met his end. Rivals of Waverly were Aleck Alley, Bull Run Alley, and Cooper's Alley, better known as Ragpickers' Alley. The denizens of the latter were of the lowest coolie class. They were the only Chinese who were personally dirty; gleaners who sold everything except the filthy and tattered rags they wore, for a handful of brass cash. With the irony so consistent with pre-earthquake Chinatown, filthy Ragpickers' Alley was the site of one of the primitive Chinese hospitals of the period.

The alleys already had a bad name by the 1880s, when the screams of tong victims thrust them onto the front pages. They had long been the avenues of commerce for both the white and yellow wantons of the city, and violence had been quick to follow vice. Their pavements were stained with the blood of crimes of passion long before the *boo how doy* were loosed in them during the tong wars. One of the first tragedies of Waverly Place occurred when it was still Pike Street. This was the murder of Marie Banier, the Parisian courtesan. As if to cleanse the street even of its horrifying memories, the city had Marie's trim little white cottage torn down. (It was replaced by a joss house.) Stout's Alley had its baptism of blood early, too, in one of the great murder cases of San Francisco's history. In 1856, obeying a whim of his girl friend Jennie French, a young black sheep named Rod Backus shot a harmless man walking down the street. "Rod," she had cried, "that fellow has insulted me. Shoot him!" Backus obliged, confident that his city hall connections would get him off. Instead, he had the scare of his life as the Vigilantes strung up his cellmate. Backus was actually relieved when the gates of San Quentin shut behind him.

It was in Bartlett Alley in the '80s that the Chinese whore Selina held court in her own three-room building. She rivaled even pioneer Ah Toy in notoriety. The little street became a combat zone in the tong wars, as did Brooklyn Alley and the bizarrely named Cum Cook Alley where more than once hatchets flashed in the moonlight.

It was in Cum Cook Alley that Sing Lum shot Ah Cheng in the head in 1880. This case differed from run-of-the-mill tong murders. In the first place, Sing was captured; in the second, he lacked the courage and stoicism of the better grade of tong assassin. He tended to worry and brood. Although convicted of murder in the first degree and his attorney's motion for a new trial denied, he appealed to the Supreme Court and won a stay of execution. But this only gave him more time to think. The chief of police ordered a death watch kept on the brooding Sing as he paced his cell. The only furnishings there were a sink, two wooden bunks and two straw mattresses. When the guard relaxed his vigil for a moment Sing hurriedly tore up the ticking of the pallets, forming two long strips; these he doubled for strength. He tied one end around his neck and the other around a small sag in the gas pipe which ran along the ceiling. Sing Lum, murderer of Cum Cook Alley, then stepped off the sink into eternity, cheating the hangman. As his body swung back and forth the hammers could be heard outside his cell as the construction of a new gallows—just for Sing—went on.

Other dark and deadly avenues of the Quarter were Washington Alley—better known as Fish Alley or Butchers' Alley—redolent of poultry, fish, squid and shrimp. St. Louis Alley (aptly named Murderer's Alley),

St. Louis Place, and the Palace Hotel courtyard were other murderous mews. But all these were only pale imitations of a thoroughfare even more dangerous as time went on. This was Ross Alley, or Stout's Alley. Here lived Chin Tin Sen, alias Tom Chu, called the King of Gamblers. Suey Kwei lived there, too, with his white wife. Many others resided on the little street, but more important, many died there, their lives leaking away with the blood spilled on the cobbles.

If the police were puzzled and angered by the conspiracy of silence which prevailed in the streets and alleys of Chinatown, the Chinese were dumbfounded by the attitude of Chief Crowley. Instead of crushing the guilty tongs, Crowley—clearly at a loss—lashed out at the Six Companies. He publicly stated that he would put an end to what he called their oppressive jurisdiction over the population. Thanks to the pressure he and others exerted, the Felton Act was passed. This ended the traditional exit-visa power of the companies. Surreptitious methods were quickly substituted, with departing Chinese stopped on the streets on their way to the Embarcadero rather than on the docks themselves. Nevertheless, this was another body blow to the prestige of the already weakened Six Companies. In his Irish ignorance, Crowley had hurt badly the allies of whom he was yet unconscious and had strengthened the hand of his real foes—the tongs—which were still shrouded in mystery.

The bull-headed Crowley compounded his error by pasting signs in Chinese all over Chinatown. They read:

> NOTICE IS HEREBY GIVEN TO ALL CHINESE IN CALIFORNIA, WORKMEN OR MERCHANTS, THAT ANYONE WISHING TO RETURN TO CHINA MAY, HIMSELF, GO TO THE OFFICE OF THE STEAMSHIP COMPANY AND PURCHASE HIS PASSAGE TICKET. IT IS NOT NECESSARY TO GO TO ANY OF THE SIX COMPANIES TO BUY A PERMIT, BUT ANY CHINAMAN WHO HAS BOUGHT HIS PASSAGE TICKET AND HAS HIS POLL TAX RECEIPT MAY CO ABOARD THE STEAMER. IF ANYBODY IN THE LEAST OFFERS TO HINDER THEM, THEY MAY CALL UPON THE POLICE OFFICERS ON THE WHARF WHO WILL PROTECT THEM AND CERTAINLY

SEE THAT THEY MAY GO ABOARD THE STEAMER. LET
EVERYONE ACT ACCORDINGLY.

Then the chief added a stem postscript deemed necessary because of
past experience:

LET NO ONE TEAR THIS NOTICE FROM THE WALL!

The friction between the police and the Six Companies—and thereby
the merchant class and most of the decent people—now increased. The
Six Companies responded by posting a notice of their own which was
soon seen all over the Quarter. It threatened would-be absconders with
warrants and American court trials for nonpayment of debts. Greatly
excited crowds milled about in the streets opposite these broadsides.
The irritable Crowley, instead of being pleased at the Six Companies'
recourse to American courts of law, took their response as a veiled threat
not only against the poor emigrants but against law and order itself. He
speedily sent an extra force of men to Chinatown. He told the press that
he feared trouble. With this excuse, he had his squad tear down the Six
Companies' posters. They next arrested two innocent Chinese: Ah Chin,
proprietor of the Oriental Printing Office; and Sing Yee, a poor, harmless bill poster. As the two men were dragged off to the Hall of Justice to
face charges of conspiracy the officers must have almost brushed against
many of the real lords of the Chinatown underworld who lazed against
buildings on street corners. Perhaps these *boo how doy,* with hatchets up
their sleeves or revolvers concealed under their blouses, smirked at the
misguided and confused actions of the chief and the pained bewilderment of the harmless pair.

Had any of these racketeers been either interested enough, or expert
enough in English, they would have laughed over the next day's *Alta
California.* The paper paid fuzzy-headed praise to Crowley for stamping out the extortion racket attempted by the Six Companies. An anonymous Chinatown "expert" testified in a masterpiece of reverse thinking,
to Crowley's success in "breaking up the system of highbinders." One
might have thought *Alta's* editor were speaking tongue in cheek. But
they were deadly serious.

The Chinatown squad, although hampered by lack of information thanks to the conspiracy of silence in Chinatown, and in spite of the zeal with which Crowley dispatched it on fools' errands, was a rather effective police unit. The squad proved its worth in the Choy Cum case of October, 1881. Choy Cum was a prostitute who had accidentally thrown dirty water on a passer-by. This was not the simple annoyance it might have been had the pedestrian been a *fan kwei,* but the dampened stranger turned out to be a tongman. Not only did he believe in the Chinese superstition that water spilled on one meant bad luck, but he considered the wetting as an affront to his dignity—to his "face." The *Alta* described the man as Fung Ah Sing, "a chief of the society of highbinders and well known as one of the most desperate characters in the Chinese Quarter." Immediately after the drenching Fung entered the building and demanded a present from the quaking girl. She gave him what money she had and thought the matter settled. But the very next night Fung Ah Sing returned to the house. He did not upbraid the girl again; he did not say a word. Instead, he drew out a revolver and shot her in the face without warning, firing through the window of her room. Sergeant Tom Fields of the Chinatown squad started in immediate pursuit and apprehended the hatchet man on Brenham Place. His prisoner, wearing three coats' and carrying a fourth over his arm (he was either ready to go underground or else he feared a knifing), did not lapse into the traditional Chinese stoicism. Instead of the usual "Me *no sabe"* he blurted out a denial of having shot the girl. Crowley had him taken to the hospital where the wanton lay dying; she identified him as her attacker. Of course the word quickly began to go around Chinatown that anyone who testified in her behalf had better make himself scarce. Someone tipped Crowley, however, and he arrested the girl's companion and placed her in protective custody. She readily told him that she had been threatened with death by friends of Fung if she were to give any testimony. Under police protection she told the jury exactly how the gunman had fired through the window into her friend's face. A verdict of guilty was returned.

Equally shocking was the cold-blooded killing of Leong Ah Sing in Church Alley in broad daylight. This took place two weeks before Christmas of 1881. Highbinder Harm Ah Kee stepped up behind the unsuspecting pedestrian, pressed a pistol into Leong's back, and shot him.

Harm threw the pistol beside the body, as was the hatchet man's custom, and ran. His brief dash ended in the arms of two officers. Friends of the murdered man told the police that there was no reason for the shooting, but the murder proved to be the outcome of a feud which had originated with a trivial quarrel. Leong had crashed a feast at which Harm had dared him to take a seat. Harm had had his revenge.

These were highbinder crimes, not related to the burglaries, robberies and occasional assaults endemic to Chinatown; these were the harbingers of running vendettas and wars to come. The following April saw another such case, when Lee Kin and Wing Ah Bang quarreled over a woman in front of a Ross Alley bagnio. Bang hurried away, only to return with reinforcements—three highbinder pals. They grabbed Kin and held him while Wing plunged a dagger in his back. When Wing was picked up it was found that he already had a record. A year earlier he had been arrested for murder, but acquitted. One of his partners in the attack on Lee Kin was Ching Ah Too who—like Wing—typified the criminals now openly patrolling the streets of Chinatown. He had been arrested for the murder of a fellow Chinese but had escaped conviction. And although he had drawn an eight-year term in San Quentin in 1879, for grand theft, he had secured a new trial and acquittal after the complainant had conveniently left town. Already the close alliance between hatchet men and unscrupulous shysters was well established. By 1888, District Attorney E. B. Stonehill would complain to the Board of Supervisors of the extent to which Chinese criminal cases were being drawn out. He singled out the cases of two of the most desperate men to hold power over Chinatown: Lee Chuck and Little Pete. Lee Chuck the murderer, and Little Pete the briber and Lee Chuck's boss, had trials which ran to more than a month each. The attempts to wear out witnesses, juries and judges did not always completely succeed, however. Lee Chuck was unlucky enough to be the only one of six hatchet men murderers of the period to draw a death penalty, and Little Pete got a term in San Quentin for his bribes, but was soon out; Lee Chuck cheated the gallows by going insane in prison.

Symptomatic of the suspicion felt by the Chinese toward the Americans—explaining in large measure the Oriental *omertá* which prevailed—was the fantastic farrago of rumor which swept the Quarter in

June, 1882. It was started ironically, in central police station by some imaginative Bohemian, but soon had Chinatown agog. According to the story, body snatchers were after the corpse of Li Po Fun, the president of the Ning Yeung Company, who had just died and been honored with a fine funeral parade. Before the rumor was killed it had changed into a story that the body had actually been secured by ghouls. Bartlett Alley was in such an uproar that Special Officer McLaughlin came dashing up with drawn revolver. "I thought some highbinder had added to the plethoric record of Chinese crime," he explained picturesquely. Officer Selwyn of the Chinatown squad quickly organized a meeting of the officers of the Ning Yeung Company and they reported to the public on the wild rumor's complete lack of foundation. Order was restored, but company officials took the precaution of removing the body from the burial vault to an undertaking parlor over which they placed a constant guard until a steamer came to take the body home to China.

Shortly after the Li Po Fun incident dramatized the hysteria breeding in Chinatown, Abbott Kinney examined the Quarter carefully. He denounced the mounting tong feuds and particularly the role played by their killers in the black slouch hats. "In cases involving the Hip Yee tong," he said, "it is almost impossible to secure adverse testimony. This company is composed of the highbinders who import and own lewd women, control most of the gambling houses, and engage in pretty much all kinds of villainy. These men do not hesitate to raise from five hundred to three thousand dollars, and by proclamations posted on the city walls set that price on the head of an enemy...."

Because of the alarming reticence of the Chinese population, Crowley and his officers had to place great reliance on their Chinese interpreters—the main bridge over the widening gap between the two peoples. But according to Kinney these men were craven with fear. He explained how the Hip Yee tong could so brazenly operate the slave-girl ring: "The terror in which Chinese interpreters live makes this possible. About half of the linguists have thus far lost their lives by acting in cases opposed to the highbinders. Their fate has generally been to be chopped to pieces by hatchets."

The hatchet men were careful to confine their attentions to the Chinese. They left Caucasians strictly alone, perhaps fearing another sand-lot invasion by mobs or because they did not want to upset the police, who preferred to let the Chinese take care of themselves. The only member of the Chinatown squad who lost his life during this decade was Officer E. J. Norman, and it was a white hoodlum who stabbed him to death on Dupont Gai at the corner of Pacific Street; not a hatchet man. The highbinders made an exception, however, in the case of the white harlots whose places of business circled Chinatown. lanet Starr, a madame of Dupont Street, was stabbed by a highbinder in 1884, and one of her girls, Flora, was clubbed by a Chinese tough at about the same time. The police interviewed Miss Starr's girls after the stabbing, and one officer said to them, "I think you ought to give whatever assistance you can to the police so that we may find the assassin, for if he is not caught he may become emboldened by success and you may be the next one against whose life an attempt will be made." The officer spoke the truth; only a month later Lena Wallace, another of Janet Starr's outfit, was sent to the hospital with deep glass wounds in her face, hands and arms after a Chinese bomb exploded under her window.

These raids of the highbinders were as nothing compared with the event that highlighted the winter of 1884. A pitched battle was fought, and when dusk settled over the city on November 24, one hatchet man lay on a slab at the morgue while two others were being worked over by a police surgeon. The day had opened serenely enough and had continued that way until 2:30 P.M. At that exact moment the dozen Chinese quietly playing dominoes in the basement of an old brick building on the corner of Bartlett Alley and Pacific Street had looked up and frozen as a hush settled over the room. A murderous-looking trio had entered the doorway and stood mutely at the top of the stairs. A player shouted something in rapid-fire Cantonese, and players, dominoes and chairs went scattering in all directions. A single shot boomed and echoed in the basement, then a fusillade filled the room. Knives, were drawn, and a short, fierce fight ensued. Five police officers rallied to the scene and succeeded in arresting two of the several bleeding men who staggered through alleys and dived into doorways.

A search of the two men, Leong Ah Get and Young Ah Gin, dispelled any possibility of their being unlucky passers-by winged by stray shots. Each carried a heavy Colt revolver and a knife. The third man found by police lay dead in a puddle of his own gore in Baker Alley with a half-empty revolver at his side. He wore a padded cloth "coat of mail" under his blouse; it had stopped one bullet, but a second ball had severed the man's femoral artery, and he had bled to death in the street. The police followed the bloody trails of at least eight men who had been wounded, but lost them in Chinatown's maze of alleys.

When the police tried to get to the bottom of the riot, everyone in the neighbor-hood feigned innocence or refused to talk. Eventually it was decided that the trio was the same as that which had robbed a similar gaming room three weeks earlier. The response of the squad to the increasing violence was to clamp down on the Quarter. They closed the opium dens for a time, and the city put through an ordinance making it illegal to station guards or "look-see" men outside gambling houses. But tong violence not only continued, it increased its tempo. The next February saw a gang of highbinders creating a riot in the Chinese theatre on Jackson Street. The melee was brought under control by the two special officers stationed there but they feared the hatchet men would return for revenge. They were correct. Shortly after midnight a group of tong ruffians slipped into the alley entrance of the theatre to close in on the pair of special patrolmen. But they met a squad of regular police, lying in ambush. The hatchet men disappeared into the night.

By the mid-'80s the tong men were so cocksure that they drove the Chinese interpreter for the United States Customs Service out of the city, sent threatening letters to Assistant United States District Attorney MacAllister, and marched up and down the streets, armed to the teeth with concealed weapons, bullying the Chinese prostitutes who were at the moment being examined in a United States District Court case. They caused a riot in both Chinese theatres one night when the cobblers' guild took over the playhouses for an anniversary celebration. This fight ended in the streets, with the mob throwing gravel, mud and cobbles at one another and at policemen. One of the rioters arrested by Officer Shaw was a burly fellow who insolently gave his name as Fat Choy (Good Fortune—as in the Chinese New Year's greeting. *Gung hoy fat choy).* The Quarter was on the verge of anarchy.

Chief Crowley responded with his usual, if not always well-oriented, firmness. He began a program of rotating his Chinatown squad personnel. The chief's idea was to give each officer some knowledge of Chinatown crime and criminals. He kept only one of the old-timers on the squad to teach the new men the ropes. When he had his new Chinatown squad lined up for the first time Crowley addressed the detail:

"I want you to do the best you can with these Chinese. Keep your men constantly on the alert and make the rounds frequently, for I've a notion that they watch for the coming of the officers and open up their gambling houses after they have gone by. If the courts only sustain us in this last case [he was referring to a new anti-iron door ordinance] the work will be much easier... I want you to understand that you can have all the men you need to enforce the law. Get all the extra men you want from Captain Douglass—his entire watch if you need it. Mac [MacLaughlin] here will show you about. I repeat, I want you to do the very best you can at this work."

Winter always brought the Chinatown squad more trouble as Chinese from the countryside flocked to the city to hole up until spring. The winter of 1885-1886 was particularly bad. Most of those who came to town were broke. Attendance at the theatres was light, the pawnshops were full to overflowing, and some of the gambling houses actually had to close their ironclad doors for lack of trade. With so many men drifting aimlessly about Chinatown with nothing but time on their hands, violence seemed unavoidable. Yet the police held the drifters in check except for the stabbing of a woman in Cum Cook Alley.

The Chinatown squad at this time found some firm allies in the officers of the Customs House Chinese Bureau. They cracked down hard on the slave-girl trade in 1887, arresting a supposedly wealthy merchant, Wong Ah Hung, in the process. He had hardly set foot upon the Embarcadero before they were ransacking his luggage and the baggage of his female accomplice Fong Chum Shee. Wong had long been suspected of smuggling girls; now proof was available. Documents found in the luggage and translated by Customs House interpreter Lee Kan offered evidence enough for a Grand Jury indictment against the slave runner. Indicted, Wong had to pay $5,000 bail on each charge. When the *City of Peking* arrived in port, Customs Inspector Scott had his men search the baggage of Lee Ming Hing. In this merchant's gear agents found letters to a notorious slave dealer, Lee Shuey, memoranda, accounts, prices of women and drafts for the purchase of "nice young girls." The confiscated papers revealed that girls who were bought for $540 each in China were currently bringing $705 on the San Francisco market, although some purchasers were driving hard bargains. Chue Chung Shee, for example, got a halfdozen girls for only $1,846, or less than $308 a head.

Among the confiscated material were instruction sheets and "catechisms" of questions and answers which the girls memorized in order to reply correctly to Customs agents when they sought to enter San Francisco as returning, native-born, California Chinawomen. One set of instructions began in this fashion: "Get certificates [of previous residence, i.e., re-entry permits] with the correct measurements and descriptions of body marks; learn the questions to answers; learn the streets of the city in Chinatown [the girls were often supplied with street maps in Chinese] and the house and number of the streets. If you buy a certificate stating you lived in the country you must learn how much the fare is [to San Francisco] and what kind of work you did there. Learn some English words... When you come, have courage and don't be afraid. Then the officers will not be suspicious or detect you... I send you one dollar in small denominations and you better learn this—what the half dollar is, what the quarter dollar is, what ten cents is and what five cents are, in English...."

Meanwhile back in the alleys the death toll mounted. The Bo Sin Seer tong and the Gi Sin Seer tong were at one another's throats. When Lung Chee and Lee Ah Way were shot in December, 1887, a well-known but discreetly anonymous Chinese detective told the press that the crimes were Gi Sin Seer responses to the murder of Jo Sam Chong, alias Sara Chung, in November. But there were no clues and the police remained in the dark while the press direly—and as it turned out accurately—predicted a duplication in Chinatown of the historic vendettas of Corsica.

It is difficult to say whether Chinatown's hatchet men would kill for nothing. But there is evidence that they would commit murder for forty cents. Lum Ah Tie shot Sam Chung over that sum in a domino game. Of course Lum already bore a grudge against Sam who had frustrated him in an attempt to extort cash from a Chinese woman. In any case, killings continued apace although the Chinese Consul General issued a proclamation to his subjects, offering a $200 reward for the capture of anyone firing a revolver in Chinatown. Chief Crowley's response to the repeated attacks was to increase the Chinatown squad's strength from 7 men to 15. This show of force may have been responsible for the failure of a predicted tong battle to take place on December 8, 1887. The word was all over town that a full-scale tong war was to be waged that day; stores were shuttered early and sidewalks were strangely deserted. Crowley had trebled his Chinatown detail for the occasion, stationing men at the entrance to such favorite runways of the tongmen as Washington Alley, and breaking up any knots of men forming on the sidewalks of Chinatown, however peaceful their appearance. A *Call* reporter described the scene: "A dense fog settled over the city and in Chinatown was advantageous for any affray, as it was impossible to see further than a hundred yards but the wily Mongol saw too many police and little chance to escape. Some officers are of the opinion that more shooting will take place when least expected."

Apparently Chinese Consul Frederick Bee and Brigade Assistant Adjutant General Sproul of the California Militia were of this opinion. The former set up a curfew for his subjects, and Sproul offered Chief Crowley the services of the State Militia against the hatchet men if he felt they were needed. This action of Sproul's led to another rumor that the consignment of 53,000 rounds of ammunition for the Second Brigade, deposited in city prison, had been put there to be used by National Guard troopers against riotous highbinders. "Bosh!" said the *Call,* pointing out that it was just a routine delivery of ammunition to the one building safe enough to hold it. (San Francisco's armories were flimsy wooden firetraps.)

Other measures taken included the hiring of extra guards by butcher shops and other commercial houses and the issuance of a proclamation by the Six Companies, holding each family responsible for any murders committed by its members, with a large money penalty. Hostilities tapered off and the expected battle was never fought.

However, another cold-blooded murder during the bloody month of December, 1887, kept the police busy. Lee Wey, a clerk in the merchandise store of Chung Woo & Company, sold a bag of rice to a customer. It was still the tradition then for an employee to carry a purchaser's bulky or heavy goods, so Lee Wey shouldered the bag and carried it to the customer's tenement. He had climbed the stairs to the first landing when his companion pulled out a pistol and shot him in the left side. The sound of the gunshot and Lee Wey's shrieks of pain attracted many neighbors. Lee sank to the floor, the bag of rice falling on his legs. Somehow he fought his way to his feet and managed to stagger back to the store and fall inside it. The proprietor rushed to help him and called two police officers. The latter carried the wounded man to an adjoining room where he accused the rice buyer of shooting him. Within a few minutes a crowd of men gathered. Some of them tried to force their way into the room where the wounded man lay, and the two policemen had to disperse the crowd and arrest several men. A Chinese detective described the shooting as the most cold-blooded and senseless in Chinatown's history. He blamed the ruthless Gi Sin Seer tong. At 11:30 that night Officers McManus and Bermingham trapped the killer. One of the tips which from time to time leaked through the wall of silence around Chinatown led them to a Stockton Street garret. There, hiding under a bench, was the gunman. A search of his person turned up a large knife but not the murder weapon.

Considerable excitement was engendered in Chinatown the following year when the papers broke the story of the murder plot in Victoria, Canada, involving Lum Hip, the "salaried soldier" who planned to liquidate one of Her Majesty's Customs House officers in that British Columbian port.

The last year of the decade saw Lee Meriwether, Special Agent, United States Department of Labor, nosing about Chinatown. Meriwether was even more confused than Crowley at first. He considered Chinatown's tongs to be nothing more than labor unions. But even with this naivete he was forced to report to Washington, "It is said that a Chinaman who disregards an order of his union is severely punished." Meriwether was more intelligent when he suggested that the reluctance of the Chinese to be photographed was not due to superstition about the evil eye, but rather to their unwillingness to let the police acquire a well-stocked gallery of portraits for identification purposes.

The scales finally fell from Meriwether's eyes when he ran up against the Chee Kong tong which Ah Fook headed. The agent was wise enough to see that it was no labor union, and he did not need the advice of friends to penetrate the flimsy disguise of the secret society as a "Chinese Masonic Lodge." He observed: "A member of a Chinese union who disobeys orders is black-listed. If he makes himself especially obnoxious his name is handed to the Chee Kongs; then that Chinaman disappears. Nobody knows what has become of him. Perhaps he has returned to China or gone to the Eastern states, or perhaps he is dead. People do not know and do not care. Thus it is that the Chinese unions are enabled to enforce implicit obedience to their every mandate." The nearest practice in San Francisco's Caucasian society which Agent Meriwether could think of was shanghaiing. He knew that shanghaiers were sometimes used in labor troubles: "White unions attempt something of the kind. The only difference is that they do not carry it to such an extent. The white scab is not blotted off the face of the earth, as is the Chinese, but he is 'shanghaied,' boycotted, and perhaps beaten and badly bruised, until he comes to his senses.. . ."

Meriwether informed Washington of the gravity of the situation, saying in part: "Those familiar with its secret workings say that the Chee Kongs, or highbinders, as they are commonly called, are a set of thugs and blackmailers. Ah Fook levies a tribute of $5 a week on each gambling establishment in Chinatown. If a Chinaman is to be got rid of, the highbinders—for a consideration—will undertake the task of removing him. An officer of the secret police, from whom I obtained much information concerning the Chee Kongs, was himself blacklisted, a reward of $800 set on his head. Being a cool man and a good shot, and always well armed, he has thus far escaped, although two or three night attacks and broken bones have resulted in the attempt of the highbinders to remove their enemy...."

# CHAPTER ELEVEN

## THE GRAY '90s

*"Assassination is a branch of the art of murder which demands a special notice."*

—"Murder, Considered as One of the Fine
Arts," Thomas De Quincey

*"There is a reign of terror in Chinatown such as has never been known before. Despite the efficient work of the police—and their work has been marvelous, considering the difficulties they have had to contend with— the highbinders are constantly increasing in numbers in the Chinese Quarter and murders are of almost daily occurrence."*

—Anonymous San Francisco merchant,
1893

AS THE GRIP of the tongs tightened on the throat of the Chinese community in San Francisco many Chinese fled the Quarter. Those who could afford to do so left the city, or even the state. Others simply made themselves as scarce as possible. This flight was dramatized for the public by the solving of the mystery of the city's puzzling "Beach Ghost" Strollers on San Francisco's Ocean Beach hysterically reported seeing, from time to time, a man—or a ghost—gliding in and out of the sand dunes at dusk or in the morning sea mist. He, or it, never appeared on top of a dune but was always seen in the hollows between them, before vanishing. The wraith left tracks in the sand but when they were followed they always doubled back on themselves and disappeared or were covered up. But in March, 1893, a tenacious newspaperman finally stalked and trapped the beach ghost in his lair. The reporter found his prey in a cave scooped out in the dunes and braced with driftwood. Bushes covered the entrance to the dugout. Inside he found a Chinese curled up on a mat. "What do you want?" the Chinese asked. "Why are you hiding here?" countered the reporter. "Highbinder want shoot me" was the answer. The mystery was solved and the erstwhile ghost of the dunes had to find another hideout from tong vengeance as the story hit the papers.

Three years later the Chinese Consul General guessed that the population of the Quarter had sunk to 12,000. He was not far off. The population of Chinatown actually declined during these not so gay '90s from 25,833 people to 13,954. Many were ushered out by the authorities for nonregistration as aliens under the new Geary Act, or by similar provisions of the Scott and McCreary Acts which had been inadequate legislation until reinforced by the Geary Act. But many fled the anarchy which resulted from the breakdown of Six Companies' prestige in 1893 and 1894 when its anti-Geary Act position was overrun. The Six Companies lost face. The tongs were at last able to taunt the Six Companies.

The city's attempt to control the situation was ruthless but bumbling. It was the Bingham Ordinance, which would have confined *all* Chinese—good or bad—to their ghetto. The plan was to give Orientals outside the bounds and meets of Chinatown exactly sixty days in which to move inside the imaginary wall or be charged with misdemeanor. It was the concentration camp idea blossoming in San Francisco a full half century before Hitler and Stalin hit upon it, and a good half-dozen years before Spanish General Mariano Weyler pioneered it in stricken Cuba. Judge Lorenzo Sawyer would not hear of such totalitarian methods. He roughly told the Board of Supervisors that the authority to pass such an order was not within the legitimate police power of the state. The Bingham Ordinance was junked.

Luckily, before another mad scheme could be hatched in city hall, peace was declared in Chinatown. By coincidence it occurred on November 11, a day which just twenty-eight years later would become

Armistice Day. The press of San Francisco happily announced that the merchants of Chinatown and the Six Companies had prevailed upon the quarreling Hop Sings and Suey Ons to bury the hatchet, and not in each other. Certain adjustments *were* made, but the peace was superficial. The muscles of the humble Six Companies were flabby, and the feeling of security which had pervaded Chinatown evaporated rapidly. It disappeared entirely during a constitutional of a Suey On member and the first of a new series of murders and murder attempts.

Ah Tuck was taking an evening stroll down Commercial Street when a Hop Sing named Ah Lee sprang from a doorway and opened fire on him. Ah Tuck fled with his attacker in pursuit, firing wildly and scattering spectators. Suddenly the pursuer noticed that he, too, was being pursued. He ducked into Oneida Place, leaped into a bunk, and threw the bedclothes over himself. Two policemen broke into the room and yanked him from the bed. He quickly told them that he had been asleep there all evening. He clung to this story although he was gasping for breath and dripping with perspiration from his sprint. The inmates of the house told the officers that he did not belong there (which took real courage during those dark days), so the Hop Sing was taken to city prison.

The city's substitute for the foundered Bingham Ordinance was an effective and drastic one. It was the transformation of the regular Chinatown patrol into a "flying squad" such as usually dealt with riots. This reorganization was actually under way as early as 1888, under Sergeant William Price, but it was accelerated in the '90s. The technique, as developed by Price, was to make a series of sudden descents on tong headquarters, putting them to the hatchet. When Sergeant James Gillin smashed the rooms of the Bing On and Suey On tongs, Reverend Masters exulted: "As the officers went from tong to tong, Chinatown went wild with joy. The Chinese Consulate, the Six Companies, and the merchants expressed their satisfaction that the first blow had been struck at this bloody despotism under which men had groaned so long. Hundreds of Chinese who had been enforced members and had joined the societies from fear rather than love felt a sense of relief." The tongs speedily replied to this frontal assault. The Chee Kong tong—the only one as yet incorporated under the laws of California—filed a suit for damages when their rooms fell under Gillin's axes. Masters now groaned, "A victory for the highbinders in a court of law would be a calamity. Another vigilance committee will be necessary if the highbinder is ever protected by our courts." Even though Chinese businessmen offered to indemnify Crowley for any losses he might sustain in court, the chief stopped the hunt for the time being.

Reverend Masters, casting about for some alternative action to keep the tongs off balance, revived the idea of a Chinese detective force. He reminded the chief of the efficient work of the Chinese police in Hong Kong. But Crowley remembered better how timid and ineffectual they had been in the past experiments in San Francisco. He let the idea alone, although the Six Companies mustered a new all-Chinese police force of its own to help the regulars.

Peace was to be only a dream in the 1890s. War broke out in earnest in late 1892, when a pretty, seventeen-year-old slave girl was shot and seriously wounded in Cum Cook Alley. A prominent cutthroat of a new and modest-sized tong, the Mock Chin, did the honors. He was Chin Ah Chong and his secret society was so small it did not even have a meeting place. But its "soldiers" were as desperate as any *boo how doy* prowling the streets. Chin was attracted to the girl, but was thrown out of her house by bouncers when he pestered her with his attentions. He did not forget this, nor did he forgive it. Chin Ah Chung began a campaign of terrorization and soon had the girl paying him most of her earnings. Next he began on her sister. The slave girl was on her way to a little restaurant in Cum Cook Alley when Chin seized her roughly by the arm and demanded more money. When she told him that she had none with her but that she would go back to her house to get some he angrily thrust her away and shot her. Police officers rushed her to Receiving Hospital where doctors were astounded to find that her wound was painful rather than serious, although inflicted with a .45-caliber slug. Her miraculous escape from death was due to her wearing the traditional quilted costume of Old China. The heavy padding had slowed the pistol ball down so that it had done very little real damage. This incident pointed up the efficiency of the similarly quilted bulletproof vests worn by hatchet men. These were almost as effective against daggers and pistol balls as against the searching winds and cold tule fogs of San Francisco's winters. Even better protection was furnished by those of chain mail imported from China at a cost of $250 each.

Next to die was a supposedly peaceful and quiet shrimp dealer who turned out to be a Suey On tong member and who was shot down by a Bo Sin Seer hatchet man. The latter was captured but his accomplice escaped. Police could not track down another bloodthirsty' individual who shot his prey in broad daylight the next morning. He fired three bullets into his victim, calmly replaced the smoking pistol inside his blouse, and sauntered off. He was never seen again.

Chief Crowley, although stung by the lawsuits and uproar over his earlier raids, was eager to show off his new aggressive countermeasures to Chinatown crime. He called a press conference, and when reporters arrived at his office they found him studying a map of Chinatown. He touched an electric button and Captain William Douglass appeared. "Captain," said Crowley, "you will take the proper steps to prevent another encounter in Chinatown. These highbinder murders must cease, even if it takes the whole force to guard Chinatown. Place officers in the outlying sections so that none who shoot can escape by flight. Do you understand?" "Aye, aye, sir," replied the captain, commander of the department's first division.

The reporters hustled up to Chinatown to see exactly what measures Douglass would employ. They found that he had reinforced his two plain-clothes squads in the Quarter with a dozen uniformed men. That evening 7 highbinders were backed up against a wall, with their hands high, and searched. All 7 were found to be packing .45 Colts. They were disarmed and quickly put in the lockup on charges of carrying concealed weapons.

Even with this augmented police force in Chinatown, one tong dared another to meet it in battle on Jackson Street. But an officer was tipped off and a squad arrived early. The officers found only 6 On Yick toughs, who fled when they saw the bluecoats. The Chinatown squad followed them and trapped 4 in On Yick tong headquarters. Two were caught in the act of pulling off their coats of mail—padded blouses with a layer of woven steel links inside—weighing more than twenty-one pounds. The police tested them and found them impossible to penetrate with either knife blade or bullet. Three of the apprehended men had Colt revolvers.

The fourth and more pacific of the lot, carried only a knife with an eight-inch, razor-sharp blade. One more hatchet man was caught that night in Sullivan's Alley. He was a wiry little fellow who looked all swollen up, such was the character of his peculiar coat of mail. His armor was made up of nothing more than multitudinous layers of newspaper wrapped around his middle.

Up to this time the police were in the dark as to the reason for the particular war which was breaking out, but soon walls all over Chinatown were covered with posters in Chinese. These showed that the Sam Yup Company was the target. A Kwong Duck tong publicly announced its severance of any and all connections with the company and other signs proclaimed that the On Yick tong would no longer pay "tribute" to the Sam Yup Company. The Consul General of China soon got into the act by posting his own bills which ordered all Chinese, and particularly tong members, to conduct themselves in a quiet and peaceful manner. To show that their contempt for the Consulate was as complete as their disdain for the moral rule of the Six Companies, the tong men disfigured the consular posters with obscene inscriptions.

As if Crowley did not have enough trouble in trying to keep warlike Chinatown disarmed, the press and public began to clamor for a crackdown on opium dens in the early '90s. The *Californian Illustrated Magazine,* to document the evil, sent a four-man camera party to photograph the cul-de-sacs for the first time by night. Detective Chris Cox led the way. As usual, proprietors of the dens blew out the lights when uninvited guests arrived. But the cameramen took flash pictures and scared many addicts in the process. The *Call* leaped into the muckraking crusade by compiling a veritable catalogue of many of the 300 opium dens in the City. It singled out those it considered especially vicious, like Blind Annie's Cellar, which was a resort of white girls and (supposedly) under police protection. Although the city had enacted an ordinance which set up penalties of a $1,000 fine and 6 months in jail for keeping or visiting a den, reporters had no trouble in tailing visitors. The latter varied from "dude fiends," well-dressed ladies and gentlemen with diamond studs, to "20-cent-habit" addicts. These men could only afford twenty cents worth—one lichee nut shell of the drug—per day. On two occasions policemen were logged as entering dens.

When reporters descended into Blind Annie's they found it a foul-smelling place full of cats. There were only two white girls there; "Evil-looking women but still young," a reporter noted. Annie sat in a corner on a greasy mat. Tiers of bunks lined the walls, each having a supply of *ah pin yin* (opium), a *dong* (nut-oil lamp), needle, pipe and bowl. One of the girls volunteered that she never smoked more than twenty pills on any one visit. She explained, "That isn't enough to put me under the influence but it braces me up after a hard day and that's all I care about… It'd soon grow if I'd let it, but I'm not going to be a fiend. I've hit the pipes these five years now and I'm not a fiend yet. You don't catch this girl getting to be a hophead." But as she spoke her eyelids were growing heavy. "Guess I've taken a bit too much this time," she apologized. "I'll sleep it off a bit before I go."

The guide led the reporters aside. "She's good till morning," he explained. "She always talks that way about taking a little too much but she never quits till sleep comes on."

The reporters stared as two girls dropped nickels on a tray before Blind Annie. The old hag muttered "T'anks," then turned her sightless eyes on the men and asked, "Don't the gentlemen want to smoke?" Muttering "No, thanks," the press party broke up and the men went to their offices to write their experience. Many of the articles signed off in this fashion: "These are the facts regarding Chinatown. If the police have been in ignorance of these dens, as Chief Crowley has declared himself to be, at least they need no longer be in ignorance." True. Anyone with the price of a newspaper now knew the extent of the opium rottenness in Chinatown.

The press was not quite fair with Crowley. He had to operate within the law. When Captain John Short and his men arrested one opium peddler *six times over*, he did not even bother to change his beat, but returned each time to Stevenson Street after getting off with a $20 fine. He was neither keeping nor visiting an opium den—just selling it on the street.

Although Chinatown was terrorized by the tongs, the conspiracy of silence was never so complete that the police did not have stool pigeons to alert them of trouble. Dong Gong, a special officer of the force was a combination informer and detective, and Wong Sue also wore a star. But most of the tipsters were faceless, nameless men of the alleys. The press had its own informers in the Quarter, too, and one let out the story on the secret joint meeting of the Bing On and Suey On tongs in February, 1893. At this affair two men were sentenced to immediate death and two to deferred execution. Ten men from each of the usually rival tongs met in a room at 821 Washington Street, uneasy and watchful. They were not as frightened of a raid by the Chinatown squad as they were of treachery from their new "friends." Most wore mail under their regular clothing and carried hidden knives, hatchets or guns. Lots were drawn to see which society should furnish the soldiers to exterminate their common enemies; four Suey Ons and one Bing On were chosen. Next, four names of victims were drawn by lot from a considerable "waiting list." The crimes of the quartet against the fighting tongs were: informing the police of tong meeting places; refusing to swear to false certificates for slave girls; refusing to help land new slave girls from a ship; going to school to learn English; and talking to policemen. These death sentences were not just idle threats. Ten days earlier Chin Doo Doo had landed on a false certificate, then had refused to pay the fees asked by his perjuring friends. He was gunned down before he had a chance to enjoy his stay in San Francisco.

One of the intended victims of the tong trial rushed to Crowley's office, begged for protection, and asked for permission to carry a pistol and wear a coat of mail. He quickly went into hiding. A few days later a man was murdered when he was mistaken for one of the doomed four. Officers Withers and Cook of the Chinatown squad quickly arrested a hatchet man who denied everything though they found his revolver, four chambers emptied, in a ventilation hole of a staircase riser in the building where he lived. Confronted with this evidence, he still came up with the old answer *"No sabe."*

Luck was not with Chun Qui, another of the condemned four. This Hip Sing was murdered in a Sullivan's Alley gambling den on March 8, 1893. Sergeant Thomas Flanders and his posse seized the killer Han Wong and five Suey Sing accomplices in a very neat piece of police work. The hatchet man had used what would become a favorite tool of many killers, the deadly .44 Colt revolver which took Winchester rifle ammunition. The murder bullet had passed entirely through the victim's body.

The work of the police was complicated that winter because the Quarter was flooded with about 6,000 coolies from the interior. They were all strangers; the police did not have a line on any of them. At a meeting with Vice Consul King Owyang, Chief Crowley said:

> The situation is serious. Ever since we have had a China-town we have had highbinders and highbinder wars, resulting in more or less slaughter and trouble, but the present war seems to be one of the worst we have ever had, because of the numbers engaged in it. The Chinatown squad has worked faithfully and hard, but if every policeman on the force were stationed in Chinatown we could not prevent these outbreaks.
>
> What we are now trying to do is to prevent the escape of highbinders once arrested. It has not been the custom for prisonkeepers, who are permitted to take cash bail in cases of arrests for misdemeanors, to require the highest amount of bail fixed by law unless there is some evidence that the case is an aggravated one. The prisonkeepers have been in the habit of accepting the lowest cash bail fixed for the offense. In the same way it has not been the custom of police judges or the clerks of police courts in the absence of judges, to require bonds in the highest amount fixed by law for misdemeanors. The result is that the highbinders have been arrested for vagrancy time and again, but have secured a small cash bail and thereby their liberty to go right back into Chinatown and resume their devilish work. Understand, too, that it is generally the worst of the highbinders that become known to the police and are arrested. If we could only keep them in jail once we have them we might be able to handle their followers.
>
> We have dropped all pretense of handling this dangerous class with gloves. Thursday night Detectives Cox and Glennon and Sergeant Burke and his squad visited the headquarters of the Suey Sing tong on the top floor of the building at the southwest corner of Dupont and Pacific Streets and gutted the place, smashing the joss and destroying the flags and furniture. It has to be done, and the same work will be kept up wherever a high-

binder society is known to meet. The conference today was to agree upon bail in cases of arrest. Hereafter no bond will be accepted by any police judge or clerk of the police court for any Chinese arrested unless it is first accepted by the Chinese Consul General and by myself. In future, the highest cash bail will be required in all cases and we hope to be able to stop this war where it is.

The press liked Crowley's tough line of talk and predicted that no quarter would be given the hatchet men, but also guessed that despite the watchfulness of the police a score of men would be killed by summer in tong warfare. The figure was not to be that high, but there were killings.

Sergeant Burke and his squad continued their wrecking raids on the tongs and also apprehended twenty-three highbinders who had literally taken over two houses of ill fame and were compelling the inmates to entertain them and cook for them. The papers noticed a new willingness on the part of the Chinese in the street to cooperate with the police. But instead of being happy with this development, the press was frightened. It saw the cracks in the conspiracy of silence as warnings of even more deadly warfare—"When the Chinese are willing to join with the whites in prosecuting their own countrymen, the situation is far more serious than the police are willing to admit, yet this is the status of affairs today and the war is only begun."

The next incident of the tong war was a bizarre press conference called by ex-interpreter Kwan Mow, alias Kwan Yik Nam, another of those earmarked for death by the Suey Sings and Bing Ons. "By the heavens and the earth," shouted Kwan, "I swear that I am an innocent man and a Christian." He held his hand rigidly aloft as he took this oath. "They want to kill me," he continued. "The gamblers are after me and call me a stool pigeon to Chief Crowley." His eyes bulged and his lips twisted in a savage furor. "May my enemies be killed! And die, die, die in the street and lie low, low, low!" Kwan was far braver now, trapped in a Clay Street office, than when he had been in court. There he had fainted dead away in the corridor after being threatened for not securing the landing of slave girls. "The gamblers are after me," he cried again, "they want to kill me because I opposed the women's landing. Fong

Hon is no merchant as he claims, he is a gambler and has been arrested for selling and dealing in lottery tickets… The gamblers are after me for another thing. They say I go to Chief Crowley and tell him all I know about *tan* and lottery and highbinders. They call me a stool pigeon." He crashed his fist on the desk. "Yes, I *do* know Chief Crowley. I do go to see him. He is my friend. I *like* him.

The chief gave his men orders to use their clubs more liberally on highbinders, or even idlers found around highbinder haunts. But with all their vigilance and diligence, Bok Ah Chung—a Suey Sing hood from Portland—was riddled with bullets at noon and within one hundred feet of the little Waverly Place police substation the chief had set up in the heart of Chinatown. It was an insolent dare of the hatchet men. While the police could not prevent the assassination, at least they captured his murderer. He was a Hop Sing hoodlum named Li Gun. The *Call* prophesied, "He will swing for his deed, for he was caught red-handed." When the Chinese Vice-Consul tried to question him in his cell he got nowhere. All he could tell Crowley was that the man was a notorious liar, which the chief already knew. The Vice-Consul, King Owyang, praised arresting officers Phillips and Kaskell and promised them a $600 reward upon the conviction of Li.

After the murder Sergeant Burke immediately set Crowley's get-tough policy in motion again. Highbinders were hauled in for vagrancy, the highest bail was demanded, and no bonds allowed unless approved by the Consul General. The squad raided a house of ill fame and seized seven girls. The owner was taken aback when the desk sergeant answered his usual question "How much bailee?" with "Just two hundred and fifty dollars each." The small businessman choked and asked, "How so much?" "Well," said the sergeant, "there's two hundred each for visiting a house of ill fame and fifty each for vagrancy." The Chinese emptied a sack of coins on the sergeant's desk, counted out $1,750, and marched his chattels home.

The cuffs, kicks and clubbings of the Chinatown squad seemed to be working wonders. "I never saw so few highbinders on the streets," said Burke. "They know when to remain in their hiding places. But I would not be surprised to find more of them on the streets after darkness sets in." Some honest Chinese were clubbed in error, although Crowley's order was clear enough—"Be careful not to club a reputable Chinese, but show no mercy to a highbinder."

Sergeant Burke was impressed with the cooperation he was beginning to get from the mass of Chinese. The Six Companies put up handbills all over Chinatown. These ordered all shopkeepers who were members of tongs to quit in just thirty days or be classed as highbinders themselves and dealt with accordingly. The Consul General proved to be a staunch ally. He wrote to China for permission to confiscate the property of all known highbinders. But most surprising was the Vigilante-like attitude of the crowd which witnessed the cowardly killing of Bok Ah Chung. As Li Gun was led away they shouted "Hang him! Hang him!" Burke was amazed. "During all the years I have been in Chinatown," he said, "I never heard such a cry before and I honestly believe that if the murderer had been handed over to them they would have lynched him."

The courts went along with Crowley. One man, arrested on a concealed-weapons charge, pleaded that he was a labor boss in Alaska and needed a gun for protection. Instead of being left off as he expected, he received a lecture from Judge Henry L. Joachimson who pointed out the dual roles many Chinese were playing—respectable by day, hatchet man by night. Thanks to some character witnesses, the Alaskan got off with the lowest penalty under the ordinance but it was still a $250 fine or a day in jail for every dollar.

Sergeant Burke and his Chinatown squad now took axes to the flagpoles of the Suey Sing and Hop Sing tongs, transforming them into rooftop piles of kindling. It was Burke's belief that the tong members would take the destruction of their flags and flagpoles as an omen of the ultimate destruction of their secret societies.

Burke's orders to his squad were, "Whenever and wherever a known highbinder is, club him!" A hot-tempered Irishman, it is not remarkable that now and again Burke lost control of himself. When he axed the joss room of the Hop Sing tong his patience was completely exhausted. He had his squad kick and club two highbinders all the way down the stairs to the street three stories below. Burke swung his baton at one of the men again and again, swearing, "Get out of here you heathen cutthroat! You son of a bitch of a highbinder, get out!" Later in the day he sent Officer Withers back to the wrecked Hop Sing tong. Withers found that six men had drifted back, and he went through the whole operation again, kicking them downstairs and shouting, "Get out and stay out!"

During this period the San Francisco Grand Jury had to work overtime. On one day alone—March 15, 1893—it indicted nine hatchet men for murder.

The Chinatown squad signified its approval by raiding and demolishing the headquarters of the Suey Ying tong after forcing the fifteen members there to run a gantlet of billy clubs. With axes, sledges and hatchets the squad reduced the furnishings of the rooms to rubble.

At this juncture Vice-Consul Owyang reported that the merchants of the Quarter had resolved not to pay any more tribute to the tongs nor to let them have any rooms in their buildings, nor furnish them with bail or bondsmen. But the police doubted that many merchants would have the courage to go so far so fast. Nevertheless, the heads of the Six Companies solemnly announced that there would be no more tong wars in Chinatown. They reported that the Hop Sing tong was in such financial trouble that it could not pay its own salaried soldiers for their killings, and that the Suey Sings had given assurances they would make no more trouble. With a show of spunk the Six Companies told the American public that if the highbinders did not behave and go to work the respectable Chinese element would find means to convict them in court. In an editorial in one of the Chinese-language newspapers, in explaining the difficulty of eradicating them, a writer compared the tongs to lawless elements in the Caucasian American community—singling out the Ku Klux Klan and the Mafia—and then added, "I am not defending the Chinese highbinders; not a bit of it. We all wish that every highbinder on earth could be caught and hanged or beheaded." A white merchant reported that some of his Chinese colleagues had told him that they wished the city could take all hatchet men to some vacant lot and allow them to blaze away at each other until they killed each other off. The Vice-Consul expressed his regret at tong depredations but also his pride at the increasing assistance being given the police by law-abiding Chinese He admitted that Chinatown was ready to form a committee of Vigilantes if necessary, but ridiculed the tales that all Chinatown was an armed camp. "Why, for the past two weeks a squad of only six men has been raiding Chinatown [tongs]. They were only a half-dozen men

195

surrounded by thousands of Chinese and yet there has never been a hand raised against an officer of the law nor a complaint made by the Chinese officials although we know of scores of cases where innocent men were badly beaten. We realized that in order to reach the guilty some innocent men would have to suffer, as is nearly always the case...."

A Chinese vigilance committee actually was formed at this time— the Wai Leong Rung Sur—and was soon under tong fire. In April *chun hungs* appeared on walls, placing prices on the heads of the society's officers—-especially Chun Ti Chu, a prime mover in its organization as well as president of the Sam Yup Company. Detective Chris Cox described Chun as a fighter and a fine pistol shot who was more than a match for any three or four highbinders. Three hundred dollars was the sum on Chun's head, and posters denounced him for counseling the Chinese not to secure Geary Act registration certificates. (This was the blunder which cost the Six Companies so much of its prestige.) Police tore these down quickly, but they were replaced by much more insulting circulars:

THE PRESIDENT OF THE SAM YUP COMPANY CON-TAINS TWELVE STINK POTS, WHICE ARE INEXPLICA-BLE. HE HAS NO LITERARY TALENT. HE BOUGHT HIS POSITION WITH MONEY. HIS FATHER IS A REFORMED THIEF. HIS MOTHER'S FIRST HUSBAND WAS A FUNG AND HER SECOND A CHUNG [illegitimate]. HE SHIELDS GUILTY CRIMINALS AND TRIES TO FREE THEM. HE PROVOKED PEOPLE TO ANGER AT A MEETING AND TRIED TO ESCAPE. THEREFORE, ALL PERSONS HAD BETTER CLOSE THEIR NOSES BEFORE PASSING HIS DOOR.

The rewards were ostensibly offered by a new secret society, the Sing Ping Kung Sur, but Vice-Consul King said no such tong existed. He labeled the broadsides a bluff on the part of the hatchet men, to cow ignorant or timorous merchants.

Another *chun hung* was soon pasted up all over the Quarter. It read:

IT IS REPORTED LATELY THAT THERE IS A VIGI-
LANCE COMMITTEE CALLED THE LAW ABIDING PRO-
TECTIVE SOCIETY, WAI LEONG KUNG SUR. ITS OB-
JECT IS TO BREAK DOWN ALL TONGS. THIS ACTION
CANNOT HAVE BEEN TAKEN BY MEN OF ABILITY. ITS
ACTION IS TO ENCOURAGE THE WHITE PEOPLE AND
MOLEST OUR PEOPLE, MY GOOD PEOPLE, DO NOT
BLAME MEMBERS OF THE LAW ABIDING PROTECTIVE
SOCIETY. IF ANYONE IS MURDERED ON THE STREET
THE WHITE OFFICERS CAN ARREST THEM AND WIT-
NESS AGAINST THEM WITHOUT THE ASSISTANCE
OF THE PROTECTIVE ASSOCIATION. THE SOCIETY IS
GOOD FOR NOTHING BUT TO INFORM THE OFFICERS
AND ARREST PEOPLE FOR VISITING HOUSES OF ILL
REPUTE OR HAVE THEM FINED $20 APIECE. THE OR-
GANIZATION OF A PROTECTIVE UNION IS THE SAME
EVIL AS THE [WAVERLY PLACE] POLICE STATION IN
CHINATOWN. DIFFERENT COMPANIES SUBSCRIBE
MONEY FOR THE SOCIETY. WHY DO THEY NOT BET-
TER SUBSCRIBE MONEY TO SEND AGED PEOPLE TO
CHINA? THERE IS A MAN NAMED GONG TYNG. [Sug-
gested by Crowley for the task of approving bonds of arrested
Chinese.] ONE THOUSAND DOLLARS WILL BE PAID FOR
SHOOTING HIM DOWN AND $300 WILL BE PAID FOR
INFORMATION REGARDING THE VIGILANCE COM-
MITTEE'S INTERPRETER AND DIRECTOR. TWO THOU-
SAND DOLLARS WILL BE PAID FOR KILLING THE DI-
RECTOR OR INTERPRETER, $4,000 FOR THE KILLING
OF THE TWO, AND $50 FOR INFORMATION CONCERN-
ING THE MEMBERS OF THE SOCIETY. WE WILL GIVE
$1,000 TO A MAN WHO WILL KILL AN INSPECTOR OF
CHINESE BONDS. WHOEVER JOINS THIS WAI LEONG
KUNG SUR PUTS HIMSELF TO DEATH AND INTO HIS
GRAVE.

The Chinese quasi Vigilantes did not panic. They went right ahead with their plans. They drew up fourteen resolutions which spelled out in fine detail their counter offensive against the tongs. Heads of families were to keep all kin out of the fighting tongs; merchant members of tongs were to withdraw from them, being promised protection by the society; no one was to go bail for hatchet men—if one should do so the Wai Leong Kung Sur would do some posting of its own, pasting up placards accusing the bail supplier of being a highbinder at heart; if a Caucasian should supply bail for a highbinder, a complaint would be made to the authorities. The society's officers tried to cover everything. Anyone renting rooms to highbinders would be "published" in this fashion too. The Law-Abiding Protective Society promised to notify the police of rooms occupied by any hatchet men, to get landlords to oust known highbinders from rental rooms, and to set up rewards of $600, $400 and $200 for persons giving information leading to the arrest and conviction of tong murderers. Storekeepers were given police whistles to blow in case of attacks.

A regular battle of *chun hungs* now took place. With the posters of the mysterious Sing Ping King Sur tong still up in some areas, the new Chinese Vigilantes fostered by the Six Companies pasted up one of its own all over the Quarter:

NOTICE! BY THE SIX COMPANIES! WE, THE SIX COMPANIES HAVE ORGANIZED A VIGILANCE COMMITTEE FOR THE PURPOSE OF PROTECTING OUR INTERESTS. THE HIGHBINDERS ARE BECOMING TOO OPEN IN THEIR LAWLESSNESS. WE HAVE ALSO ISSUED AN APPEAL ASKING FOR THE GOOD CHINAMEN TO ASSIST US IN BREAKING OF THE HIGHBINDERS. IN RETURN, THEY HAVE ISSUED A PAPER DIRECTED AGAINST THE WAI LEONG SOCIETY. THEREFORE, WE GIVE NOTICE THAT WE WILL GIVE $100 TO ANY PERSON WHO WILL GIVE US INFORMATION AS TO WHO WROTE OR POSTED SAID INFLAMMATORY CIRCULAR, AND $200 WILL BE PAID FOR THE APPREHENSION OF THE AUTHOR AND INSTIGATOR OF ANY PAPER OF A LIKE CHARACTER. WE WILL ALSO GIVE $100 FOR THE

ARREST OF THE PERSON WHO FORGED THE NAME OF
THE SIX COMPANIES TO THE LATE PAPER.

The next broadside to be plastered on walls bore the Consular seal.
Consul General Li Wang Yu posted copies of a notice stating that he
had received authority from the Chinese Minister in Washington to send
highbinders home for beheading by Governor Kwong Si of Canton.
Whether this was bluff or not, the *chun hung* which ended: YOU WILL
NOT ONLY BE BEHEADED BUT YOU WILL BRING DISGRACE
ON YOUR OWN FAMILY, FATHERS, BROTHERS AND SISTERS
intimidated many *boo how doy.*

Chief Crowley was asked about the Consul General's *chun hung.*
"This much I know," said Crowley. "That the Chinese Consul General
told me recently that he has communicated with the Chinese Minister
at Washington with the view of getting him to obtain power from the
Chinese Government to confiscate all property belonging to highbinders
arrested for a crime, and (if they have no property) suggesting that the
Chinese Government should behead the relatives of these highbinders
so as to make an end to these murders which are disgracing the whole
Chinese population in this country. Whether the Consul General has obtained this power I do not know... If the Consul General would send the
highbinders to China to be beheaded, I think it would be a mighty good
thing and would please me very much."

When the new president of the Yeong Wo Company arrived he
brought with him from China a document printed by order of His Imperial Majesty, the Emperor of China. It deplored the fact that "Certain
classes of Chinese have persisted in maintaining societies to carry on
blackmail" and ordered all Chinese to obey the laws of their new land.
But it had little effect. Just before Thanksgiving Day another Chinese
was murdered in the Jackson Street theatre for informing the Immigration Bureau that the girls coming to the Omaha Exposition, ostensibly for the Chinese pavilion there, were in fact en route to Chinatown
whorehouses.

Crowley kept his own "hatchet men" busy. The keen blades wielded
by the Chinatown squad sent six more tong flagpoles crashing, including those of two new rising stars among the tongs—the Gee Sin Seer

199

and the Bo Sin Seer. Sergeant Burke said, "The work will be continued till not a single flagpole, surmounting a place where highbinders have been in the habit of meeting, is left standing." A quixotic campaign perhaps, but it appeared to have a calming effect on the tongs. Rumors of peace began to waft about the Quarter. A Chinatown police officer was not sanguine, however, of peace between the quarreling Hop Sing and Suey Sing tongs. The officer said: "I believe it is only a temporary truce forced upon the highbinders by the vigorous actions of Chief Crowley. They will wait till the present excitement blows over and will break out shortly, worse than ever. The clubbing by police and the destruction of their headquarters have had the effect of driving a number of the highbinders out of the city. But, as soon as things quiet down again, they will return and will be found in new headquarters, ready for offensive operations. In fact," he added, "I have heard it rumored that a new highbinder society has been formed, even more powerful than any one of those known to the police."

Proof that the highbinders had not gone underground was shortly supplied Crowley. Mrs. Annie Leonard complained to authorities of tong bribery attempts. Murder witness Annie told the court, "Last night two Chinese called at my residence and asked to speak to me. I asked them what they wanted. They said they had come to see me about Lee Sing who was on trial for murder. They said they knew that I was going to testify against him. Then one of them told me that Lee Sing was not a member of the highbinder society and had no authority from the society to kill the man, that he did it for private reasons and could expect no aid from the society-but that his friends had undertaken his defense. They then offered me a sum of money if I would leave the state and not testify here today. Of course, I showed them the door at once."

As if the position of the Six Companies was not insecure enough after the Geary Act loss of face, in 1894 it split right down the middle when a See Yup was arrested for murder. He was acquitted by the jury, and the Sam Yups—who had not only refused to help his case financially but who had indicated that they thought him guilty—were ridiculed unmercifully by the other company. The result was a war of sorts between Sam Yups and See Yups: a lack of confidence in American law and justice on the part of the former; and a long-drawn-out boycott on Sam Yup stores by the much more numerous members of the See Yup Company. The on-again, off-again boycott did not end for four years. Stores went bankrupt; commercial stagnation added its woes to the political anarchy of the Quarter. The fighting tongs were delighted as the pressure was shifted from them after the Chinese vigilance committee had all but frightened them out of their coats of mail.

Hatchet men hired out to either or both sides and were generally quick to stir up what trouble they could. They mixed into Chinese "union" (guild) squabbles at this time, too, indulging their talent for arson in attempts to burn down two factories. They also bullied Chinese capitalists, but in one case picked a tartar. When Chun Mon, overall factory owner, learned that the factory workers' guild had put a $1,000 price on his head after he had fired his whole labor force and substituted the Chinatown equivalent of scabs, he armed himself and marched into the guild's headquarters. He saw that his executioner, hired from a tong, was there. He coolly walked up to him and said, "Well, here I am. Why don't you earn your money? One thousand dollars does not grow on bushes to be picked so easily every day." While the highbinder was slinking away Chun notified the Six Companies. Pressure was brought to bear and the hatchet man left on the next steamer for the Old Country.

More and more people fled Chinatown. The Chinese Government tried to stablilize the situation through the Consulate General. A succession of consuls and vice-consuls was tried. Each failed to end the boycott and was recalled. Finally Wu Ting Fang, Chinese Minister in Washington, sent his brother-in-law Ho Yow to San Francisco as Vice-Consul. He got the two companies to come to terms with one another and to jury rig a peace of a kind. As a tribute to his success, the Emperor made him Consul General. But his labors in this area had to go on for months to preserve even the shakiest peace.

Ho Yow also had a radical plan for exorcising the tongs. He put his plan to city authorities. By it he would have a say in determining which officers, Chinese or others, should be detailed to the Chinatown squad. He would coordinate police judges' jurisdiction over Chinatown. Ho Yow urged the abolition of jury trials of arrested Chinese, in order to stop bribery. He asked for the deportation of convicted Chinese felons rather than their imprisonment in California. "In this manner," he said, "the United States would be rid rapidly of the Chinese criminal class and the sources of the disturbing tong wars removed." Inspector Frank Schuyler of the Chinese Bureau of the Customs House went further. He urged that the Chinese Consul General be made head of a court to deport aliens found "guilty" of membership in any of the fighting tongs.

The city was not about to surrender its hegemony—even over Chinatown—to the Chinese Empire's representative, but it did adopt some of Ho Yow's ideas. When the Chinatown squad smashed the Ross Alley gang, for example, the quartet of burglar-robbers was given the choice of imprisonment or deportation. One chose the latter course and was soon joined by three more felons aboard the *Gothic,* bound for China. This was a good beginning. By a revival of the half-forgotten McCreary Act, deportation of Chinese criminals was made feasible, and the Consul General prepared a list of potential deportees for the police department. Typical of the kind of men picked up in the ensuing dragnet was an ex-con named Jeong Woo. Walking down Washington Street one lazy day, Jeong felt a gentle but firm pressure on his arm. He saw Detective Chris Cox. "I'd like to talk to you," said Cox. "Where you takee me?" asked Jeong. Soothingly Cox responded, "We'll just drop down to the Old Prison where we can talk without fear of interruption. I think you'll see some of your old friends in China before long, Jeong, my boy." The face of the highbinder fell. He protested, "Why you takee me? Me been out of San Quentin ten years." "That's a fact," agreed Cox, "and you've made lots of trouble during those years. Now you've got to go home."

Another symptom of the sickness afflicting Chinatown in the mid-'90s was the police shakeup of 1894. A number of men were discharged from the department, for corruption. Chief Crowley, too "sick" to go before the Grand Jury, sent his able aide Captain Isaiah Lees to appear in his place. The captain explained that the evidence against Police Clerk William E. Hall and the others was enough to show their guilt but was not enough for a court conviction. After leaving the Grand Jury room he was pressed by reporters for a fuller explanation. Lees said, "I explained to the Grand Jury the difficulty with which the information was obtained which led to the dismissal of delinquent officers in the department. But I could not go into it all. It would be the part of idiocy for us to give all our sources of information and the methods pursued to obtain evidence against the corrupt ones. This would prevent us from getting any more information from these quarters and the guilty ones might escape. It would be foolish to tip our hands."

By the time of the police scandals the Chinatown squad had become a potent factor in controlling crime. It remained so as long as it stayed honest. After the scandal broke, Lieutenant William Price explained how it had come into being:

> When I first went into the Chinatown district in 1888, things were in a very bad condition. There was hardly a day that someone was not killed, even white people killed by accident, as shot was flying everywhere. One afternoon there were seventy-five shots fired on the street from one faction toward another... One night about eleven o'clock I was on the corner of Spofford Alley and Washington Street when the people were coming out of the Chinese theatre. A shot was fired and it struck a woman who was passing... The man who fired the shot was not more than one foot away from me but... turned so quickly and got away in some alley that I could not find him... Once I had two officers with me and there were two more across the street in uniform, though we did not usually wear uniforms in the Chinese Quarter. Notwithstanding all this, the murderer walked deliberately out into the middle of the street, and surrounded as he was by all those officers when it was impossible for a man to escape, he killed his man...
>
> I went to Chief Crowley and said, "Chief, when any one of these Chinamen commit deeds of violence they run into the numerous small alleys of Chinatown and get beyond our reach, and after being once lost sight of it is impossible to identify them unless by some peculiar mark about them." [In later years Price used to boast he could tell a hatchet man from a peaceful Chinese by the former's "fluffed" hair, not so well kept as others, his round, stiff-brimmed felt fedora, and the little piece of red silk he carried on his person somewhere which identified him as one of the *bow how doy.*]

These societies are unlawful and organized for unlawful

purposes. They do not recognize our laws and to compete with them we have to go beyond our present laws. They are not sufficient. I can put a stop to these societies if you will give me my own way.

Crowley had responded, "I am under bonds here, of course. They will sue me if I do as you suggest." But Price had gone to the Chinese Consulate and when officials there spoke to the chief, agreeing to stand by him financially if sued, he came around.

The chief had allowed Price to reorganize the Chinatown squad of 7 or 8 officers. With this force Price gave all of Chinatown's myriad societies a careful scrutiny. When he was ready, Price struck. He enlarged his force to 16 uniformed men and a police surgeon, armed them with axes, and set off. He marched them from one tong to another and literally cut them to pieces. He bragged that he broke up $180,000 worth of property and did not leave a piece of furniture over five inches in length. "Wherever we went, we got arms, ammunition, bowie knifes two feet long in the blade, iron bars done up in braided cord, and so forth. Also chain and steel armor."

Price began the technique of kicking downstairs any members found in tong quarters, a procedure in which he was soon excelled by his brother officers, mainly Sergeant Jesse Cook. The better class of Chinese—even those forced into tong membership by fear or other circumstance—praised his drastic action and secretly informed him of tongs he had missed. Informants came to his home secretly by night. He was able to close in on the Hop Sing tong, giving its officials one hour's notice to remove their furnishings. They ignored his threat, so he led his infantry in and tore the interior of the four-story building to pieces, smashing seven josses in the process. With no place to meet, the tong men had to disperse. Price recalled his next move. "I then went around to all the stores, houses of prostitution... and notified these people that if I found out that they were aiding these highbinder societies in any way, manner or form, by giving them money, I would demolish their places. If they wanted protection, I would furnish it to them. If one officer would not do, we would give them forty." Price was sued for his blitzkrieg raid on the tongs, but he just laughed and said, "All the prosecutors make out of me is the experience they desire."

His ruthlessness paid off. Although there were some thirty tong murders in Chinatown's streets and alleys between 1880 and 1898, for about three years after Price's initial raids there was not a tong killing in the Quarter. But his strong measures were not always kept up after his transfer to other duty, and corruption as well as flaccidity crept into the squad. It had deteriorated so much at one point that the chief felt it safe to tell only the sergeant in command of the exact locality of the gambling den or tong to be raided. Even so, the Chinese were rarely taken by surprise. The 1897 Grand Jury's raids on gambling hells were frustrated, for example, by the eternal vigilance of the sentinels and the multiplicity of trap doors and secret panels through which players and gambling devices were spirited away. Of course there was more to it than the leaks in the squad. When Immigration Commissioner Hart North asked "Do any of the white men who are employed by the Chinese as guards, and so on, ever render any aid to the highbinders?" Lieutenant Price made this point. "They destroy the whole business because they will never give any information to anybody. They are working for those people and shield them. Of course the worst houses pay these guards the most money, so naturally they are willing and glad to work for them. This ought to be done away with, by all means. Some of them collect seven or eight hundred dollars a month and would not give it up. As soon as an officer appears, and these guards do not like him, you cannot turn a corner before signals are given. The highbinders also are assisted by Chinatown guides...."

When heads rolled in 1894, they rolled on the Chinatown squad too. The press claimed that Chinese gamblers subsidized the squad's sergeants by the most systematic method of corrupting officials ever brought to light in the city. With all Chinatown under tribute to the police to the tune of $500 a week, the pockets of the half-dozen policemen were jingling. The Chinese were willing to pay much more liberally than the white gamblers of South of Market. The Quarter was split into 5 divisions. Each of these were presided over by a Chinese boss and all 5 formed a sort of board of corruption. The bosses collected a certain amount from each gambling house and held weekly meetings at which the money was divided between themselves and the squad sergeant who in turn paid off his men.

But the Chinese gamblers did not trust the patrolmen "in their employ." They kept the Chinatown squad under surveillance, using a well-organized squad of spotters. This counterespionage corps tailed even the heads of the department. All the gambling houses were wired with alarms, and as soon as a "tipper-offer" officer appeared the panic button was pushed. This did not close the doors of the dens; ax-splintered doors were expensive and hard to replace. Instead the doors were thrown wide open and groups innocently playing dominoes replaced the *tan* gamesters. When the all-clear signal was sounded and the coast was clear again the "stage set" would be struck and out would come the sticks and buttons and a return to normality.

Shortly after the Chinatown squad scandal broke, the corruption syndrome reappeared and this time in the Customs House. Customs Inspector Richard Williams was summarily dismissed from the service on charges of sneaking girls ashore to the Jackson Street slave mart, and Interpreter Louis Quong was suspended. Perhaps because he did not have enough faith in the Chinese Bureau after these developments, United States Commissioner of Immigration Hart H. North, when he wanted *expertise* on crime along Dupont Gai, turned to Lieutenant Price.

Price evaluated the situation at the time of the police and Customs scandals. He told him first that the merchants were not yet brave enough to cut loose from their enforced tong connections. He cited one man, Fong Wing, as an example. Fong had paid protection money to *all* of the tongs to absolutely guarantee the safety of his skin. (But even this did not work and he was shot down in Waverly Place by someone he had overlooked or offended.) Price went into details.

> The merchants are obliged to belong to these societies for the sake of protection. They cannot get out of it. Although belonging to the society, they are always willing to furnish me with information to aid in my breaking them, but they would not be seen speaking to me on the street. They are members of the highbinder societies in fact but not in spirit. But the merchants are so entirely under the control of these societies and are so dominated by fear that any demand that is made upon them they

pay without question. I'll tell you of an instance of this. There was a butcher on Washington Street. One evening he threw a little clean water out onto the street. A Chinese highbinder who was standing nearby got the water on the sleeve of his coat. I happened to be there at the time and when I had passed by, this highbinder went to the butcher and demanded a hundred dollars for the offense, and said he would call again. I told the butcher not to pay the money but to make an arrangement to meet him at a certain place and I would be there. ? He promised to do so, and would you believe it, before I got back there he had paid the highbinder the hundred dollars? That is too show you that anything the highbinders demand they get.

As if to disown themselves from their corruption-tainted predecessors, certain Chinatown squad sergeants went out of their way after the scandals broke in order to do an excessively brutal policing job on Chinatown. For a time Sergeants Witham, Gillin and Esola were more the terrors of Chinatown than the tong killers. They did an efficient job of erasing tong headquarters and gambling hells from the face of Chinatown. They had learned well from the example of Sergeants Burke and Price. They were so thorough that they soon had five damage suits simmering against them in the United States District Court. Some of the injured people were innocent, for the squad did step out of line as it overcompensated after the bribery scandals broke. Bystanders were roughed up; property was wantonly destroyed even if only thought to be connected with a tong or gambling den. But the raids continued. The Chinese Consulate tipped Sergeant C. H. Witham off to the location of seventeen tongs. He gave them twenty-four hours to vacate their premises. Of those who were tardy, Witham wryly reported to the chief, "We gave them very material assistance in removing not only their furniture but themselves."

Sergeant James W. Gillin, when in command of the Chinatown squad further refined the techniques of the other sergeants. He had patrolmen Lynch and Ellis report to a Market Street costumer before one of his raids. They were decked out in slouch hats, Chinese blouses and breeches, and their skins were dyed an almond hue. Gillin toyed with the idea of disguising himself but he was too vain of his red beard to shave it off and knew no way to camouflage it. So good was Ellis's disguise that a hoodlum called him a coolie and chucked a rock at him. He could only dodge, swear silently under his breath, and grip his club the more tightly up his sleeve. He and Lynch met in Washington Alley, gained entrance to a fan-tan den, pulled off their hats and false queues, and arrested eighteen gamblers.

The squad used disguise several times thereafter with varying effectiveness. Officer Galloway got inside a new club which fronted as a merchants' association and was able to let his comrades through the barred door to seize twenty visitors, but in another raid Officer Morton had his disguise penetrated after he had sneaked into the Oriental Pacific Club—one of Little Pete's properties. He was assaulted by some of the gamblers and roughed up. By clubbing his pistol he drove them off, and blowing his whistle, secured reinforcements waiting in the alley outside. Morton's maneuver netted about $300 in cash, sixty players and a complete fan-tan outfit.

At the end of the decade, Lieutenant Price hit upon the idea of equipping two men of the squad with cameras. They "shot" all well-known highbinders, and the photographs were placed in an album at police headquarters—a tong rogues' gallery. These Chinese were notified to leave town or be arrested for vagrancy. Many were taken in by this latest tactic and did leave, reducing further the population of *boo how doy.*

It was Sergeant Gillin who not only wrecked local tongs but ousted highbinders drifting in from interior cities for the Chinese New Year's celebrations in San Francisco. Among them were a large number of undesirables run out of the State Capital by a committee of safety.

It was Gillin who rated the tongs publicly in terms of their bloodthirstiness in 1895. He gave the Bing On and Gee Sin Seer top honors. Of each tong he said, "Its hatchet men bear a reputation for absolute disregard for life and law." Gillin was tough and courageous. The very day after being sued for $5,000 damages for his raids he descended upon thirteen more tongs. He was praised by the public. (The only violence was a rash of robberies and raids on some whorehouses by Alaska fishermen who doubled as highbinders during their winter layovers in San Francisco.) But he shrugged off the praise, saying, "The highbinders are such a bloodthirsty lot that no dependence can be placed on them and they may break out again at any time."

Of all the Chinatown squad sergeants, Jesse Cook was the most hated. When he had been only two months in the Quarter he had already earned a bad reputation for poking Chinese in the ribs gratuitously with his stick. He also punched a number in the face. He paid little heed to the first part of Crowley's edict—"Be careful not to club a reputable Chinese, but show no mercy to a highbinder." When he led raids on gambling dens and was unable to make any arrests he took his anger out on anyone at hand, beating up on the closest Chinese. All Chinatown and the city at large was shocked when he threw a Chinese down a staircase of a joss house next door to a gambling house. Cook claimed that the man was a lookout who had "slipped" on the stairs. In so doing the man collected a broken arm, bruises and internal injuries. Complaints poured in against the sergeant who apparently felt that he was a law unto himself. (For all his threats and violence, he took fewer cases to police court than any of the other sergeants handling the squad.) Heading the complaints of individuals were those of the Consulate General and the Six Companies. Representing the latter, Jee Chong Tone said, "This beating of Chinese in the street and in the stores has to be stopped. Gambling and other crimes against the law should be suppressed, and we will help the authorities, but beating a suspected Chinese because there is no evidence against him has to be stopped. I am free to confess that Sergeant Cook is the most brutal officer we have ever had in Chinatown." Cook was relieved of his post.

Another more successful and less brutal Chinatown squad sergeant was Patrick Shea. He was most effective in stamping out gambling. He usually bagged a half dozen or so players when he raided a den, but on January 4, 1898, he astounded the department by marching in eighty offenders at one time. He also enriched the city treasury by $500, since the Chinese gamblers never defended themselves, preferring to pay their $5 or so in fines and then hurry back to another game elsewhere.

The public's attention was turned away from the troubles of the squad when another tong war broke out. When a Bing On man sold a slave girl to a member of the Wah Ting San Fung tong but was not paid the full amount agreed upon he turned the bill over to his collection agency—the tong. The Wah Tings treated the demand with contempt. They heaped insult upon insult, saying the girl was not worth $1,000— not even $500—and if the Bing On tong wanted to make something of it they were welcome to try at their own peril. The Bing Ons decided to wipe out the debt in blood. The police learned that something was up but not exactly what. Merchants on Jackson Street between Dupont and Stockton were observed hurriedly securing the iron shutters over their shop windows, so there was no doubt as to the location of the chosen battlefield. Consul General Chang tried to stop the fray by ordering the new Six Companies' police to locate all ex-convicts and turn them over to regular patrolmen for arrest and/or deportation. He quickly posted a large proclamation bearing his consular seal which read:

LATELY THERE HAVE BEEN MANY ROBBERIES AND MORE CRIME THREATENED. THE LAW OF ALL LANDS FORBID SUCH CRIMES. THE CRIMINAL ELE-MENT CANNOT BE ALLOWED TO GO ON UNCHECKED. IT WILL SURELY BE SUPPRESSED AND THE LAW-ABID-ING PEOPLE WILL BE PROTECTED. HEREAFTER, NO CRIMINAL ARRESTED FOR ROBBING OR SHOOTING WILL BE BAILED OUT. IGNORANCE OF THE LAWS WILL NOT BE ACCEPTED AS AN EXCUSE. ALL SHOULD RE-MEMBER THE UNIVERSAL LAW FORBIDDING CRIME. MY PEOPLE MUST QUICKLY REPENT AND NOT MAKE TROUBLE FOR THEMSELVES IN THIS LAND.

Chang was intelligent enough to know that his proclamation would not cause the city's hatchet men to repent their evil ways, but he hoped his action might frighten them into at least postponing their street battle. He was right.

Such crowds gathered in Chinatown's streets on a late April day of 1895 that cable cars were stopped until police could clear the tracks. The cause of the commotion was a new rash of signs posted on tele-phone poles on the major corners of the Quarter. Only when Sergeant Christensen ordered the placards torn down did the crowds disperse. The small unsigned posters denounced the special police squad reorganized by the Six Companies as a worse evil than the grafting white special police force of earlier years. The signs read:

> TAKE NOTICE, THE WHITE DEVILS SENT INTO CHINATOWN BY CHIEF CROWLEY HAVE LATELY BEEN HELD IN CHECK. THEY DO NO MORE BLACKMAILING. BUT WE ARE ONLY RELIEVED OF ONE CLASS OF BLOOD-SUCKERS TO BE AFFLICTED WITH ANOTHER. THE CAPTAIN AND EIGHT MEN APPOINTED BY THE SIX COMPANIES TO KEEP ORDER ARE NOW WORSE THAN EVER THE WHITE DEVILS WERE. THEY ARE BLACKMAILING THE WOMEN, THE OPIUM SELLERS AND THE LOTTERY GAMES. NONE OF US ARE SAFE FROM THEM AND IT IS TIME THEY WERE DONE AWAY WITH. WE HAD TO PUT UP WITH THE WHITE DEVILS BUT WE WON'T PUT UP WITH THE SIX COMPANIES' DEVILS.

"I don't know who was the author of this notice," said Vice-Consul Owyang to reporters. "It was some scurrilous denunciation, I suppose, and as the police tore it down, no attention will be paid to it. If the men appointed by the Six Companies to act as policemen have been blackmailing anyone, we don't know anything about it." The reporters dutifully returned to grinding out the traditional predictions of more tong wars. And as usual they were right, as Murderer's Alley—Baker Alley—lived up to its reputation again. A man was shot to death by a highbinder for kicking a dog. But a really explosive incident was the Mook Tai case.

A Chinatown guide claimed, "In fifteen years, I have never seen Chinatown so worked up over anything. If some agreement is not reached in a day or two, there will be the bloodiest war ever seen in the Chinese Quarter." A member of the Ning Yeung Company was murdered, presumably by Mook Tai. Immediately the boycott was increased as the dead man's company joined the embargo on the Sam Yup commercial houses and butcher shops. The angered meat cutters retaliated by declaring war on the See Yup Company, which led in the boycotting, but their inflammatory posters were torn down by police. The tongs put up posters egging on both sides as fast as the police tore them down. A small riot erupted when the butchers had a rally. Cartoons accusing the Consul General, Li Wing Yu, of bribery in the Mook Tai case were the next to bloom on the brick walls of Chinatown. These caused another riot. Once again the fighting tongs had real cause to rejoice. The already tottering business community appeared to be intent on self-destruction as it shattered itself further by dissension. An old Chinatown expert, throwing his hands up in despair, commented: "This is no war of rival tongs. In fact, the most reputable and wealthy portion of the Chinese community is involved, including the Consul General. Neither Chong Wai, the murdered man, nor Mook Tai, the alleged assassin, belongs to the highbinder class."

Crowley, more exasperated than ever by the spreading of this contagion, hurried new posters up over those of the quarreling factions and the trouble-stirring tongs. They read:

NOTICE TO THE CHINESE POPULATION OF THIS CITY AND TO THOSE OF THE STATE THAT MAY CONGREGATE HERE. WHEREAS ON THE 12TH DAY OF JULY, 1895, ONE CHONG WAI WAS MURDERED IN THIS CITY IN COLD BLOOD AND ONE MOOK TAI IS NOW UNDER ARREST BECAUSE IT IS BELIEVED THAT HE IS THE MURDERER, AND THE FRIENDS OF MOOS TAI THREATEN TO COMMIT VIOLENCE ON THE PERSONS OF THE FRIENDS OF THE DECEASED SHOULD THE SAID MOOS TAI BE CONVICTED FOR HAVING COMMITTED SAID MURDER, I DO THEREFORE WARN ALL CONCERNED IN THIS MATTER, IF THE SAID MOOK TAISHOULD BE HELD ON THE PRELIMINARY EXAMINATION ON A CHARGE *OF* MURDER, THAT THE GUILT OR INNOCENCE OF SAID MOOK TAI WILL BE DECIDED BY A JURY OF UNBIASED CITIZENS OF THIS CITY AND COUNTY. IN THE MEANTIME, SHOULD ANY UNLAWFUL ACTS BE COMMITTED BY ANY OF THE MEMBERS OF THE CHINESE FACTIONS CONCERNED IN THIS MATTER, THE STRONG ARM OF THE LAW WILL BE BROUGHT TO BEAR TO SUPPRESS ANY OVERT ACTS

THAT MAY OCCUR IN THIS CASE, AS I WILL BE PRE-
PARED TO TAKE ACTION WITH THE POLICE RIFLE BAT-
TALION AT ONCE AND IF I AM COMPELLED TO ACT, I
ASSURE YOU, THE LAW BREAKERS WILL BE TAUGHT A
LESSON THAT WILL BE REMEMBERED FOR ALL TIME.


It took Crowley a long time to make his postered point but when he did there was no doubt that he was ready to shift to an even more drastic policing of the Quarter.

The rifle-bearing squad did not march through Chinatown, but the San Francisco board of health sent an expeditionary force. This team was guided by members of the Chinese vigilance committee and Sergeant Owens of the Chinatown squad. They looked into rookeries two stories underground, and shudderingly examined the hole called The Last Chance or Leprosy Hall. Here they threw into the street sides of beef "in advanced stages of decay," and carcasses of two "pea-green sheep." But their main purpose was to earmark shanties for destruction as health hazards. They had the cooperation of Chief Crowley, who saw the physical destruction of ghetto Chinatown and the warrens of the highbinders as the only sure way to rid the city of them.

As the year came to a close there was a rash of tong fights caused by the desertion of one tong for another by a hatchet man; a small riot connected with the Sam Yup-See Yup rivalry; and two skirmishes between the Suey On and the Wah Ting San Fung tongs. The following year saw the powerful Wong family association try to break the boycott, but it failed. Some of the Bo On tong countered with a poster campaign and Sergeant Harper and his squad were kept busy de-posting *chun hungs*. Summer saw more deaths from shootings and stabbings. Many thought these were connected with the boycott. Meetings were held between police and Sam Yup officials to try to end the violence, but all were fruitless. A hatchet man and his stooge were captured after gunning a Chinese druggist to death; a Bo On tong member was shot and killed, and while the search for the assailant was on, still another man was shot in reprisal. A Chinese who called at Receiving Hospital to see the victims went- away shaking his head and muttering, "Lots more be killed tomorrow. Big fight now."

Some of the tongs connected with the See Yups were cowed by a telegram which reached the Consulate from Chinese Minister Yang in Washington and which was immediately made public: YOU ARE TO DISSOLVE THE HIGHBINDER ASSOCIATIONS AND THE SEE YUP ASSOCIATION WITHOUT DELAY. NONCOMPLIANCE WILL SUBJECT YOU TO IMPEACHMENT AND DEGRADATION FROM OFFICE. But there was no possible way in which the new Consul General, Fung Yung Heng, could dissolve the See Yup Company— or the tongs. Other tongs threatened consular officers. Reporters found the Vice-Consul willing to speak for the Consul General and himself. The press knew that police had received reports that both officials were scheduled to die at the hands of salaried soldiers on October 17, 1896. King Owyang said, "It is a mistake to suppose that the present trouble lies between the See Yups and the Sam Yups... The real status of the case is that trouble exists *in* the See Yup Company alone. It is composed of twelve highbinder organizations of whom ten are now neutral, while two—the Bo On tong and the Bo Leong tong—are at war. The Bo Ons are assisted by the Suey Sing tong and the Hip Sing tong, the Bo Leongs by the On Yick tong and the Hop Sing tong. As regards the cause, you know as much as I do..." A reporter asked, "Do you realize the danger you are in?" "Certainly," said the Vice-Consul. "But it will do no good to kill us. New men will take our place at once."

Concealed riflemen guarded the See Yup headquarters. Consul General Fung's maneuver of securing twenty John Doe warrants for his special police—to be used to arrest See Yup highbinders for vagrancy—was thwarted by the See Yups obtaining a restraining order on him. At least, groaned Crowley, the warring factions were making use of legal weapons. There was another poster war of course, with *chun hungs* going up every day. Vice-Consul King was accused of almost every crime, and Six Companies' police officer Lee Fook Ning was denounced as the fomenter of all the trouble between the Bo Leong and Bo On tongs. Of the Consul General himself, the posters read: TAKING THESE MURDERS AS A PRETEXT THE CONSUL TELLS HIS SUPERIORS THAT HE IS MERELY DESTROYING THE ABODES OF MURDEROUS HIGHBINDERS. WHERE IS HIS LOVE FOR HIS COUNTRYMEN? WITH BUDDA-LIKE LIPS, HE HAS A WOLF'S NATURE.

More murders ensued. A See Yup, discovered hanging in a stable next door to the Consulate, an apparent suicide, was found to have been shot before being lynched. In reprisal a Wah Ting San Fung highbinder shot down a Bo Leong before his brother and other witnesses. The brother, who swore revenge, told police, "These three men came across to where he was. They said not a word but one suddenly drew a large revolver from under his blouse and handed it to one of the others and at the same time pointed at Ging. The man took the revolver and shot my brother. As he fell, he stepped up and shot him three more times...."

Vendetta followed vendetta. The Suey Sing ranks were thinned by one with only hours left in the (Christian) year. According to a witness, the victim was sighted by eight men at Jackson Street and St. Louis Alley. One pointed at him dramatically. Another, the stooge, drew a pistol and handed it to a third. The latter fired one shot into the air to scatter the crowd and to give himself a better target, then lowered his weapon methodically and fired twice, killing the Suey Sing.

While the war continued there were those—even among the tong membership—who sought peace. The powerful Bo Ons were tired of war. Perhaps peace was in sight that Christmas of 1896. But hopes were dashed and for years by the event which made 1897 a critical year in Chinatown's history. The murder of powerful Little Pete on January 3, 1897, marked the high point of tong violence. The effects of the crime were lasting; there was no quick tapering off of violence. Rather, it crystallized the professionalism of murder in Chinatown and had an effect like the booster charge of a modern rocket. The tong wars were continued on a high plateau of incidence. But in its way the murder of Little Pete was the beginning of the end, too, although San Francisco had to wait nine years for the San Andreas fault and the earthquake and fire to put an end to tong rule in Chinatown.

# CHAPTER TWELVE

# LITTLE PETE: KING OF CHINATOWN

*"Pete was square. When he said 'You shall have your cut,' that was enough. He never threw me down yet."*

—James B. Ranier, San Francisco
horse trainer, 1897

*"Little Pete was unquestionably the cleverest Chinaman on the Pacific Coast and probably in the United States. He was a born organizer and was full of schemes and deviltry... Until his advent there were no highbinder societies or tongs and the Chinese were quiet, orderly and peaceable."*

—Chief of Police Patrick Crowley, 1897

THOMAS DE QUINCEY, the opium addict essayist, would have enjoyed sitting in on the 1897 murder of Little Pete, Chinatown's tong-war boss. The case became a *cause célèbre* of all time in that area. It is the only Chinatown homicide which has come to be considered an unsolved "classic" in the annals of San Francisco crime. It was a skillfully planned and executed assassination, and, as De Quincey wrote, "Assassination is a branch of the art of murder which demands a special notice." He was a keen student of homicide, his concern being entirely with the "taste" with which it was conceived, planned and carried out. Like Samuel T.

Coleridge, he argued that once the act—murder or arson—was consummated the question of the morality of it was ended and there was left only the matter of the style of its execution.

The erasure of Little Pete was accomplished with daring, imagination and style. The assassins were in danger of being killed themselves; they made a clean getaway.

Much lore and legend have encrusted the facts about Fong Ching, alias Little Pete. Even his name varies from account to account because of the inflective idiosyncrasies of Cantonese dialects and usage. In one account he may be Fung Ching; in another Fung Jing Doy. His business alias—F. C. Peters—is often mistakenly rendered J. C. Peters. Some say he did not know a word of Chinese; others that he spoke fluent Chinese but could neither read nor write a word of it except to sign his name. Still others insist he was so highly literate that he wrote Chinese operas which were performed on the stage of his own Jackson Street theatre. There may be truth in the latter, for Pete was a theatre enthusiast. He posted a standing offer of $1,000 per month, for example, for Poi Loi—China's outstanding actor—if he would perform in San Francisco. This was no small sum in those days.

There is confusion as to the site of his murder. Actually he was shot down around the corner from Waverly Place on Washington Street, almost on the doorstep of his home. This was ironical, for he had extraordinary protection there. Two vicious police dogs kept watch, along with a large group of Chinese hatchet-men bodyguards and one or two white bodyguards.

The chief suspect in the crime is another source of confusion. He has been called Wing Sing, Woon Sing, Chun Wing Sing, Chin Woon Sing, and Chun Woon. His supposed accomplice was Chin Poy or Chan Ah Chuey. The name of Pete's ubiquitous white bodyguard on the night of his murder is sometimes given as Ed Murray, whereas it was actually C. H. Hunter. (Murray was an earlier aide of Pete's.) And finally, while most students of Chinatown history feel that Pete was earmarked for murder early and stalked long, a minority believe that his killing was a spur-of-the-moment revenge action demanded by the See Yup Company for the assassination of one of its men immediately after a disagreement with some of Little Pete's cohorts in one of his gambling dens.

*Richard H. Dillon*

What we do know of Little Pete is that he was a strange admixture of East and West. He was a well-to-do businessman, yet a boss of Chinatown crime. He was both respected and hated but also genuinely liked by many. His passing posed a problem to law-abiding members of both races. Should they attend ceremonies honoring a business magnate who doubled as the rackets' boss of Chinatown?

When Little Pete was killed he got the entire front page of the *Call,* including three line drawings and six headlines or subheads. The story of his life was told in thumbnail fashion in a welter of uppercase type which festooned page One:

## Little Pete Murdered by His Enemies

CHINESE HIGHBINDERS ASSASSINATE THE MOST FAMOUS
OF LOCAL MONGOLIANS

GRAND JURY BRIBER SHOT DOWN BY SEE YUP ASSASSINS

KING OWYANG, THE CHINESE VICE-CONSUL SAID TO BE
NEXT ON LIST OF DOOMED SAM YUPS

THE GREAT LEADER KILLED IN BARBERSHOP FOR PRICE
SET ON HIS HEAD

NOTORIOUS VICTIM WAS ONCE MILLIONAIRE, RACE-
JOBBER, IMPORTER OF SLAVES AND THE MAN
WHO GAVE CHRIS BUCKLEY THE TITLE OF BUND
WHITE DEVIL

Little Pete enjoyed neither a long nor an honorable life. But it was an exciting one. He was born in Kow Gong, about ten miles out of Canton, in 1864, and came to San Francisco when he was ten years old. In his

218

early teens he became an errand boy for a Sacramento Street shoe factory. Hard working and ambitious, Pete was also loyal to his family; when
he was making only $10 a month as a shoestore clerk he contributed part
of his wages to the support of his relatives, including an aged mother in
Canton. By attending the Sunday school of the Methodist Chinese Mission as well as a grammar school (and some say high school too), Pete
learned to be fluent and proficient in the English language. He joined the
Sam Yup Company and while still a youth became involved in Chinatown and city-wide politics. Although a young man of taste, breeding,
grace and gentility amounting almost to delicacy, his was a ruthlessly
materialistic philosophy. His story was Horatio Alger, Dupont Gai style,
but with sinister overtones.

As interpreter for the Sam Yup Company, Little Pete was privy to
all sorts of business information which could make a smart man into a
powerful and rich man. Handsome, intelligent and always immaculate
in appearance, he became so well-liked by the Caucasians with whom
he did business that he was Mr. Chinatown to them. He was perhaps the
most thoroughly Americanized Chinese of his day, despite his fondness
for Chinese costume and theatre and his retention of his queue. He was
a great lover of American methods, and these helped him to get ahead
in the Quarter. He took excellent care of his health and was bright eyed
and clear skinned—the direct antithesis of the sallow, tubercular (and
possibly leprous) coolie of sand-lotter tradition. Pete dressed richly and
well; his Oriental clothing was expensive and in the best of taste. He
appeared to indulge in none of the vices for which his countrymen were
condemned at the time. Little Pete combined Oriental cunning and sa-
gacity with Occidental friendliness and business acumen.

In short, the cultured, Westernized Little Pete would seem to have
been the ideal man to lead Chinatown toward a better day; to integrate it
and its people into American life. Unfortunately Little Pete had a serious
flaw in his diamond-hard character. He did not know the difference—or
at least he cared to draw no distinction—between good and evil. He
knew what was legal and what was illegal, but instead of a true sense
of right and wrong, Pete had only an egocentric philosophy. What was
good for Little Pete was *good*. This ambition, power hunger and super-
pragmatic philosophy would lead him to success. But it would also drag

him to an untimely death on the floor of a barber shop. When his time came, at thirty-three, the people of Chinatown were ready to forgive him for his sins. His success story and his personal charm and charity had made him their idol.

Pete saved his money until he had accumulated what he needed and then borrowed a few hundred dollars more on his good name. The diligent young Sam Yup was obviously an excellent credit risk. Had he not become a broker, landing both goods and persons (including many illegal immigrants and prostitutes) in San Francisco while still only a very young man? With this capital Little Pete established himself in the shoe business with his uncle Fong Yuen, his brother Fong Shun, and some forty employees. To fool his Caucasian customers, many of whom belonged to the union-labor class, Pete gave his shoes the brand name of F. C. Peters & Company. San Franciscans who were in on the joke—F. (Fong) C. (Ching) Peters—named him Little Pete because of the Occidental pseudonym he had chosen. He built up a big wholesale business and hired a white bookkeeper and white salesmen to sell his shoes from Puget Sound to San Diego. He paid his help the highest salaries in the business. Within a very short time he was independently wealthy. But he was not content; he began to conduct several lucrative gambling dens on the side. He married Chun Li and took very good care of her and the three children she bore. Although still only a youth, Little Pete came to be looked to for legal counsel and general advice by the whole Chinese community. This was a rare honor in a society in which, traditionally, young people—even bright young people—must defer to their elders for wisdom and advice.

According to Police Captain Thomas S. Duke, Little Pete was the founder of the new fighting tong, the Gee Sin Seer, before he was even of age. There is confusion here, too, for Pete admitted tong membership in court but stated he was a member of the rival Bo Sin Seer. In either case, the men he recruited were young toughs of the criminal class who were a world apart from their cultivated leader, with his native intelligence and dignity, but they were dedicated and dangerous. Pete's tong machinations were soon so successful that tribute began to pour in. Hatchet men who were jealous of his success formed rival secret societies and bided their time to topple the new King of Chinatown.

Enmity festered, particularly between the Gee Sin Seer and Bo Sin Seer tongs. Finally the headmen of the latter society decided that the only way to conquer their bitter rival was to eliminate the gentlemanly and rich leader of it. Word of the plot reached Pete's ears, for he was close to every shoot and tendril of the Chinatown grapevine. He took immediate action. One of his precautions was to hire Lee Chuck, the deadliest *boo how doy* in San Francisco, as his bodyguard.

On July 23, 1886, Detective William Glennon was tipped off that an attempt was about to be made to kill Lee Chuck in order to clear the way to Little Pete. The detective obligingly warned the highbinder to be on his guard. Lee Chuck grunted his thanks for the warning and told Pete. The latter secured an extra heavy coat of mail for them both. These bulletproof vests of steel chains weighed thirty-five pounds each. Hatchet men then stalked hatchet men for the next several months in a cat-and-mouse game. On October 28, Lee Chuck finally ran into his executioner, face to face. It was Yen Yuen of the Bo Sin Seer tong. The two pigtailed highbinders exchanged angry words preliminary to Teaching for their pistols. Little Pete had chosen well. While Yen was still tugging at the weapon in his waistband Lee Chuck was firing five rounds into his body, killing him instantly.

Officer John B. Martin, who was later to be chief of police, rushed to the scene of the vendetta when he heard the close-spaced fusillade. Lee Chuck was already in flight, but Martin pounded after him in scalding pursuit. Suddenly Lee Chuck stopped, turned, and aimed his pistol at Martin's chest. The officer saw the muzzle of the gun bearing down on him; he had no time to draw and aim his own weapon as he ran. There was not even time to dodge. But miraculously the gun failed to explode. The sixth cartridge, after five perfect ones, was a dud. Lee Chuck snapped the hammer twice, then Martin collided with him, grappling for his gun arm. He was about to overpower the hatchet man when he saw that with his free hand Lee Chuck had extracted a second revolver and was cocking it to fire into Martin's side as the two men struggled. As the hatchet man's finger squeezed the trigger Officer Maurice J. Sullivan ran up and tore the weapon from his grasp. The two policemen snapped the cuffs on Lee Chuck and hustled the armored highbinder down to headquarters.

At this point Little Pete made the first of only two major mistakes of his career. (The second one would prove fatal.) Shortly after his body-guard was arrested, Pete—perhaps bereft of his usual common sense and in a fit of panic because he was unprotected—approached Policemen Burr Love and Con O'Sullivan in the back room of a saloon at Clay and Stockton Streets. He offered them $400 each to help Lee Chuck. Next he hunted up Officer Martin himself and offered him $400 to perjure him-self at the trial and give testimony favorable to the gunman. Pete wanted Martin to say that several men had attacked Lee Chuck and that the latter had fired in self-defense. To Pete's surprise and consternation, Martin was indignant. Instead of quietly pocketing the graft, as Pete had been sure he would do, Martin reported the bribe attempt to the Chief. Stewart Menzies, foreman of the Grand Jury, secured a warrant for Pete's arrest. On August 5, 1886, Little Pete was indicted by the Grand Jury for at-tempted bribery of officers of the police department.

Pete quickly rounded up a number of shysters, the best in town, and was not above hiring an honest lawyer or two for prestige and for their skill. One of these was Hall MacAllister whose bronze effigy still stands facing MacAllister Street from a sidewalk pedestal opposite one wing of city hall. MacAllister was astonished at Pete's plea. The King of Chi-natown told his counselors, "Now I will tell you, gentlemen, I'm no lawyer and that's why I retain you. But I do know that I stand alone against two policemen who will swear I offered them four hundred dol-lars. Therefore, I will not be believed. Now, I want you to go on the stand and confess that I not only offered them the money but that they took it." MacAllister and the other lawyers told him such a plan was out of the question. But the clever Chinese insisted. "Gentlemen, you are not as well acquainted with the police department as I am. They have been blackmailing every Chinaman in Chinatown for years, and it is not a question of right or wrong with them, it is 'how much money do we get?'" Pete managed to convince his attorneys. They did it his way.

Judge Dennis J. Toohy and the jury heard the polished, slender young Chinese address them in perfect English on January 7, 1887. "Yes, gen-tlemen, I paid those officers a bribe but it was honestly done, as I asked them to take the money and only testify to the truth. The truth is all that I wanted of them, and I thought four hundred dollars would be enough for them to tell that, but it was not. They came back for more money, and when I refused their demands they not only convicted my friend but arrested me." Little Pete proved himself to be an astute judge of human nature. The jury disagreed on the 18th and was dismissed, and Little Pete was released on $5,000 bail pending a new trial.

This second trial was held on May 16. Testimony closed on the 24th and was argued before the jury on the following day. Chief Crowley, Sergeant Thomas W. Bethell, and Detective William Glennon all testified to the bad reputation Pete bore, and Crowley related that Policeman Martin had reported the bribery attempt immediately and in complete detail. Both Martin and Love denied, with some heat, that they had ever accepted any money from Pete or any other Chinese.

Proof that Little Pete had labored long and hard in preparing for his second trial was soon evident, but it was revealed in an unexpected quarter. A prosecution subpoena brought in a surprise witness. He was Gus Williams and his temporary abode was Point San Quentin where he was resting from the strenuous life of a professional burglar. Little Pete's emissaries had approached him while he was still "outside" and had offered him money to swear that he saw Martin taking a bribe from the defendant. He was only too willing and dutifully jotted down fictitious memos of dates and places—all furnished by Little Pete—where he had supposedly been a witness to the paying off of Martin. Unfortunately for him and for Pete, his burgling proclivities landed him in the State penitentiary. To say that his word was discredited would be understatement. On the other hand, Pete rounded up a number of Chinese who testified to his sterling character.

Finally Little Pete himself appeared, testifying in his own behalf. He had little to say other than that he was twenty-three years old and had been in San Francisco for thirteen years. He was not as glib as he had been in the earlier trial, and admitted that both he and Lee Chuck were members of the Bo Sin Seer tong. Presumably this was to disavow any hatred for this tong. It was, after all, a Bo Sin Seer—Yen Yuen—who had been shot down by his bodyguard who was also a Bo Sin Seer. It was all in the family. Pete denied all allegations made against him, categorically, and swore that it was the Bo Sin Seer's rival, the Gee Sin Seer tong, which had desired Lee Chuck's death. This was a real tangle.

223

Captain Duke insisted that Pete had been the founder of the Gee Sin Seer and that both he and Lee Chuck were members. Pete claimed membership in the rival tong. Thus he and his hatchet man were comrades of the murdered Yen Yuen.

About four in the afternoon of the 27th, the jury shuffled into court, yawning, unkempt and bleary of eye. The sleepy foreman reported that they were unable to agree after more than twenty-five hours of continuous argument. No verdict was possible, he said. The jury differed on a question of fact. Nonsense, insisted Judge Toohy. He did not think it proper to discharge them yet; he sent them back to consider the case further. They were to render a sealed verdict or to remain locked up for another night. At 5:15 they were back. The foreman again announced that agreement was utterly impossible no matter how long Toohy might choose to keep them out. The judge discharged the panel and set a date for Little Pete's third trial. He admitted Pete to $5,000 bail again and the weary jury of nine for conviction and three for acquittal trudged out.

At this time Foreman Stewart Menzies of the Grand Jury heard that incriminating papers belonging to Pete were in the safe of a business house on Montgomery Street. Word of this had leaked out when Pete, in jail, tried to get one of his attorneys to use the documents to lever Boss Buckley into action. Pete wanted Buckley to get him off. He had paid the acknowledged boss of San Francisco $4,500 in advance for just that. Pete had little use for the blind boss, and when it appeared that Buckley might double-cross him, the keen-eyed Chinatown boss was ready and willing to drag him along to prison too. Buckley became frightened and promised to return the money. But Attorney Mowry obtained a search warrant and rounded up two detectives and a locksmith, and the latter drilled the safe open. The men were in the act of extracting the papers when one of Pete's stable of attorneys, Henry H. Lowenthal, walked in. He demanded to know by what right they had broken into Ung Sing & Company's safe. Lowenthal scouted out the sheriff and his deputies and got them aligned with him—and Pete—in a civil war of the law-and-order bodies of the city against the police department and the Grand Jury. The legality and propriety of the search and seizure of the documents was hotly argued for days, and accusations, counteraccusations and contempt charges were hurled back and forth in broadsides. As the papers passed through so many hands, filching was carried on and many of the prized documents disappeared forever. The Grand Jury tried to persuade the Sam Yup Company to turn over all of Little Pete's business papers but the company refused. The officers said that they were afraid that Buckley would buy up the court and send them all to jail.

The contents of enough papers were made public to provide a journalistic blockbuster. Chris Buckley, Joe Cochrane, Jerry Driscoll and Henry Lowenthal were disclosed to be friends, at least fair-weather friends, of Pete. One communication from Little Pete to Buckley read: "Must see you on important business before Sunday at 12 o'clock. Can I come up to see you? Answer yes or no. I have some new business for you which is very important." Other documents showed Pete's dislike for Buckley by his use of the term the Blind White Devil. The newspapers gleefully snapped up this synonym. In one letter to a friend Pete said he was no longer going to submit to Buckley's demands. In another to Kwan Shan he wrote:

> I write this letter to let you know if you, sir, with Lowenthal, will go to see the blind white man and get him to see No. 11 Court to get the judge to set aside the sentence passed by him and not have a new trial. Get it changed to one or two years. Get the judge to give his decision to pardon this crime because this is my first wrongdoing and I will avoid doing wrong in future. In America it is thought an ordinary affair to pardon a man after sentence has been passed. If this judge is willing, it can be done and if it can be done it will be better than having a new trial. A new trial is a long business. I hear Lowenthal wants $1,000 fee to get bail and then wait a year or six months before the case conies up. This would make it too long. If you can get the blind white devil to get to the judge and get him to pardon me, then expend whatever money is needed. This will save a lot of bother. When you go to the blind devil, you take Joe Cochrane. He is better than Lowenthal, for the latter is a swindler. If the blind man will guarantee to arrange this case, all right. The money that was put ready the other day may be paid to Lowenthal, but if they can't fix it up they must refund the $4,500....

An examination of Pete's careful accounts by Foreman Menzies revealed that he was a "benefactor" of Dupont Street. He had made "presents" of $200 to District Attorney Edward B. Stonehill ("An unmitigated lie!" said Stonehill) and $600 to Judge Toohy ("An infamous lie!" roared the jurist), while the various shysters' receipts were topped by the $11,000 given Lowenthal over a three months' period. Pete's records were so minute and meticulous that the exact cost of the armor he had bought for Lee Chuck and himself was determined—$264. He had also spent $191 for revolvers.

Although Pete had claimed in court that he was a Bo Sin Seer, a Gee Sin Seer document turned up in his papers. It did not connect him directly with that tong, since it was an appeal for a general tithe from a committee of the "United Villagers" of the tong. It might have been sent him by one of his espionage corps who was charged with keeping him posted on the activities of the (presumably) rival tong. The document read:

> Suddenly calm is disturbed by a wave of adversity, and numerous foes gather together to insult and to annoy our tong. We meet together in justice to ourselves to consider what to do. All men from our locality now settled in America should help. Every man ought, as a rule, to help to the extent of subscribing half a month's wages—if more than this sum, all the better. No matter whether merchant or laborer, all ought to help to this extent. We hope that you will remember that we are brother villagers and the course of justice should be of more importance than money. Every person should be eager and so preserve the honor of our tons and check those outsiders who insult us. You cannot excuse yourself from giving because you are in a store in which your partners belong to other tongs.

The Sam Yup Company scrutinized Pete's records carefully and found them extremely accurate. They learned that he had spent $75,000 so far to corrupt justice in San Francisco. The businesslike attitude of the racketeer more than restored him to favor amongst his erstwhile commercial friends; it practically endeared him to them. The *Chronicle* observed that Pete was far from being ruined. It predicted that "the honest corruptionist" would be well taken care of by his associates upon his release from prison.

The third trial was as much a sensation as the disclosure of the Little Pete papers. This was due mostly to the many attempts to bribe veniremen. A Chinese first approached Juror M. M. Feder with a proposition; then Juror Abraham Mayfield was tampered with. He reported that a mysterious white man had showed him $250 which would be his if he would but "look after Pete's interests." Next, Juror Blanchard swore out a warrant for the arrest of J. T. Emerson, charging him with offering a bribe. (Emerson was already in trouble for testifying in behalf of witness-con Gus Williams in the prior trial.) Assistant District Attorney Joseph J. Dunne was furious at the press for the publicity given the jury-rigging attempts. He claimed that it scared off those responsible just when he was about to close the trap on them and produce what he said would have been "one of the greatest sensations in the criminal history of San Francisco." After all the furor had died, Pete heard a verdict (August 24) of guilty after a deliberation of only thirty minutes by the jury.

A key date in Little Pete's life was Saturday, September 7, 1887. On that day he heard Judge Toohy intone sentence upon him. From his bench Toohy lectured the archcriminal of Chinatown:

> No one is more familiar with the facts and circumstances attending your case than you are and no one knows better of your guilt than you. I must say that you have displayed remarkable intellect and activity. You have taken advantage of the institutions of this country and have become acquainted with its customs and language... By reason of being master of the language you raised yourself to an exalted position and you magnified that position in the eyes of your countrymen by making them believe that you have power and could corrupt officials.
>
> At a very early age you became prosperous and at the head of a large manufacturing house. It is very strange that you should have entered upon a course that aroused such enmity against you that it was at your instigation that Lee Chuck assumed a panoply of mail to act as your bodyguard. It is my opinion that

227

had it not been for the fact that Lee Chuck was so armed, the killing of Yen Yuen would not have occurred.

Before Yen Yuen's body had been removed from the morgue, before the breath had more than left his body, you began the attempt to corrupt officials. For that offense you have had three trials. I believe that either of the other juries before whom you were tried would have convicted you but for your emissaries and agents.

At the last trial you could not submit your case to your attorneys but tried to again interfere with justice. I hope, for the glory of this State, that others who are your accomplices will have to join you in the investigation brought about by the Grand Jury.

You have been the studied traducer of every official from myself down. You did this to create the impression that there was *no* justice for a man without money. If you had left gambling debts alone and had not made yourself the subagent of shysters, you would have been a prosperous businessman.

Pete bore this scathing denunciation without flinching. His face was a mask. The crafty King of Chinatown was turning new ideas over and over in his mind and seeking new ways out of his predicament. His agents used every means to attempt to circumvent the law. A request for postponement of sentence having been refused, Lowenthal next made a motion for a new trial. Toohy told him that if he could find one shred of error to warrant a new trial, he should have it. Lowenthal argued that the verdict was based on hearsay evidence. He read part of Chief Crowley's testimony as an example. But he was overruled by the court on all points.

When the Judge asked Little Pete if he had anything to say as to why sentence should not be passed upon him, Pete answered by requesting that the court not pronounce sentence in the absence of Hall MacAllister whom he had retained to argue a motion for a new trial. He asked that MacAllister be sent for, but Judge Toohy declined to permit any further delays. Notice of appeal was given, and Little Pete was removed to the county jail to await trial for the attempted bribery of Juror Feder. On September 7, 1887, he stoically went off to Folsom Prison to begin serving a sentence of five years.

Although safely put away in Folsom, Little Pete's power was not entirely broken. Of all the Oriental prisoners in State penal institutions he alone was allowed to keep the queue of which he was so vain and which was contrary to institutional rules. However, his being sent to prison did cause astonishment in most Chinese quarters and consternation in some. His power at fixing raps had seemed supreme.

District Attorney Stonehill complained loudly to the supervisors about the lengthiness of such trials as those of Lee Chuck and Little Pete. Both had had multiple trials up to a month each in length. Stonehill's complaint reminded the public of Lee Chuck who had been pushed pretty much into the background by a troubled Little Pete. On August 23, 1886, Lee was held to answer before Superior Court Justice Rix. On January 23 of the next year the trial began before Judge Toohy, and on February 4 Lee Chuck was found guilty of murder. He was sentenced on March 29 to be hanged—the only hatchet-man murderer of six then in detention to be given the death penalty. For the others the sentences were life imprisonments. Lee Chuck, too, had to undergo a tongue lashing from Judge Toohy:

> On the 28th of July, 1886, having with settled determination and malice aforethought first accoutred yourself in a coat of mail, two large revolvers and a brace of huge pistols... in company with other Chinamen no better than yourself, you tarried in a place of ambush on Washington Street at a point about four hundred yards from where you now stand. This was just before noon on that summer day ... your unsuspecting victim Yen Yuen, passing from his shop to his dinner, was shot down in cold blood, without the slightest provocation by you and your dastardly accomplices. Your helpless countryman, who never did you wrong, was slain in a manner which denoted that you were endowed with more sanguinary cruelty than generally falls to the lot of ordinary assassins. As he lay, gasping in the throes of death... you and your gang of cutthroats perforated his prostrate body with bullets... you next sought safety in flight to some refuge where you might at once begin the training of false wit-

nesses to prove your innocence of this atrocious crime... The judgment of the law and the sentence of the court is now, here in open court and in your presence, pronounced against you, which is that you, Lee Chuck, suffer the punishment of death and that you be hanged by the neck until you are dead.

The same maneuvers which were tried in Little Pete's case were used in Lee Chuck's. His case was appealed to the Supreme Court and a new trial granted, but with the same result as the first. He was found guilty after six hours of deliberation by the jury. Judge Toohy refused a motion for a new trial and an insanity plea, too, but the case was again appealed and Lee Chuck was given a third chance. This time he was sentenced to five years' imprisonment. But on February 10, 1892, Lee Chuck was pronounced insane. He was committed to Agnews Asylum. There he remained until May 30, 1904, when Governor George C. Pardee agreed to pardon him on condition that he be deported. (He was now said to have recovered his mind.) The steamship companies balked at taking him aboard, however, fearing that the Chinese Government would not permit him to land. So Lee Chuck was returned *to* prison and in the spring of 1905, had to be recommitted to Agnews Asylum.

Little Pete's long years of imprisonment did not make him repentant or honest; they only made him wary. He was more careful and more cautious, but unchastened. He made his way back to Chinatown after serving his term, and it did not take him long to regain a position of power. His name was in the news in February, 1893, when Yick Kee refused to accept a bribe of $80 from him or from one of his cohorts to swear that a slave girl who was trying to land was the wife of one of his partners. His declining led Pete to raise the offer to $80 for himself and $80 for his firm. When he again refused, Pete offered $100 and $100. He then warned the obstinate Yick Kee not to interfere and swore that he would land the woman if it cost him $5,000. But Yick Kee testified against the slave girl. As a result, at a joint meeting of the Bing On and Suey On tongs a death sentence was pronounced upon Yick and another merchant. The police refused to divulge the second man's name in hopes of safeguarding his life, but he fatalistically made plans for his death and said that he would do all he could to help the police, since he was to be killed in any case. Hia information was that two Customs officers could be prevailed upon to land Chinese prostitutes and that certain whites and Chinese whom he knew gave false certificates in behalf of such women for $30 each.

The next year saw great preparations in the city for San Francisco's exposition, the Midwinter Fair, in Golden Gate Park. When the *Gaelic* arrived in port she bore 103 Chinese, mostly women, for the Chinese pavilion. The press was suspicious. The girls' chaperone turned out to be Chung Ying, a cousin of Little Pete's. The newspapers protested the landing of these people without examinations or certificates, since they were sure they meant to desert the Fair and enjoy comfortable and illegal lives in Chinatown. The *Call* said: "The fact that Little Pete, who has been known here for years as the head and front of almost every crooked piece of work of any magnitude in which the Chinese have engaged, is engineering the importation of the Midwinter Fair Chinese is, alone, enough to make the Customs officials believe that a repetition of the [Chicago] World's Fair business is intended. The Customs officials believe that Little Pete or his agents or his cousins in China have collected, for every one of the Chinese brought here for the Fair, a fee...."

Sam Ruddell, Deputy Surveyor of the Port, inspected the *Gaelic's* passengers with Collector of the Port John H. Wise. "I'm satisfied, Mr. Collector," said Ruddell, "that all of these people have come to stay." The collector swore. "But, Sam," he said, "what can I do? Congress has said they can come in. Even if Little Pete is bringing them over, what can we do?" Each knew the answer—nothing.

The newspapers prophesied that the illegal immigrants would comply with the McCreary Registration Act later in order to save themselves trouble, while Little Pete would grow richer day by day. In June of 1894, the Treasury Department sent Special Agent John Phoenix to the Chinese village of the fairgrounds. He found that all but 37 of the 257 Chinese had already disappeared. The papers said, in effect, "We told you so" and guessed that Pete had netted $50,000 through his female imports.

Little Pete was a fan of expositions. When a slave girl fled to the security of the Presbyterian Mission in 1895, she turned out to be an actress imported by Pete for the Atlanta Exposition. After doing business in Georgia for a brief time she had been removed to a den in Chinatown. The girl named Pete's associates in the slave-girl traffic—an unsavory group that included Madame Choy, Chan Yeung, Charley Ah Him and Tom Hung. Charley was a knowing ex-interpreter in Los Angeles courts. Tom was a genuine *kwei chan,* or villain—an ex-convict (manslaughter) and blackmailer who lived with an elderly madame, Dan Pak Tsin, in the Church Alley den she ran for him and his brother. Hung was a brag-gart who claimed that he had enough money to win any court case and a quack con man who sold an opium-cure concoction as a front. Hung was an interpreter for the Bing Kong tong and a member of at least two other tongs. Trying to get the runaway girl back from the mission by means of shysters and legal trickery, he applied for a writ of *habeas corpus,* swearing that she was being unlawfully detained. Miss Williams fought the case successfully and Hung—or one of his gang—retaliated by shooting at a window of the mission.

That same year of 1895, the police heard a rumor that Pete was be-hind the murder of Chew Ging, a member of the Suey Sing tong. The tong claimed that Little Pete had hired a decoy named Do Ming, who was actually arrested for the murder, in order to get the heat off the real killer whose identity was unknown. They were probably right; the po-lice had to let Do go for lack of evidence. Undoubtedly the real assassin made his escape.

Besides the Suey Sings, Little Pete had other rivals and enemies. Lee Gee and Lee Hoy were competitors in the slave-girl trade, and from him they picked up the custom of forging Revenue Agent B. M. Thomas's name to revenue stamps on opium. Another rival, though not really an enemy, was Chen Hen Shin, alias Chin Tan Sun or Big Jim. He ran gambling dens in Chinatown and Oakland and owned banks, restaurants and other property in San Francisco plus property in China. Big Jim was even better off financially than Pete (Pete's income had fallen off dur-ing his stretch in Folsom), and was often described as a millionaire. He was the inventor of the "no-see-'um" lottery. His Chinatown office had a blind, windowless face on the street—the facade being broken only by a small aperture. Money was pushed through this hole by customers and tickets pushed back out by a hidden cashier. The buyer never saw the vendor, and thus could not identify him in court. One May evening the department decided to put an end to Big Jim's operation. A detective pushed some money through the opening. When the hand came out with the tickets, the officer snapped one of a pair of handcuffs over its wrist and hung on. He braced himself against the building but the hand got away. There must have been a half-dozen men pulling on the unfortunate member. Big Jim courteously returned the detective's property, pushing the manacles gingerly through the opening after they had been worked off the trapped teller's wrist.

Expositions and the slave trade were not Little Pete's only hobbies. When he was thirty-one he became a horseracing fan and enjoyed the easy money he made at it. He took in $100,000 within a few weeks. He would bet up to $6,000 a day and would seldom lose any large amount on any one race. His profits came to be enormous, even after he had greased the palms of innumerable fixed jockeys, bookmakers, hostlers and stableboys of all categories. It was no surprise, therefore, that Pete developed a sure-fire system of picking winners, even in a closely matched race of favorites. He generously shared his track knowledge with others, giving his friends good tips on the horses. A typical race fixed by Pete was the one in which all the experts had figured Wheel of Fortune as a sure thing. But Pete put his money on a horse named Rosebud. Miraculously—or so it seemed—the judgment of the green track fan from Chinatown proved to be superior to that of race-goers of many years' standing. Rosebud came in well ahead of the favorite—ridden by Pete's good friend Jockey Chorn.

It was not until March, 1896, that bookmakers and public alike realized that they were being systematically plundered at the Bay District track. They could not figure out just who was responsible or how it was being done. They did not yet suspect the Chinese newcomer. But Pete, if he did not know horses, knew people and their weak points. He had made "arrangements" with as many as ten jockeys. It was Jockey Arthur Hinrichs, a mild-looking, blue-eyed lad from St. Louis, who informed on Pete. Hinrichs was an artist in the saddle and a demon finisher in the stretch, but he ratted on Pete, claiming that he was not getting his share; he was probably panicky because he had double-crossed his fixed comrades of the track. In a race in which Pete had selected Jerry Chorn

233

*Richard H. Dillon*

to win, the greedy Hinrichs declined to lay back. Instead, he whipped up his 10-to-1 shot and came home in first place past a startled Chorn. Hinrichs had $800 of his own money on the nose of his own mount. The other jockeys were so bitter about his double-dealing that he thought it best to hire a bodyguard.

Finally Hinrichs's nerve deserted him entirely and he confessed to Tom Williams, president of the Jockey club. Hippolyte Chevalier, Chorn and Hinrichs usually rode the three fastest horses in any race, so Pete "fixed" all three possible winners, arranging in advance who would come in first. Because he knew that suspicions would be aroused if he was seen talking to the horsemen, he used Dow Williams as a gobetween, telling him the horse chosen to win on a particular day and having the trainer whisper the password to the jockeys at the last moment.

Tales of Pete's big winnings had begun to spread even before Hinrichs confessed, but he laughed them off, saying each time, "I backed two or three in the race but only won a trifle." Elated at his success, Little Pete tried his hand at bookmaking, but was only partially successful. One or two of the horses laid up in his book as "dead ones" suddenly revived and his book lost heavily.

When Hinrichs confessed, Williams called a meeting of the board of stewards. After hearing the evidence, that body directed that the California Jockey club expel Chorn, Chevalier and Pete from the tracks for conspiracy and fraud, and refuse permission to Hinrichs to ride in any races. Pete's bribes ruined a number of reputations and probably lives. Hinrichs, Chevalier and Chorn were ruined as jockeys.

Supposedly Pete was *tabu* at all tracks after this, but following his death, James B. Ranier, a trainer, came forward to reveal that the track boycott on Pete had never been effective. He said:

> I understand that someone got hold of part of the story so I thought it best to make a clean breast of it. After Pete got ruled off, I operated for him on the race track, and while he was not betting heavily—only a hundred or two at a time—he was working in other ways. At his suggestion I bought three horses. I bought them at a good price on the condition that the people in whose names they stood would go on racing them in their

234

colors but at my orders... If Fete had lived only a week longer the bookkeepers out on the track next Saturday would not have had sufficient money to pay their carfares home. We would have cleaned up at least two hundred thousand dollars. Why, I gave his widow eighteen hundred dollars today—the proceeds of one winning on one of our horses on Friday in Oakland... Pete's play was this. He gave me a note or power of attorney six months ago, saying "Anything this man does or says for me I will stand by." Well, I always had some money on hand to treat the "push" and the jockeys and I would put up champagne for the high-toned ones and perhaps steer them into good feminine company. Then when my man was mellow I would suggest he wasn't riding for his health and that all I wanted him to do was to ride one race for me—he to get fifty percent of the money. They all knew Little Pete would divide fairly ...

One crackerjack jock came into town, and when I broached the proposition to him and showed him Little Pete's note he was a little leery. He said he never did business with any but the principals. "Very well," I said... I took him to Chinatown and got Pete and introduced them... when I next saw the jockey... he said, "It's all right. Whenever you want me to ride for you just give me the word."

I tell you, we have five of them—the jockeys—sure. It was the greatest thing ever done. There was no playing for place, but just straight money. The names of the jockeys are known everywhere and the alleged owners of the horses are some of the biggest people on the turf.

I have documentary evidence of what I saw, including some interesting letters. My arrangement with Little Pete was to be paid for running expenses and wages for the time being. We were looking for the big cleanup on Saturday. When that came I was to have fifty percent of the total profits... and I would have got it sure. Pete was square....

With Lee Chuck in the insane asylum after being released from Folsom, Little Pete had to look for a new bodyguard. He chose well in selecting Ed Murray. The strapping Murray was to be his shadow and the start of a vogue among highbinders. Pete's idea was that any hatchet man would think twice before gunning down a white man to get at his Chinese enemy. If one did, he just might have a lynch mob of *fan kwei* after him. The killing of whites would certainly mean an end to the casual attitude of the public which permitted Chinatown crime to flourish. White bodyguards for the Mandarins, as Chinese big businessmen and bosses came to be called, became quite a fad.

C. H. Hunter later replaced Murray as Pete's bodyguard. And on the evening of January 23, 1897—exactly eleven years to the day after Detective Glennon warned Lee Chuck of the plot on his life—Little Pete made his second major mistake. His first had been to try to bribe Officer Martin in the Lee Chuck case. His second—and last—was to let his Chinese bodyguards off for a pre-Chinese New Year's revel and to separate himself briefly from Hunter.

From his home upstairs over his shoe factory Pete sent Hunter on an errand, saying "I'll go downstairs and get shaved while you are gone." Hunter advised him not to be so rash but Pete laughed. "That's all right, I'll take care of myself." It was about 9:05 P.M. Pete proceeded downstairs, secure in his own building and with his bodyguard only a few blocks away on a ten-minute errand. He walked through the ground floor and turned into the barbershop next door. In the meantime Hunter sauntered down to the New Western Hotel to pick up a copy of the *Sporting World* so that Pete could learn the results of the day's races. He passed within a few feet of two young men idling against the corner of a building; he may even have brushed against them. Once he was well past, the two loungers separated themselves from the black shadows, straightened up, and reached inside their blouses and drew out pistols. They hurried to the doorway of the barbershop. Their long, patient tailing of Pete had paid off at last.

An unarmed, unguarded King of Chinatown had taken a straight chair in the shop, only four feet from the front door. For the first time in months—perhaps years—Pete was briefly defenseless. The timing of the shadowy figures was perfect. In the shop with Pete were two barbers, and one other customer who was having his head shaved.

At approximately 9:10 P.M. the two hatchet men, fedoras pulled low over their faces, strode into the barbershop. At the exact moment that Hunter was fumbling with a handful of coins to pay the newspaper vendor at the New Western Hotel, a pistol shot echoed in the barbershop, followed by three more. Smoke and the smell of cordite filled the room. The men spun on their heels and were gone. In the rear of the shop barbers Wong Chong and Won Chick Cheong were emptying basins of water. They saw nothing.

Hunter came hurrying up the hill, pistol in hand, but he was too late. Much too late. He stared in disbelief at the crumpled form on the blood-soaked floor of the barbershop. Two of the assassins' bullets had torn into Pete's head and a third into his chest. Hunter was out of a job, and some Chinese was richer by the price ($3,000) on Little Pete's head.

Reporters questioned Hunter the next morning. "Of late," said the bodyguard, "I'd been contemplating giving up my job because of Pete's recklessness and his often expressed contempt of the value of my service. There is no more danger of my being hurt than there is of you being hurt,' he would say. But several times men tried to get the drop on Pete. Only last week a man rubbed up against me to see if I had a weapon. I gave him a shove, and four other men showed hostility. I had to hit one on the head with my revolver before he would quit." Hunter added, "In spite of this, the fact that a price was on his head worried him, and of late he was rather ill tempered." Hunter could tell them no more.

Even before the Chinatown squad sped to the murder scene Special Officer George Welch arrived. He had been quick enough to see two men flee from the doorway of the barbershop. He pursued them as they ran into Waverly Place. (Waverly was also known as Ho Boon Gai—Fifteen Cent Street—because that was the cost of "haircuts" [shaving] in the many barbershops which lined the street.) Policeman Murty Callinan came up at that moment and Welch pointed to No. 123 Waverly into which the duo had fled. The two officers entered the building, and Callinan arrested two men, Chin Poy and Wing Sing, upon Welch's identification. In their room Callinan found a chest containing a box of loose pistol cartridges, a dagger with a three-edged blade, and two pairs of homemade "brass" knuckles made of solder.

Sergeant John Mooney and his Chinatown posse arrived shortly after Callinan. Mooney himself picked up the murder weapon—a modern

Colt Storekeeper revolver. He found that four chambers were emptied. Mooney had officer Myler arrest the barber Wong Ching as a witness before he could drop from sight. Within a few moments Mooney was joined by Sergeant Wollweber and fourteen more men. Wollweber had his men frisk all the curious Chinese who pushed up close to the barbershop to peer inside; not a weapon was found on anyone. The lone customer, Wong Lung, was detained for questioning although he insisted that he had seen nothing. He was marched off to city prison.

At California Street Station the two suspects were given a thorough grilling. They denied any complicity in, or even knowledge of the crime. In fact they swore that they were unaware of the murder until arrested and that they had neither heard the shots nor left their room that evening. Wing Sing affected a *no-sabe* attitude but Chin Poy was glib enough. He told his interrogators that he was a cook who had just arrived from Portland two weeks earlier and had been hired by an insurance agent who was living in a local hotel until he could secure a new home. Of Wing Sing, Chin Poy said that he had come to San Francisco from an Alaskan cannery about a month earlier. The police thought that Wing was very well dressed for an ex-laborer. He did not resemble the coolie type of cannery worker who drifted into Chinatown each winter.

Attorneys secured the release of the barber witness on a writ of *habeas corpus* but the two men from the North were held. The arsenal found in their room, together with Welch's identification of them as the men he saw fleeing the barbershop area, was damning. They were formally charged with murder. It soon became obvious that the department had the wrong men.

An anonymous merchant told a reporter that he had spoken to Pete just before the murder and that the latter had winked slyly at him and showed him $2,000 in gold—the result of a "good business deal." The informant said the deal was the framing of an honest man for the murder of a Suey Sing while the real culprit, probably a Wah Ting San Fong tong hatchet man, got away. The talkative merchant insisted that Pete was killed by Suey Sings intent on evening up the score. Then, too, Little Pete's nephew Chung Ying was reported boarding the steamer *China* in Hong Kong to come to San Francisco to find his uncle's real murderers. The best evidence that the real murderers had escaped was the *chun hing* posted by Pete's widow after the arrest of the suspects. It offered a reward of $2,000 for the capture and conviction of the murderers of Little Pete.

But the police were stuck with Chin Poy and Wing Sing. New witnesses appeared to identify them as the killers. One man, D. S. Hutchings, repeated his story time after time without deviating; right up through the course of the trial his account never varied. Chief Crowley placed great faith in this witness. Hutchings's story went as follows: "I was in Chinatown on the night of the shooting when Little Pete, otherwise known as Fong Ching, was killed. I saw the defendant [Wing Sing] standing in the door of the barbershop and heard the shots fired... As soon as the shooting was over, the defendant here ran by me. He had on a Chinese-made blouse with long sleeves... I did not see a pistol in his hand and did not see the flash of the shots. As soon as the shooting was over I started toward the barbershop and met this man Sing. He was wearing a fedora hat. There was another man with him, a Chinaman who also had on a fedora hat. [Hutchings never did positively identify the other man as Chin Poy.] When the shooting was finished, the defendant ran away rapidly."

Hutchings was apparently an honest man. He told the court what he saw as he remembered it. He never did say he actually saw Wing in the act of shooting Pete, for all the coaxing he received in that direction. He refused to incriminate Chin Poy. But he did stress the point that Wing Sing was at the scene of the crime and that he had hurried away immediately after the shooting occurred. Hutchings had had a good vantage point on the northwest corner of Washington and Waverly when the murder was committed and when he saw Wing fleeing from the shop.

The fact that Wing and Chin Poy would hurry away from a shooting was not surprising. Hutchings admitted that practically everybody broke into a run in one direction or another when the shots were fired. He had done so himself. But the two suspects doggedly stuck to their story that they had not even left their lodging that evening. Special Officer Welch could add little information. He had followed two men in fedoras from the scene of the crime and had arrested the only two men in the rooming house who were wearing slouch hats.

Two more men, a Pullman porter named James Briggs and a dishwasher and bartender, James Daly, then came forth to corroborate

Hutchings's testimony. During the trial both Daly and Briggs were able to single out Wing Sing from the numerous Chinese in the courtroom, as the man they had seen fleeing the murder scene. But when Counsel Murphy asked Daly if he had actually seen pistols in the men's hands he admitted that he had not. He said their hands were concealed by the sleeves of their blouses. "Then, how do you know that one of them dropped a pistol?" asked Murphy. "Because I saw it dropped. The man in front—the smaller of the two—dropped it." The defense scored by weakening Daly's testimony at this juncture. Two brothers, Edward and Charles Johnseon, were called as surprise witnesses. They made it clear to the jury that Daly was remembering more and more as time wore on. Immediately after the murder he had said to them, "I was in Chinatown last night and if I had been five minutes earlier, I would have seen the shooting."

Before the trial of Wing Sing and Chin Poy began, four other Chinese were arrested. The police collected a small arsenal from them—three knives, a cleaver, a .45 Colt, and two hatchets—but could not implicate them. Still another suspect was found in late January—Gee Pon Jin, a Suey Sing member with a reputation for recklessness. He was identified by another new witness, Frank Mason, as one of two men he had seen fleeing the barbershop as he emerged from Ross Alley to see what had happened after he heard the shots.

Crowley, who would have been content with one killer, now found himself with an embarrassment of riches. He had seven suspects. But not one of them was ever to be convicted of a part in the crime. The solution of the murder of Little Pete remains a mystery to this day.

The really hot suspect was never arrested. He was Big Jim. Although he was a See Yup and a social and business rival of Pete, he was thought by most people to have been friendly with him. But many, including Captain Thomas S. Duke of the police department, considered him the chief conspirator in the crime, if not the executioner. The press, on the other hand, felt the friendship between Little Pete and Big Jim to have been genuine and that Big Jim was not implicated. Guilty or not, Big Jim soon found himself in grave danger as a scapegoat at least. Rumor was that there was a price of $5,000 on his head immediately after Pete's murder. On Wednesday, January 26, in fear for his life at the hands of

Little Pete's hatchet men, he fled the city, taking only his bodyguard along. He hid out on a farm near Fresno, but when word trickled into Fresno's China Alley that there was $1,000 available for anyone who would do Big Jim in, he did not wait. He left the Fresno area on February 23, on the Oregon express. His departure, though hurried, was a well-kept secret, as he did a masterful job of covering his tracks. While he quietly converted his bulky cash into checks at two different banks— one for $50,000 and the other for $44,000—he let a story circulate that he was going to visit a Northern California mine in which he had an interest. Instead he went straight to Victoria with his white wife and family. There he caught a steamer for China and safety.

Both friends and rivals of Pete's either fled town or secured bodyguards after his death. One of the former, Ung Hung—nicknamed the Russian—was warned of a $2,500 reward for his life. He had to die, it was said, because he knew too much about the murder. The Russian did not leave town but he did hire Tom Douglass, son of Police Captain Douglass, as his personal bodyguard. Another close friend of Pete's, Sin Goon, learned that there was a $2,000 price on his head. Like the Russian, he hired a white gunman for a shield.

Just four days after Pete's death the rumor swept Chinatown that Dong Gong, police interpreter and informant, had been shot to death. A later report had him only shot in the leg. When Sergeant Jesse Cook investigated he found Dong at home unharmed, but under guard. He was a frightened man. He never went out without his bodyguard and was seldom seen in the streets in the future.

While Dr. Morgan was performing the autopsy on Little Pete the Sam Yups were hurriedly holding a powwow. They met in the rooms of the Wah Ting San Fong tong at 820 Jackson Street. Couriers had sped throughout the Quarter to round up members for the strategy meeting. Soon the rooms were crowded. The conference lasted all night and ended with the declaration that some prominent See Yups would have to die to expiate the murder of Little Pete.

Meanwhile the rumor was spreading that Pete's assassins were after Vice-Consul King Owyang. The latter, an old hand at being death-listed, smiled stoically when he heard of it.

More and more rumors rolled into the police department. Crowley was soon swamped with them: Pete had been murdered for accepting a $40,000 fee for destroying the See Yup Company, and had already been paid $10,000 on account; Vice-Consul Owyang had been backing him, as he had the Sam Yup Company; Pete was to have taken the Sam Yup Company from the defensive in the boycott and put it on the offensive. There were many more and there may have been a grain of truth in each. For one thing, a completely illegal raid reminiscent of the Chinatown squad's savage forays had made a shambles of the See Yup Company headquarters before Pete's death. The ax-wielding raiders had been led by a private eye named Ferdinand Callundan. The police had quickly arrested him but the See Yups were convinced that Pete, not Callundan, had brainstormed the raid. Whether he was guilty or not, Pete had found *chun hungs* posted with rewards for his head. But there had been no takers at the $1,000 price. The figure was doubled but without success. The price was upped to $3,000. This brought results. Pete was shot to death the next night.

Other stories noised abroad were that the Sam Yups had hired hatchet men to man the roofs of Chinatown after Pete's death and to shoot down a policeman and see to it that the See Yups were blamed. This was a good story. It was so good that it was shortly revived, but with the roles reversed. This time the See Yups were said to be on the roofs and the Sam Yups destined for trouble. Another startling rumor was that certain highbinders were building up a cache of arms and ammunition in a Pacific Street basement. According to the tale, these underground stores were for the use of a subterranean army which would spring up should the *fan kwei* dare to interfere in the blood bath which would have to follow Pete's murder. The police found this to be completely untrue.

Both the white community and Chinatown were of two minds over Little Pete's passing. But it was a eulogy of sorts which *The Chinese Recorder* printed right after his death: "Little Pete, as he was commonly known, was the most famous man among us. He may have had his faults, and more than the average man, but his good qualities were more than sufficient to counterbalance the evil part of his nature. He has furnished more work to those in need than any man that can be named. When he had no work to give he furnished sustenance to the needy. The list of his bad traits does nowhere contain the word 'miser.' It is to be hoped that the police will succeed in catching the murderers and that they will meet with speedy punishment. It is not generally believed, however, that the two men under arrest are the guilty ones."

But Crowley was not about to accept a Robin Hood characterization of Little Pete. He agreed more with the *Call* which said: "Little Pete had not been a credit to the city in which he lived." And with the French language paper *l'Impartial* which stated that "characters of his stamp will not be missed." Indeed, Crowley went far in damning Pete. He blamed him for *all* of the trouble in Chinatown since he had reached a position of power, saying:

> Little Pete was unquestionably the cleverest Chinaman on the Pacific Coast and probably in the United States. He was a born organizer and was full of schemes and deviltry. Until his advent there were no highbinder societies or tongs and the Chinese were quiet, orderly and peaceable. He was the first to organize a tong and finally he had fifteen or sixteen of them at his command. They levied blackmail upon houses of ill fame and upon inoffensive merchants, and by that means Little Pete became a rich man.
>
> He was at the bottom of every blackmailing scheme and held absolute power over the highbinders of Chinatown. Four years ago when Sergeant Price and his squad demolished the headquarters of the different tongs it was Little Pete who instigated the damage suits against me and the squad in the United States District Court because, as he said, it would deter me from any further attempts to repeat the dose. In that, Little Pete made a mistake and he came to recognize the fact.
>
> Five years ago I prevailed upon the Six Companies to employ eight responsible Chinese to act as policemen, and each of the eight carried a tag signed by me, showing their authority. By that means I thought they would be able to keep the Six Companies and myself posted as to any proposed action of the highbinders to commit murder. I have found out my mistake, as they have been utterly useless, and I will ask the Six Companies to discontinue employing them.

> It has always been the case that while there was an extra force of police in Chinatown there was no shooting, but as soon as the extra force was withdrawn trouble recommenced. I have about twenty men in Chinatown now and I will keep them there… till the present trouble blows over. I can do no more with the force at my command.

Crowley's mention of Sergeant Price, who had earned the title the American Terror from the Chinese as a result of his ax raids, sent newsmen scurrying to him for interviews. Price had no reluctance to comment, and had his own ready prescription for ending the reign of terror in Chinatown:

> I regard the situation here as most serious but do not look for any great trouble until after the funeral. I understand that the Sam Yup men have imported the most desperate rascals belonging to the highbinder tongs found in the interior and coast towns to carry on the feud. One thing is certain; there was a time when I knew every highbinder in Chinatown and where nearly every individual could be found. But I can't now. The streets are filled with strange faces. At one time I arrested thirty-five men in one day and did not make a single mistake. I was always careful not to arrest innocent men and give cause for complaint. Why, once we smashed eight thousand dollars' worth of property in breaking up a tong meeting. It was a long time before they dared to come together again. But, you see, all these clubs are incorporated now. That is what balks us in disturbing them. When we do manage to get through to where the rascals are playing forbidden games and hatching deviltry of all kinds, they have had plenty of time to start in on some innocent game. When the police leave they return to what they were doing before.
>
> Give me men and I can break up these tongs in two days. No jury on earth would convict a man for taking summary action in stopping such a reign of terror. They never have in the past and they will not now.

Although the large damage suits for the earlier raids were still pending in United States' courts, Crowley gave Price the men he needed. The latter embarked on a new series of tong raids with the usual destruction of josses and furniture. First to be destroyed was the headquarters of the Suey Sing tong, for it was thought by many on the force to be responsible for Pete's murder. Over the years both uniformed men and plainclothes' details had been used in Chinatown, with the latter the more effective. But right after Pete's death, to make a stronger show of force, Price outfitted his men in new bright-blue uniforms in place of the former quiet gray color. Within an hour of the resplendent squad's lockstep entry in Chinatown *chun hungs* blossomed on brick walls, reading LOOK OUT FOR SERGEANT PRICE AND HIS MEN! THEY ARE DRESSED LIKE PEACOCKS AND ARE COMING TO STOP THE WAR AMONG THE CHINESE.

In death Little Pete was even more of a celebrity than in life, and crowds of Chinese and Caucasians gathered to see the corpse. Not all came out of morbid curiosity. Robert Ferral, one of his friends, said, "I've known Little Pete for years. I've prosecuted him and he has been my client and I have never known him to break his word."

Pete's widow and little son came with Pete's brother Fong Shun to receive the deceased property. Coroner William J. Hawkins was afraid to turn over Little Petes' magnificent diamond ring, gold watch and other jewelry to anyone else. He gave Chun Li a paper bag of belongings and then slipped the ring on her finger. As she gazed at it her composure was shattered and she sank to the floor, shrieking with grief. Her female companions and Pete's brother were in tears, and even Coroner Hawkins was much moved by their emotion.

The body was taken from the funeral parlor in the finest casket Fong Shun could buy—one of metal covered with broadcloth. On the 25th it was moved to the morgue and there Hawkins empaneled a jury for a coroner's inquest. The body, dressed in fine Chinese burial raiment including the so-called consular cap with gold knob worn by nobility in the Old Country, was then moved to Pete's shoe factory. An area had been cleared where Pete could lie in state only thirty feet from where he had met his death. The building was quickly besieged by curiosity seekers. The gloomy building was bright with a profusion of flowers; colored candles and incense burned at the foot of the coffin and before an altar erected in the rear. In one corner the bereaved family and hired mourners, in blue wrappers and flowering white headdresses, kept up a continuous lament.

According to Price, highbinders were shadowing all Chinese who entered to view the corpse and were preparing a fate similar to Pete's for them: "These fellows," he said, "want to see who offers condolences to the relatives. When it comes to a feud they will have such persons marked." The ceremonies began with the cooking of ritual meats, the burning of punk and candles in front of the barbershop of death, and the clanging of cymbals and incantations of priests. The procession got under way at 1 P.M. on January 26, with a platoon of police leading. With the help of exploding firecrackers and clanging gongs they managed to force a path through the press of people to the Sam Yup cemetery at the far end of the Richmond district, adjacent to the Jewish cemetery. Here the funeral ceremonies were held, but Pete's body was not buried. It was returned to the undertaker's vault to be kept there until the estate could be settled and the widow could return with it to China.

The entire population of Chinatown plus curious tourists and hordes from inland Chinatowns turned out en masse to see the floral tributes, brass bands, marching mourners, and the ornate hearse drawn by six black horses in royal black trappings. Rumors that the See Yups would interfere with the ceremony were completely unfounded. Everyone in Chinatown—friend or enemy—was an interested spectator. A goodly portion of Caucasian San Francisco was on hand too. One hundred and twelve carriages took mourners to the cemetery. Roofs, windows, balconies and lampposts were alive with people watching the parade. Little Pete's funeral dwarfed all others before or since, and became a measuring stick against which other public events in the Quarter would be compared; there were 31,000 Chinese spectators alone.

Among the spectators was a prematurely gray young man with a slight look of distaste on his handsome face. He made notes as he eyed the antics of the mob scrambling for a better view of the procession. Frank Norris was the top reporter on San Francisco's fine literary magazine, the *Wave*. (Talent abounded in the office of this journal which

John O'Hara Cosgrave pioneered—and included Ambrose Bierce, Jack London and George Sterling.) And this was future novelist Frank Norris, who within the next seven years would write the highly successful *McTeague, The Octopus* and *The Pit*. His story of Little Pete's funeral was a fine piece of incisive reporting:

...Perhaps I have seen a more disgusting spectacle than that which took place at "Little Pete's" funeral ceremonies, but I cannot recall it now. A reckless, conscienceless mob of about two thousand, mostly women, crowded into the Chinese Cemetery. There was but one policeman to control them and they took advantage of the fact. The women thronged about the raised platform and looted everything they could lay their hands on; China bowls, punk, tissue-paper ornaments, even the cooked chickens and bottles of gin. This, mind you, before the procession had as much as arrived.

The procession itself was rather disappointing—from a picturesque point of view. Perhaps one expected too much. There might possibly have been a greater display of color and a greater number of bands...

At the cemetery, however, things were different. There was & certain attempt here at rites and observances and customs that would have been picturesque had it not been for the shameless, the unspeakable shamelessness, of the civilized women of the crowd.

A few mandarins came first, heads no doubt of the Sam Yup, one of them in particular with all the dignity and imposing carriage of a Senator. He was really grand, this mandarin, calm, austere, unmoved amidst this red-faced, scrambling mob. A band of women followed, the female relatives of the deceased.

"Here comes his wife!" screamed half-a-dozen white women in chorus.

Pete's widow was wrapped from head to foot in what might have been the sackcloth of the Bible stories; certainly it had the look of jute. A vast hood of the stuff covered her whole face, and was tied about the neck. Two other women, similarly dressed, but without the hood, were supporting her. A mat was unrolled, and after the white women had been driven back from the platform by the main strength of two or three men, not yet lost to the sense of decency, the mourners kneeled upon it, forehead to the ground, and began a chant, or rather a series of lamentable cries and plaints, *"Ai-yah, ai-yah, yah."*

A gong beat. A priest in robes and octagon cap persistently jingled a little bell and droned under his breath. There was a smell of punk and sandalwood in the air. The crouching women, mere bundles of clothes, rocked to and fro and wailed louder and louder.

Suddenly the coffin arrived, brought up by staggering hack drivers and assistants, a magnificent affair of heavy black cloth and heavy silver appointments. The white women of the crowd made the discovery that Little Pete's powder-marked face could be seen. They surged forward in the instant. The droning priest was hustled sharply. He dropped his little bell, which was promptly stolen. The mourners on the mat, almost under foot, were jostled and pushed from their place, or bundled themselves out of the way, hurriedly, to escape trampling.

Just what followed after this I do not know. A mob of red-faced, pushing women thronged about the coffin and interrupted everything that went on. There was confusion and cries in Cantonese and English; a mounted policeman appeared and was railed at. There can be no doubt that more ceremonies were to follow, but that those in charge preferred to cut short the revolting scene.

The coffin was carried back to the hearse, a passage at length being forced through the crowd, and the Chinese returned to the city. Then the civilized Americans, some thousand of them, descended upon the raised platform, where the funeral meats were placed—pigs and sheep roasted whole, and chickens and bowls of gin and rice. Four men seized a roast pig by either leg and made off with it; were pursued by the mounted police and made to return the loot. Then the crowd found amusement in throwing bowlfuls of gin at each other. The roast chickens were hurled back and forth in the air. The women scrambled for the China bowls for souvenirs of the occasion, as though the occasion were something to be remembered.

The single mounted police, red-faced and overworked, rode his horse into the crowd and after long effort at last succeeded in thrusting it back from the plundered altar and in keeping it at a distance. But still it remained upon the spot, this throng, this crowd, this shameless mob, that was mostly of women. There was nothing more to happen, the ceremony was over, but still these people stayed and stayed.

This was the last impression one received of Little Pete's funeral—a crowd of men and women, standing in a huge circle, stupidly staring at the remains of a roasted pig.

The following June the jury in Judge Carroll Cook's Superior Court failed to agree in the trial of Wing Sing for the murder of Little Pete. In November a jury returned a not-guilty verdict after the defense, led by General A. L. Hart and Colonel T. V. Eddy, proved to its satisfaction that Wing Sing was nowhere near the scene of the tragedy when Pete was shot. Chin Poy had earlier been released because of insufficient evidence.

Eddie Gong, writing thirty-five years after the assassination, stated that the murderers were two Suey Sings named Lem Jung and Chew Tin Gop. They were in San Francisco on a stopover while en route to China and were chosen for the task because they were unknown to Pete, his bodyguard and the police. However, Gong is so often wrong in describing details of the Little Pete case that this convenient solution of the perfect Chinatown crime must be viewed suspiciously.

It is much safer to consider the case as still unsolved and to accept the verdict of the coroner's jury at the inquest: "We find that Fong Ching, aged 34 years, nativity China, occupation merchant, residence 819 Washington Street, City and County of San Francisco, came to his death January 23, 1897, at 817 Washington Street, said City and County, from shock of gunshot wounds and we further find the wounds were inflicted by persons or a person unknown to us."

# CHAPTER THIRTEEN

# AFTERMATH: CHINATOWN IN RUINS

*"The strange, mysterious old Chinatown
of San Francisco is gone and never more will
be. Heaps of sand and colored ashes mark the
once densely populated, gaily painted, and
proverbially wicked haunts of highbinders and
slave dealers."*

—Donaldina Cameron, 1906

IMMEDIATELY after Little Pete's murder, the police clamped a tight lid on Chinatown. It was lucky for the Quarter that the force's repressive measures were so effective. Chief Lees thundered, "I will end highbinderism in San Francisco if I have to call out the entire police force to do so." Even though he did not end it, there was no war and those who were calling for the razing of the Canton of the West, like Editor Charles Shortridge of the *Call,* found little real support. Shortridge hoped that Pete's murder would rouse the entire city to action, but to his disgust the citizens were moved only to sign a petition to President McKinley, urging him to put a stop to slavery in Chinatown.

The Chinatown squad rousted about 300 men in 22 tong raids and arrested almost 50 of them, besides hitting opium dens and slave-girl dealers. They had one less headache when Loo Fook Yeung, called King of the Highbinders, was killed. Sergeant Price again took over the Chinatown detail during the day and Sergeant Cook was put in command of the squad at night. Captain Wittman created a special striking force of 55 policemen, which he split into 15 different "boarding parties," struck at the gambling dens run by the tongs, and dragnetted 242 gamblers.

The police were helped in their cleanup by the successor to the Chinese Vigilance committee, the Chinese Society for English Education. Many of the leaders of this society found prices placed on their heads by the tongs, as a result.

A neutralist Consul General, Ho Yow, favoring neither See Yups nor Sam Yups—although leaning toward the latter—almost secured an end to the boycott which was a major factor in the persistence of the tongs. The politico-economic chaos in Chinatown, as a result of the boycott, extended the life of the fighting societies by many years. Chinese Minister Wu Ting Fang tried to help stabilize Chinatown by approaching the United States Government in regard to . a formal extradition treaty between the two countries to permit the expulsion from the United States of hatchet men; but the United States did not warm to it, since Yankee and Chinese judicial processes were so different. Wu Ting Fang finally did act in the way the *Examiner* had claimed he had on the night of Pete's murder. He secured the arrest and imprisonment of relatives of See Yups in China. Shortly, however, he traded their release for a cessation of the boycott by the See Yup Company.

But as spring gave place to summer and fall the tong wars began to spread. The Wah Ting San Fongs and Sen Suey Yings joined the Hop Sings against the Suey Sings. As the hatchet men began to take their toll once more, headlines screamed MURDER AGAIN STALKS ABROAD IN CHINATOWN. The chief of police, confronted with a dozen or more murder attempts and half of them successful, laid down an ultimatum to Chinatown. He notified the Six Companies and the Consulate General that if the tong murders did not cease he would not only increase the strength of police patrols in Chinatown, but would personally start an agitation for the expulsion of *all* Chinese from San Francisco. A naturally disturbed Ho Yow replied, "I will do everything in my power to prevent further trouble, and I will lend my support to any measure which will assist in suppressing crime. I define my official capacity in this city as being consular and commercial, however, and I am not a detective, hence I cannot ferret out crime. This duty rests with the police. Understand, I do not mean to refuse to give the police any assistance I can but the bulk of the responsibility must not be placed on me." Ho Yow did get the Six Companies and the Merchants Association to post rewards for the leaders and hatchet men of the warring tongs, to hire Chinese private detectives, and to pay rewards to Chinese who would give testimony in court. Ironically, the sums were based on a figure which would allow a person to flee the city. The Six Companies made another of its threatening but not very effective pronunciamientos—"If the tongs do not cease the taking of life, the highbinders will be turned over to the police by the Chinese themselves." All in all, Ho Yow was the most effective Consul General the city had seen and his actions (particularly his pressure on Minister Wu to put the squeeze on Kwangtung relatives) earned applause from the *Wave* and other important publications.

Of course the tongs did not cease the taking of lives. All efforts to end the Hop Sing-Suey Sing war failed despite several abortive peace proclamations, the fleeing of nineteen hatchet men from San Francisco, and the death of the Suey Sings' president in December. Hundreds of innocent people fled the city. Many preferred to return home to China. Chinatown was terrified. Between 1890 and 1900, the population of the Quarter dropped from 25,000 to only 14,000, and the Chinese population of the United States, largely in California, declined by a full 16 percent.

At the end of 1898, with the boycott not yet dead, Chief Lees put up a *chun hung* of his own which garbled the facts of life in Chinatown badly but which made clear his determination to clean up the district:

> TO THE CHINESE: REPORTS COME TO MY OFFICE OF MUCH TROUBLE EXISTING IN THE CHINESE QUARTER IN THE PAST THREE OR FOUR WEEKS RELATIVE TO THE HIGHBINDERS SOCIETIES. IT APPEARS THAT THE SEE YUP TONG [sic], WHOSE HEADQUARTERS ARE ON CLAY STREET, DETAIL MEMBERS OF THEIR SOCIETY TO ROB, BLACKMAIL AND BOYCOTT THE SAM YUPS AND OTHER SOCIETIES; ALSO, MURDERS HAVE BEEN TOO FREQUENT LATELY. I, AS CHIEF OF POLICE OF THIS COUNTY, WARN AND CAUTION SUCH SOCIETIES THAT ARE ENGAGED IN BOYCOTTING, ROBBING, AND MURDER, THAT SUCH ACTS ARE CONTRARY TO THE LAW OF THIS STATE, WILL NOT BE TOLERATED ANY

LONGER, AND MUST BE STOPPED, AND IT WILL BE MY DUTY TO CAUSE THE ARREST OF EACH AND EVERY ONE WHO COMMITS OR IS SUSPECTED OF COMMITTING ANY OFFENSE AS STATED ABOVE. IT IS HOPED THAT ALL CHINESE SOCIETIES WILL HENCEFORTH RESPECT THE LAWS OF THIS COUNTRY, OTHERWISE THEY WILL HAVE TO TAKE THE CONSEQUENCES.

The tongs, of course, preferred to take their chances on the consequences. The chief continued the old blitzkrieg-style raids, still the most effective deterrent, and in 1899 had the Chinese Society for English Education raided along with the tongs. It was believed by many in the department that the society had succumbed to temptation and become nothing more than a front for tong activities or even a supertong itself. Its officers vehemently denied all charges, and portions of the press backed them up. But the police lost confidence in them, convinced that they informed on illegal gambling dens or prostitution only to move in themselves to take over once the police raiders had left. The raid on the society turned up nothing incriminating, and the piling up of damage suits led Lees to relax for a time. The blitzkrieg raids were stopped, and tough Lieutenant Price was shifted from Chinatown to other duty, even though a Suey Sing vs. Sen Suey Ying war broke out with the usual shootings and hatchetings. While the former posted a lopsided score of killings (4-0 in their favor over the Sen Suey Yings), the police appeared to be helpless.

The lid really blew off in 1900. Police frustrated Hop Sing attempts to dynamite several buildings including the Suey Sing tong headquarters and an attempt on the life of the president of that tong was thwarted in March. But on the very day after the attack a Hop Sing was slashed terribly with a cleaver and almost decapitated in reprisal. More arson attempts were made that spring, and the Bing Kongs were next on the warpath, at the throats of the Suey Dongs. Police had to batter down the doors of a tong building to rescue a man from a makeshift debtors' prison there, and the *Call* published its shocking roll call, the "Record of Blood," listing the seven men murdered and four wounded in the preceding three months of the Hop Sing-Suey Sing feud.

*Richard H. Dillon*

A bubonic plague scare that year deepened the hard times in Chinatown. The area was literally roped off and all traffic in and out was forbidden, although street cars Were permitted to pass through if they did not stop to either pick up or let off passengers. The situation was not improved when the public learned that the scare was a false one. Ho Yow had been approached by a man who offered to lift the quarantine for $10,000. "I do not know for whom this man was acting," said the Consul General.

The California writer, Will Irwin, who felt that the Bo On and Suey Sing tongs were the bloodiest of all, at least as of 1900—had some harsh words for the police too: "In this development of civilization, we are as children beside the Chinese, and out of this situation grew the highbinders, adventurers in crime. For they were not only criminals, they were formal and recognized agents of justice. Crime and punishment had become tangled and involved beyond any power of ours to separate them and straighten them out. The constituted police of San Francisco struggled with this paradox for a generation long, and finally, perceiving that the Chinese would settle their own affairs their own way, gave it up and let things go. They kept only such interest in the Quarter, these Caucasian police, as would permit them to gather that rich graft which made a Chinatown beat a step toward fortune." Irwin's cynicism was well merited but he was wrong in one respect. The police department never gave up trying to wrestle down the tong war problem.

More and more murders were committed. Four men were killed in the ten days of November 4-14, 1901, alone. An angry Chinese Exclusion convention met at the end of the year to demand the total obliteration of Chinatown, with colonization of its people to some distant portion of the peninsula. Reverend William Rader's words were typical of the impassioned thinking (and oratory) of the convention: "Crime is bred in Chinatown. Highbinders execute their own laws of vengeance. Murders are frequently committed. In thirty years, 1,645 [Chinese] felons have served time. During the last six months 1,140 arrests were made in Chinatown. It breeds murder, crime, licentiousness, slavery. Destroy it! Let the plow run through the filthy streets! Plant corn where vice grows! Let the fountains splash where opium fumes fill the air!"

The next year, the *Chronicle's* solution for the Chinatown problem

254

was lifted bodily from the convention's prescriptions. The paper asked that Chinatown be improved out of existence by running Grant Avenue right through the district, atop Dupont Street, from Market Street to North Beach.

The usual round robin of murders in 1902 led to more criticism of the police for their ineffectiveness. The *Chronicle* reminded its readers that twenty tong murders had taken place in only a few years without a single highbinder being forced to pay the extreme penalty. Hatchet men were so bold that they marched into stores openly to demand money. In a brazen stroke one invaded the home of Dr. George Palmer and chopped his Chinese cook badly about the head. Typical of a dozen ante-mortem statements given police was that of Little Louie, struck down in the street: "My bodyguard and I were about to enter my gambling house when somebody fired a shot at me. I turned around and was again fired at, the bullet striking me in the groin. As I fell three more shots were fired at me, one of which took effect. The last shot struck my bodyguard, preventing him from using his revolver."

A Bing Kong-Suey Dong truce failed. The police padlocked the Bing Kong headquarters. The Consul General and Six Companies revived the special Chinatown force of twelve heavily armed white policemen, their morale presumably boosted by liberal rewards for tong killers. But still the tong wars continued.

As the early years of the new century rolled on it became evident that some restorative had been applied to the tongs to prolong their lives. Men on the inside knew the magic ingredient—graft. Before the earthquake and fire San Francisco had been riddled with graft, from the Embarcadero to Seal Rocks. Chief William Sullivan, alarmed at the continuing growth of crime in Chinatown, did his best by removing Sergeant Patrick Mahoney and his entire Chinatown squad and replacing them with a brand-new, untainted squad under Sergeant Bernard McManus. He told the city "I made the change in the Chinatown Detail because I believe it will be beneficial to the service. I discovered conditions in Chinatown which convinced me that the squad was not as aggressive as it should be...." But graft continued and crime went on.

Each year tong troubles appeared to increase. The Chinese New Year celebration of 1903, for example, was spoiled by several murders as the Hop Sing vs. Suey Sing feud continued. That year Mayor Eugene Schmitz raided six notorious hangouts, seized documents, and pored over them to try to find out who was demanding and getting protection money from Chinese gamblers and others. Little evidence seems to have been found by Schmitz, but one lead was discovered in a payoff man—a Chinese gambler named Buck Guy. Schmitz pledged, "I mean to push this matter and to learn all that I can concerning the charges that have been made to me that money is being extorted from Chinese gamblers for police protection. The story the two men told me was that they were informed that their new club must pay to Buck Guy for police protection $400 or their new club would be raided. They refused to pay and the club was raided. They then paid the amount and have not since been molested."

While the mayor was making reform noises war broke out between the Hop Sings and Hip Sings. A prominent Hop Sing was interviewed and boasted, "We will not allow our rivals to insult us in this way and as they have threatened to put me out of the way, I will state that we maintain the same attitude toward the members of the Hip Sing tong. We can shoot as well as they and our aim is just as good. For every Hop Sing man that falls, we will demand that two of our rivals give up their lives."

One of these turned out to be a Sen Suey Ying member as well as a Hip Sing, so the Sen Sueys joined the fracas, shooting up the Hop Sing headquarters. Reporters counted twenty-two bullet holes in doors, windows and walls but not one Hop Sing was hurt by the barrage. Two days later a second fusillade was directed at the building after a member of that tong bungled an assassination attempt on one of the enemy. The Chinatown squad now took a hand and raided the place, seizing revolvers, ammunition and slung shots. The squad arrested seven men found there, and obliging Sen Suey Yings identified three of them as murderers.

When a Sen Suey Ying went to a joss house to call down a curse on the Hop Sing tong he found three killers from that society waiting for him in ambush in the temple. They wounded him and in so doing brought the Chee Kongs into the wars, for he was also a member of that tong. There were killings within the Suey Dong tong, and the Si On tong almost entered the frays when one of its gunmen shot the outstanding female singer in Chinatown. But this tong sensibly paid a sum of money in damages and averted further bloodshed. Usually all tongs involved in warfare were anathema to the public, but increasingly the Hop Sings were becoming the villains of the battles after the turn of the century.

By late 1903, the situation was more grave than at any time since Little Pete's murder. A hatchet man stepped on the stage of the Washington Street Chinese theatre, and in full view of a packed house shot down a well-named (Gong) cymbalist. The audience panicked and stampeded. Not one person who had been present could be persuaded to give testimony as a witness. A policeman with many years of duty on Dupont Gai shook his head and observed: "There has seldom been a time when Chinatown has been so thoroughly cowed as at present." The Six Companies' rewards for information on murderers were finding no takers. The all-white police force the Six Companies had set up was scrapped as useless and Chinatown's merchants hired a force of Pinkerton-like private police, the Morse Patrol. This force soon proved its worth. One of the patrol captured Yee Foo, a Suey Dong highbinder long wanted by police, and in one of the pitched battles between tongs Morse Patrolman Thomas P. Spellman was shot in the leg. For once, a force of specials was earning its pay—on the side of the law.

The tong wars continued. Truces were made and broken. The long-smoldering war between the Hop Sings and the Wah Ting San Fongs broke into flame again in 1904, with a battle at Waverly and Washington Street. The Wah Tings soon struck by stealth too. A Hop Sing told police of the death of his roommate: "I was sleeping with my friend when three men entered the room. One held a pistol to my head while the other two proceeded to kill Muck Ling. They struck him on the head with a butcher's cleaver and then stabbed him through the lung with a long knife. I was powerless to assist him for I feared if I made an outcry they would also kill me." All San Francisco was shocked by the retaliatory attack of the Hop Sings, for they got the wrong man—not a Wah Ting at all—and hatcheted him so badly he was scalped of his queue.

The police did their best. They kept all pedestrians on the go, broke up all gatherings—no matter how peaceful—and repeatedly searched suspects for weapons. To add to their troubles there was a revival in the slave-girl trade because of a new exposition, the St. Louis Fair, and be-

*Richard H. Dillon*

cause of corruption in the Chinese bureau of the Customs House.

Indeed, things were breaking so well for the tongs and illegality in general by 1904, that there was a successor to Little Pete and Big Jim. He was Wong Yow, called King of the Chinese Gamblers, the director of five clubs and Chinatown's richest citizen. His abode on Waverly was luxuriously furnished and had all the latest improvements including a telephone, electric lights, and a Victrola. His silk curtains were decorated with precious stones. On a wall of the reception room of the former cook of Deadwood, South Dakota, was a silken banner made by Imperial embroiderers in Peking at a cost of $20,000. His home was his office, and Wong directed his gambling empire from there by telephone. Like Pete, Wong Yow was no hatchet man. He was said to despise the *boo how doy,* in fact, but there was a truce between them. They did not bother him and he allowed them the run of his clubs. They respected him, although they did not actually fear him as they had Little Pete.

The unusual and welcome sight of tong toughs turning state's evidence occurred in 1904. Nine tong leaders were indicted and one of them convicted in the Tom Yick murder case. Yick was a member of the Chinese Society for English Education—the sometimes trusted, sometimes suspect organization. (In the latter case, the police derisively called them the Reform Highbinders.)

At the moment of upswing in tong troubles one of California's giants decided to take a hand in the game. Fremont Older, crusading editor of the *Bulletin* and muckraker extraordinary, was not so much a new Crusader Farwell as he was a man beset with the idea of *using* Chinatown to topple the crooks of city hall. He thought he could crack the hard shell of Chinese criminality and expose it and the roots which ran to the mayor's office. Older printed the pictures of the men he called the Unholy Four (Mayor Eugene Schmitz, Boss Abe Ruef, Police Commissioner J. A. Drink-house and Chief of Police George Wittman) on the front page of his paper. He surrounded their pictures with a frieze of human hands and ran a caption which read ONE OR MORE OF THESE MEN ARE TAKING BRIBES IN CHINATOWN. Corner newsboys were almost mobbed as the public bought up the edition. Ruef ordered the police commissioner to subpoena Older to appear and testify before the commission as to what evidence he had of bribe-taking in Chinatown. Older blithely told them that as yet he had no information, only belief—but added that he was positive some of them were taking money and that he was going to prove it.

Older sat tight and waited for a break. At last it came when Grant Carpenter, attorney for the Six Companies, came to his office and told him that Chan Cheung, or Big Cheung, was the police paymaster. Carpenter also had the idea that Cheung had commissioned several of the recent hatchet-man murders. The lawyer thought that if Older could pressure Cheung enough on these killings he might get him to squeal on police graft. The editor was delighted. This was just the break he had been waiting for. His first step was to work over Sergeant Tom Ellis of the Chinatown squad. Older got ex-Police Chief John Seymour to contact Ellis and give him Older's promise of two years on the *Bulletin's* payroll at $120 a month if he would confess to having accepted bribes in Chinatown. Seymour got a statement from Ellis that Big Cheung had paid him $200 a week for seven weeks. But Ellis did not know who had paid other policemen, how much, or even which patrolmen—or so he said. He reported to Older that he was sure that a number of ordinary officers were getting a "blind man's bonus," as he put it, of $40 per week. Ellis assumed that Schmitz, Ruef and Wittman were taking payoffs, but though he had no proof he was quite willing to go before the Grand Jury and make a statement. One day Ellis dramatically entered a Grand Jury session, walked to a table, and threw down $1,400 in bills. He said, "I received that from Chan in Chinatown. That's seven weeks' pay to ignore Chinatown gambling." This was good theatre, but it did not involve the city's leaders. The Grand Jury could do nothing.

Older had an ace up his sleeve in the person of Ed Bowes, later Major Edward Bowes of radio amateur hour fame. Bowes was not only his friend, he was head of the police committee of the Grand Jury. Like Older, he was willing to cut corners if the goal was important enough. Bowes helped Older plan a campaign. They decided to drag hatchet men before Chan and the Grand Jury, getting them to testify against him. They plotted another scare they would throw into Big Cheung. Older would take him to the Grand Jury room in absolute, frightening silence. Then the carefully coached district attorney would walk in and threaten Chan with hanging. Next, the hatchet men would be led in, one at a time, and asked the same question—"Is this the man who hired you to kill?" Older was sure Cheung would weaken after several of these accusations. Then the district attorney would promise him complete freedom *if* he would tell them whom he paid off regularly.

The stage was set but the "star" did not appear. Someone had tipped off Chan. Older had a private detective look for him, but he had disappeared. Older phoned Bowes and told him to ask a friend of Chan's to call him. A meeting was arranged; Bowes kidnapped Chan in a hack and drove off, telling him that he was an officer of the Grand Jury. He took Chan to the Occidental Hotel and stood guard over him, keeping him in the dark as to what was going on and keeping him off opium. The next day he brought Chan to the Grand Jury room, the Chinese shaking from nervousness, fright and the effects of opium deprivation.

The district attorney knew his lines perfectly. "Chan Cheung, you think that you are going back to China to live the rest of your days in comfort and prosperity with your children. This will never happen. You will be hanged." The impassive Chinese did not blink an eye. The highbinders entered, identified Chan as their murder broker, and were excused. The district attorney then went into his carefully rehearsed speech. "Chan Cheung, we don't want to hang you. We don't want you to die in prison, on a scaffold with a rope around your neck. Tell us who takes the money from you for protecting the gambling and we will let you go. You can go back to China and live in peace and comfort and plenty all your days... We know how much you paid to Chief Wittman and how much you paid to the officers. But you are a merchant, a man of standing in the community, and your word will go far and will help us. The police have told us, but we want your word. If you tell, you will not be hurt and you will not suffer. You will simply be called as a witness. But unless you tell us what we wish, we will indict you for murder."

All eyes were on the gambler. Those watching him leaned forward expectantly as he began to speak. He looked at the police committee of the Grand Jury and said, "Where you nineteen men? One, two, three, four... Grand Jury nineteen men. I *no sabe.*" Chan would not say another word.

The news was rushed to Fremont Older. The latter was far from nonplussed. "Give him his nineteen men," he said. Older secured the use of a Superior courtroom to impress Chan, seated the nineteen Grand Jurymen with Foreman Andrews on the judge's bench. The foreman demanded that Big Cheung tell them about the payoffs to Chief Wittman. But he refused to speak. "All right," snapped Andrews, "you don't tell us; we will indict you for those murders and hang you." Handcuffs were clamped on Chan's wrists and he was loudly and dramatically indicted for a part in the murder of Tom Yick. But the wily Chan would not be tricked. He said only, "Gentlemen, this is your country and if you can indict me for murder, go ahead." No threats could elicit anything further from him. Chan was not long in jail.

San Francisco's great crusader appeared to have been routed. He had to watch Ellis go before the Grand Jury and demand his bribe money back, and get it. But Ellis was found guilty of bribe-taking and was dismissed from the police department in 1905. Shortly thereafter Chief Wittman was also dismissed. Ruef and Schmitz themselves were evicted by Older with the help of Hiram Johnson and Francis J. Heney.

In 1905, Lieutenant Price, the Terror of Chinatown and the White Devil to the tongs, retired. The *boo how doy* breathed sighs of relief. But they had little time left. Neither they nor *Lo Mo* herself could guess that another female would align herself with the latter in her crusade against Chinatown vice and crime. It was Mother Nature. On April 18 of that year she rearranged the city of San Francisco more to her satisfaction with the help of the San Andreas Fault which underlies the city. In purging San Francisco with earthquake and fire she cleansed it of its blighted Chinatown by wiping out the Queen's Room, the tongs, every sorry brothel—and everything else—in the Quarter. Like the very tongs which controlled them and waxed fat upon their profits, the bagnios and gambling dens were never able to make a comeback.

The exact number of dead in the 28,000 structures destroyed in San Francisco's four days of tribulation is not known but is estimated to have totaled 450. Undoubtedly a good number of these were Chinese trapped in their tenements and warrens.

Chinatown would have been wiped out no matter what steps might have been taken, but its actual destruction on the first night of the four days of fire was accidental. In an attempt to stop the blaze from spreading west of Kearny Street—one of several thoroughfares vainly designated as firebreaks—a demolition crew planted a charge of black powder in a drugstore on the corner of Kearny and Clay Streets when they ran out of dynamite. When the charge was ignited the blast sent burning grains of powder and shredded, blazing bedding flying across Kearny Street from the windows of an upstairs room. The far side of the street was quickly aflame and Chinatown was doomed. It was a tinder-dry wooden city. The heat was so intense across Kearny from Chinatown that a group of prominent citizens who gathered in the Hall of Justice to offer their help in the emergency had to leave the oppressive, stifling building and make their way via Portsmouth Square to Chinatown and then to the Fairmont Hotel on Nob Hill. There they perfected their plans for the Relief Committee of Fifty which was to do yeoman work during the days of crisis.

Witnesses to the fire's leapfrogging across Kearny were Frank W. Aitken and Edward Hilton, who described the scene: "Quickly it crossed from Kearny to the little arm of Chinatown that reached down the hill beside Portsmouth Square, and beyond Chinatown with its huddled houses and narrow passages and overhanging porches... During the evening, too, the fire from the wholesale district, having thrust out an arm into Chinatown, stretched down along Montgomery Street... Before the night was far advanced Chinatown was in the grasp of the destroying flames and the Chinese joined the throng. It was a motley procession, sprung from many places, its ranks filling with homeless, footsore legions, orderly and nearly silent... By midnight a solid wall of fire stretching from Market Street to Chinatown was working steadily out toward Powell Street and Nob Hill."

Charles Keeler recalled that "Chinatown was ablaze early in the evening and had burned throughout the night, the fire sweeping fiercely through the flimsy Oriental city, scattering the inhabitants... in helpless bands. Out of the narrow alleyways and streets they swarmed like processions of black ants. With bundles swung on poles across their shoulders, they retreated, their helpless little women in pantaloons following with the children, all passive and uncomplaining... [though] in every quarter the night was full of terror. The mighty column of smoke rose thousands of feet in the air, crimsoned by the wild sea of flame below it."

Exhausted after trudging about the city all day, James B. Stetson had gone to bed at 1 A.M. on the first night of the fire; but he could only sleep until 2:30. He got up, pulled on his clothes again, and went out to see what was left of his city. He stood at the corner of California and Mason Streets. "From there I could see that Old St. Mary's Church and Grace Cathedral were on fire. To the north, Chinatown was in a whirlpool of fire."

California author Mary Hunter Austin wrote: "I remember the sigh of the wind through windows of desolate walls, and the screech and clack of ruined cornices in the red, noisy night, and the cheerful banging of pianos in the camps, the burials in trenches and the little, bluish, grave-long heaps of burning among the ruins of Chinatown."

Before midnight of that terror-filled first day 10,000 Chinese had fled the Quarter. Soon the remainder would follow. Donaldina Cameron saw sharp-eyed highbinders watching for their prey among the refugees driven from hiding, even in the midst of the confusion and chaos. They fled to Washington Square in North Beach, to Fort Point, to the Ferry Building and across the bay to Oakland. A special camp was set up for Chinese at Fort Winfield Scott and most of the refugees ended up there. The Chinese Minister came from Washington to tour the camp with agents of the Six Companies and was completely satisfied with the care and help being given his nationals. Major General Adolphus W. Greeley, in a special report to Washington on relief operations, said, "It is gratifying to report that neither in San Francisco nor in Oakland has any relief committee showed discrimination against the Chinese, and this line of action of the civilian organization has been consistently followed by the Army." Another observer also remarked on this point. Edward Livingstone, a San Francisco businessman wiped out by the fire, said, "I was impressed by the fact that caste and creed were thrown to the winds. There were no rich, no poor, no capitalists and laborers, no oppressed and oppressors. All facing a common peril, men and women who had lived in elegance stood in the breadline with Chinese and colored people."

Many of the Chinese servants who lived in Chinatown rushed to rejoin their white households out of loyalty. They proved of great aid in salvaging valuables, bedding and clothing. Twenty years later James W. Byrne recalled that "Chinese servants rose nobly to the exigencies' of the catastrophe. We had no vehicle, no means of transporting the mattresses and commissariat otherwise than in our arms or on our backs until the Chinese boys solved the difficulty. They went out foraging in their own quiet way and presently returned to the house with a couple of children's four-wheeled wagons... [which] we piled with mattresses, bedding, hams and other essentials, and then we started out with the convoy, up and down hill to the Presidio, as the Chinamen pulled...."

On the second day anything that had escaped the earlier flames was destroyed as the fire fanned back over the skeleton of Chinatown again. Aitken and Hilton wrote, "Soon the flames were racing down the western slope of Nob Hill, racing across California Street to meet the fire on the south, racing pellmell beyond Sacramento Street and back to the purlieus of the destroyed Chinatown. There was no wind to drive them [back], and no man there to stay them...." By the fourth day the Quarter was a blackened ruin. The two men wrote: "The bright lanterns, the little grated windows, the balconies that whispered of romance, the flaring dragons, were gone. Gone, too, the ill-smelling fish markets and cellar shops, the bazaars, the gambling dens, the places where opium was smoked in guarded secrecy. Everything that had made the little foreign section a tradition throughout the world had disappeared."

Amidst the general sorrowing, the erasure of Chinatown was hailed as a blessing. In the *Overland Monthly* a writer exclaimed: "Fire has reclaimed to civilization and cleanliness the Chinese ghetto, and no Chinatown will be permitted in the borders of the city. Some provision will be made for the caring of the Orientals." The *Independent* thought that they would be settled at Hunter's Point. In Britain *Blackwood's Magazine,* in commenting upon what it called the purification of San Francisco, applauded Chinatown's disappearance: "...a sink and sewer of the city, tainted in every vein and vessel, a relic of a former existence nourished solely on the evil traditions of the past... The maze of ramshackle tenements, lean-to joss houses, gaudy brothels and disgusting dives is no more."

True. Gone were the houses of the singsong girls, the opium dens, the fan-tan parlors, the packed tenements and the moldy Globe Hotel and decaying Mansion House. The headquarters of every tong were completely demolished too. Most of them never came back. It is said of the Kwong Duck tong, for example, that it boasted only one member after the earthquake and fire—Wong Sing, a man who guarded the tong seal, the society's flag and its book of oaths, and held all offices. The ranks of the hatchet men, already thinned by old age, extradition, voluntary return to China, and death, scattered after 1906. Some went to Oakland; others to Portland and Seattle. Many went to San Jose or south to Los Angeles, and a considerable number went on East to Chicago or New York to cause trouble there. Many never returned to plague San Francisco again. When the San Francisco police force had to be reduced by one-fifth as an economy measure after the disaster (most of the taxable property had been destroyed) there was a crime wave, but not in Chinatown. It was the quietest sector in the city. The slate had been wiped clean and a fresh start made possible.

The Chinese drifted back to Dupont Gai and its smoking rubble. They shrugged off the demands that they move to the periphery of the city. The *Overland Monthly* recognized the inevitable and predicted a better Chinatown. "It may lack the familiar holes, corners and smells... but it will be more agreeable to the eye if not so piquant to the nose... Possibly the new San Francisco will not be so joyous a place to the unregenerate nor so painful a spot to the pious as formerly...."

Fine, handsome buildings of Oriental design, many with pagoda-like roofs, were designed by men like T. Patterson Ross and A. W. Burgren and built along what was coming to be called Grant Avenue (old Dupont Street). The structure at Grant and California, kitty-cornered from Old St. Mary's, for example, was constructed at a cost of $135,000 and leased to the Sing Fat Company. At 32 Spofford Alley, Charles M. Rousseau designed a new $25,000 home for the Chinese Society of Free Masons, the Chee Kong tong, with much Oriental detail and Chinese tile. Apartments and hotels sprang up and the population crowded back into the Quarter. With the tong ranks thinned, many people lost their fear and the population began to curve upward again until it would reach 25,000 in 1950 and 36,445 in 1960.

But the tongs and tong violence were not completely dead. A Suey Sing vs. Bing Kong war flared up; then a two-year struggle between the Hop Sings and Bing Kongs. As late as 1914, the Hop Sings and Suey

Sings were even using motor cars and a machine gun to try to settle their quarrel. But these were the last spams of dying organisms. By 1909, the Chinese League of Justice in America was taking up problems of concern to the Chinese and settling them via legal means. The days of the tongs were numbered. The formation of the Chinese Republic in 1912, World War I and America's entry into it in 1917, all speeded up the integration process. These factors finally forced the citizens of Chinatown to make up their minds whether to return to China or to become Americans. Most chose the latter course, abandoned their queues and Oriental costumes and habits to a large degree, and acclimatized. They turned their backs on the old vendetta codes. The heads of the tongs—older men now—saw the handwriting on the walls of Chinatown, and in 1913 the tong chiefs themselves formed a Peace Association—the Wo Ping Woey—to end intertong strife.

It can almost be said that from this time on the tongs became poker, *pai gow* and pinochle societies. Families became the rule rather than the exception in Chinatown. Americanized Chinese were displacing the old-timers in positions of influence, as well as in sheer numbers. By 1910, American-born Chinese numbered 14,935—a thousand more than the entire population of Chinatown of 1900. They were now the distinct majority in Chinatown and they asserted their rights. Merchants no longer felt it necessary to become (grudging) members of tongs for reason of "protection." The tongs had to be content with the leavings of their former illegal empire—largely *do far* (lottery), fan-tan and *pai gow* parlors.

As early as 1909 the Six Companies began to foster tourism in the new Quarter. During the city's Portola Festival of that year their guidebook, *San Francisco's Chinatown,* was published. The editors assured travelers of their personal safety. "Visitors in Chinatown need fear no harm from members of the Chinese race. As to members of other races who often haunt Chinatown's streets, the visitor must use ordinary prudence." Tourists were urged to see (and smell) Fish Alley, off Washington Street just below Grant, but were warned, "Visit this part only in the daytime, as white 'sporting women' live on this street in considerable numbers." Although the Six Companies had to admit that some tongs had come back, it was no longer afraid of them—"There are some highbinder societies, which the better class of Chinese regret." The editors boasted of how clean Chinatown had become. "San Francisco's *reconstructed* Chinatown is composed of modern sanitary and attractive buildings. A Chinese lodging house recently constructed by Chinese owners on Clay Street has bathtubs on each floor—something novel in Chinatown." The editors added, "There are no underground opium dens in Chinatown—haven't been any since the fire." Opium had been practically taxed and priced out of existence by the time of the Opium Act of 1923. The State Legislature's Red Light Abatement Act of 1914 was practically the death blow for the singsong girl industry, although the last slave-girl raids were not made until 1925.

After the fire all of the major newspapers ran articles urging the resettlement of the city's Chinese elsewhere than in their old area along the Street of a Thousand Lanterns (Dupont). But nothing came of this idea. The Chinese were obstinate in their desire to return to their old precincts and they did so. Students of Chinatown like Hartwell Davis soon noted that: "Since the great San Francisco fire, a change has come over the Chinese in San Francisco. The merchant, realizing that this fire has removed much of the filth incidental to the Chinese section, has turned his face against the re-establishment of the sinister and crime-breeding conditions."

The *coup de grace* was administered to the fighting tongs by a now legendary figure—Inspector Jack Manion, who died in 1959 at the age of eighty-two years. Born in Ross, Marin County, he moved to San Francisco, joined the force in 1907, and served in the police department until his retirement in 1946. From the moment he took over the Chinatown squad on March 28, 1921, he became the unofficial chief of police of Chinatown. The last six tongs—the Hop Sings, Suey Sings, Suey Dongs, Sen Suey Yings, Jun Yings and Bing Kongs—were trying to turn back the clock to a time when assassinations, slave girls and gambling were the rule. But Manion would have none of it. "No more killings; no more shakedowns; no more opium or slave girls." These were his orders. But six men were killed. Manion put pressure on the tongs. He got their heads to meet together in an unwilling peace conference and bulldozed them into signing a treaty pledging peace. He threatened them with deportation if they did not sign. Manion's firm but fair methods

*Richard H. Dillon*

worked and it was he who finally pacified Chinatown. There were no more tong killings after 1922 (and few murders or manslaughter cases of any kind), although in the rare crimes of violence in later years the newspapers could be counted on to rush a headline on the streets reading TONG KILLING! no matter how far from the truth it might be. (This was even the case in 1961.)

Manion won the nickname *Mau Yee,* the Cat, because of his cunning and apparent knowledge of everything that went on in the Quarter. The last of the hatchet men were convinced that he not only had eyes in the back of his head but that he never slept. He used to fool them by standing in a crowd, reading the Chinese newspapers posted on the walls, apparently studying and digesting the calligraphic information. Actually he could read hardly a word of Chinese, but the highbinders did not know this. All of his psychology was simple but effective. When a show of force was needed he had only to march into a tong headquarters, listen silently and intently to what was but gibberish to him (though never showing this), then violently whip out his handcuffs and slam them on the table in front of the startled tong officers. Manion had a temper too. More than once he returned the thinly veiled bribes of costly presents by flinging them at the donors before kicking them out of Chinatown. One such gift was a complete dinner set in gold plate—the cups and bowls stuffed with currency.

But he was liked, even loved, by the common people of Chinatown, the merchants, and especially by the children. They did not call him *Mau Yee* but *Min Bok,* Old Uncle. The Americanized children liked him for the kindness beneath his rough exterior. Small Orientals would cry out as he passed. "Hello, Daddy!" He was repeatedly asked to be a best man or a godfather. For twenty-five years he headed the Chinatown squad and only once asked for a transfer to other duty. When the word got around, a large crowd of Chinese gathered with petitions demanding that "Sergeant Jack" stay on where he belonged. Although no braggart, Jack Manion did allow himself one boast in the beginning: "Ours will be the cleanest Chinatown in the United States." He was right, because he saw to it himself.

By 1925, when the last slave-girl raids were made in Portola Alley (renamed Cameron Alley, renamed Old Chinatown Lane), Manion's firm policing had paid off. He could explain why there were no more tong wars: "You see, there can't very well be any tong killings unless there are tong gunmen on hand to make them. The first thing I did when I took over the Chinatown detail was to make it hot for gunmen. All those without visible means of support I arrested on charges of vagrancy. The gunmen had social clubs and hang-outs. I arrested them for loitering around these clubrooms. I wasn't always able to secure convictions or sentences that amounted to very much. But I kept on arresting them and I gave them to understand that things would continue to be hot for them in San Francisco indefinitely. I succeeded in driving them out of the city and I've kept them out. I closed up the hang-out places and I've kept them closed."

By suppressing gambling and prostitution, Sergeant (later Inspector) Manion deprived the tongs of their last sources of revenue and power. This crippled them. He put the fear of God into the *boo how doy* by telling them, face to face, when he heard a rumor of a war between tongs, that he would try every one of them for conspiracy in murder should a single man be killed. He thought nothing of dropping through skylights or shinnying down ventilator shafts to rescue slave girls or seize hatchet men. Donaldina Cameron, his firm friend, said of him, "He has the support of the better elements in Chinatown and I think he has the respect of the worse elements."

For all its dark alleys, there is nothing sinister about modern 1962 Chinatown. Only on foggy nights when veils of sea mist obscure Spofford Alley and Waverly Place does the Quarter assume something of an air of mystery and an evocation of its turbulent past.

There is overcrowding in Chinatown, TB, and ironically, a tendency toward juvenile delinquency as today's Chinatown children become so completely Americanized. But little psychological damage appears to have been done by the years of persecution—internal and external. The long suffering, patient community has overcome its legacy of violence in magnificent fashion. Other than the deeply ingrained love of gambling, the almost sole survivor of tong-days traditions is a sort of secretiveness, perhaps a vestigial remnant of the conspiracy of silence of a century ago. Chinatown still keeps its own counsel as a community, perhaps for fear of embarrassing a citizen of Grant Avenue by causing him to be confronted unexpectedly by a tax collector or an immigration inspector.

But Chinatown is no longer the chaotic no man's land of a ghetto in transition. The quarter is so law-abiding today that sociologists study it in hopes of finding a cure for the increasing lawlessness of other areas of the city, state and nation.

According to the 1960-1961 annual report of Chief of Police Thomas J. Cahill, only one of 26 men arrested during the year for murder or manslaughter was an Oriental. (The statistics do not distinguish between Chinese and others of Oriental descent.) Of 22 rape arrests none was of Chinese, of 243 robbery arrests only 2 were of Orientals. The Quarter which once had a monopoly on street warfare was represented in the fiscal year of 1960 by only 7 cases of assault with a deadly weapon of the city's total of 177. There were no arrests of Orientals for prostitution and only 30 (out of 652) on narcotics charges. Only in terms of gambling is Chinatown well represented in Chief Cahill's reports. There were 276 such arrests of Orientals in 1960-61, for the Chinese still love the clatter of *pai gow* tiles and the clink of silver dollars.

Chinatown today remains the most colorful district of a colorful city. And few if any lament the passing of the lawless city within a city of yesterday. Most of us are content to accept the obituary which Donaldina Cameron pronounced, with no regret for its demise, back in 1906: "The strange, mysterious old Chinatown is gone and never more will be.

Heaps of sand and colored ashes mark the once densely populated, gaily painted, and proverbially wicked haunts of highbinders and slave dealers."

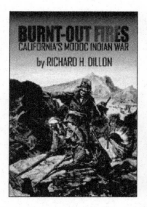
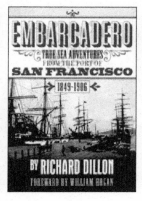
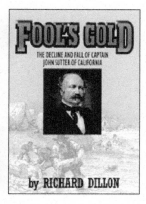

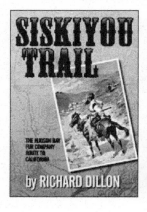
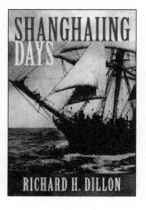

CPSIA information can be obtained
at www.ICGtesting.com
Printed in the USA
BVOW05s1603231216
471481BV00001B/71/P